THE ILLUSTRATED ENCYCLOPAEDIA OF ARTHURIAN LEGENDS

Ronan Coghlan

ELEMENT

Shaftesbury, Dorset ✦ Rockport, Massachusetts ✦ Brisbane, Queensland

For Mourna

© Ronan Coghlan 1991, 1993
Compilation © Element Books Ltd. 1993

This edition published in Great Britain in 1993 by
ELEMENT BOOKS LIMITED
Longmead, Shaftesbury, Dorset

Published in the USA in 1993 by ELEMENT INC
42 Broadway, Rockport, MA 01966

Published in Australia in 1993 by
ELEMENT BOOKS LIMITED for JACARANDA WILEY LIMITED
33 Park Road, Milton, Brisbane 4064

Designed by Bridgewater Books
Typeset by Chris Lanaway
Picture research by Julia Hanson
Printed and bound in Great Britain by the Bath Press

British Library Cataloguing in Publication
Data available

Library of Congress Cataloging in Publication
Data available

ISBN 1-85230-428-6

RIGHT *Guinevere and ladies of the Court, detail from* LANCELOT AND GUINEVERE, *Herbert Draper (1864-1920).*

FOREWORD

VERYONE who has approached the Arthurian legends with a view to finding out more about them is struck at once by their sheer breadth and complexity. Many turn away at this point, or content themselves with reading Sir Thomas Malory's *Le Morte d'Arthur.* In so doing they miss a great deal. Wonderful though Malory's retelling of the legends is, it is only one among many. To have failed to discover the fourteenth-century poem of *Sir Gawain and the Green Knight*, or the mysterious pageantry of the mighty *Vulgate Version* from which Malory himself drew extensively, is to have missed a wondrous experience. ⋎

Even if the intrepid reader does find his way to Wolfram von Eschenbach's *Parzival* and discovers how it differs from *Perlesvaus*, he will almost certainly reel back at the welter of names – people, places and things – which are part of the magic of the Arthurian world but which change, overlap and sometimes contradict each other outright. ⋎

In twenty odd years of writing about, and teaching, the Arthurian legends the question I am still most frequently asked is this: What book should I read first to give me an overview of the legends? That book has now arrived. Ronan Coghlan's *Encyclopaedia of Arthurian Legends* is both timely and useful. It gives brief entries on all the major themes and characters of the legends, as well as on many minor figures whose identities will have remained, at best, shadowy and, at worst, completely obscured to most readers unfamiliar with Medieval French, Middle High German, Old Spanish or, indeed, any one of the half dozen antique tongues in which the Matter of Britain, the corpus of Arthurian legends, was composed. ⋎

With this book, which is both scholarly and readable, you can discover the identity, and the story, of such exotic people as Bishop Baldwin of Britain, Bran the Blessed, Claris and Laris, Garlon the Invisible Knight, Dame Ragnell, Meliant de Lis, Wrnach the Giant and Ysaie the Sad, as well as the castles, forests, weapons, horses, dogs and all the other wonderful paraphernalia which make the Arthurian legends among the most riveting and fascinating of all such collections. You will also be given clues to help you follow up such recondite matters as the Quest for the Grail, the identity of the Lady of the Lake and the fate of Merlin. ↓

Towards the end of the twelfth century, the poet and philosopher Alain de Lille wrote:

Whither has not the flying flame spread and familiarized the name of Arthur the Briton, even as far as the empire of Christendom extends? ↓

That 'flying fame' has continued to spread into the twentieth century which has seen probably the largest explosion of interest in the matter of Arthur since the Middle Ages. Novels such as Rosemary Sutcliffe's *Sword at Sunset*, Henry Treece's *The Great Captains* and, most recently, Marion Zimmer Bradley's *Mists of Avalon* have helped keep the legends alive; now those who have longed to discover for themselves the older stories behind these fictional re-tellings, can take the first steps upon their own Arthurian quest. ↓

Ronan Coghlan is to be congratulated on producing a book which should be on the shelves of everyone who shares his love of the myths and legends of the British Isles. ↓

JOHN MATTHEWS

AUTHOR'S NOTE At the time when the Arthurian romances were written, spelling had not been standardized. In the text of this work, considerable effort has been made to achieve consistency in the spelling of proper names, but occasionally the same name may unavoidably be represented by variants.

INTRODUCTION

BOOKSHELVES everywhere creak under the weight of books on the Arthurian legends and if there is to be another it must either open up new ground on the subject or provide information that is difficult to find elsewhere.

This book is primarily intended as a reference book and its main aim is to provide a detailed 'who's who', 'what's what' and 'where's where' covering all the different strands of the Arthurian legends, something which no book has hitherto achieved.

There have, of course, been other less comprehensive books with a similar aim; for example, P.A. Karr's *King Arthur Companion* (Reston Book Co., Reston, VA), but this confines itself largely to Malory and certain French writings. N.J. Lacey has edited *The Arthurian Encyclopedia* (Garland Press, New York, 1986), but this is not a detailed index of persons, places and things; most of the articles therein concern the romances themselves, their writers and the development of the legend in general.

There is, then, a real need for a book such as this – a book in which the basic stories of the main heroes and villains, locations and objects of the Arthurian legends are to be found listed in alphabetical order.

One of the main issues to be addressed in compiling this work was that of the potentially tremendous scope within the Arthurian field. A huge number of names occur in the vast corpus of Arthurian literature and selective choice was a necessity. It became apparent that the best approach was to cover the following aspects:

⚜ the heroes and heroines of the main romances;

⚜ Arthur's family, immediate and extended, including a number of his ancestors;

⚜ the chief place names of the Arthurian tales and Grail romances;

⚜ historical topics relevant to the legend;

⚜ theories about the legends, including a number of unorthodox theories which the general reader may have encountered.

Modern Arthurian literature is outside the scope of the book and, while there are a few references to such latter-day compositions, they have for the most part been set aside. ✧

THE LEGEND OF KING ARTHUR

BELOW *Sir Galahad*, *George Frederick Watts (1817-1904). The Arthurian Legends have been a rich source of inspiration for writers, artists and poets throughout the ages, and were particularly influential during the nineteenth century.* ~

Who is this Arthur who has fascinated people for so long? Did he ever exist? And are even half the things told about him true? ✧

The answer is that, if Arthur indeed lived, he did so at a time when British history was hardly documented at all, a time of historical shadow-lands of which all manner of tales and fables could be told without fear of contradiction. This was the time when the Romans had left Britain and the Britons – ancestors of the modern Welsh and Cornish – had to fall back on their own resources to counter the onslaughts of the Picts, the Irish and the Anglo-Saxons, the latter being the forebears of the present-day English. ✧

Arthur is supposed to have lived in this period of upheaval and turbulence and to have been a leader of the Britons, but there is no direct evidence that he ever lived at all. There may be one near-contemporary reference to him: the poem *Gododdin* (*c.* AD 600)[1] tells of a certain hero who, though valiant, was not as valiant as Arthur. Unfortunately, it has been suggested that the line in question may be an interpolation, so it forms no solid foundation for belief in Arthur's existence. Irritatingly, Saint Gildas, writing in sixth-century Britain, would have known all about Arthur if, in fact, he existed, but Saint Gildas, dubbed 'the Wise' or Badonicus, because of a reference he makes to the battle of Badon, does not mention him. Gildas is not writing a history, but a 'grumbling book' (*liber querulus*)! It is, in fact, a kind of sermon in which he bemoans the woes that have overtaken his land – due, he informs

us, to sin, of which he felt there was a great deal amongst the British princes whom he upbraids with an acid tongue. He remarks that the Saxon ravages had been stayed for a time by Ambrosius Aurelianus and that afterwards the Saxons were defeated at Mount Badon, but he does not identify the British leader. Later legend was to claim it was Arthur. ✧

But, if we have no direct indication of Arthur's existence, some circumstantial evidence is to be found. Shortly after the time when Arthur would have lived, were he a historical character, a group of people are found bearing the name Arthur, previously unknown, as though in honour of some illustrious personage. Aedan mac Gabrán, king of Dalriada, had a son so named who died in AD 596. Arthur, son of Peter, was a ruler in Dyfed in the early seventh century and Arthur, son of Bicuir, flourished in AD 625. An Irish Arthur of about the same time is also noted.

The first undisputed mention of Arthur occurs a long time afterwards in the *Historia Brittonum* of Nennius, which appeared about the year AD 800, leaving much time for Arthurian fancy to combine with any Arthurian facts that might have existed. Whether the work was in fact compiled by Nennius has been queried, but the writer, whoever he may have been, makes no pretensions to being one of the world's great historians. Instead, he says he simply made a random collection of the various data he had to hand. On the face of it, this does not sound very promising material. He says that Arthur fought alongside the British kings, but was himself the war leader (*dux bellorum*). Nennius does not say that Arthur is a king, though his phraseology does not entirely preclude his having been one. It does, however, suggest the possibility that he held some Roman designation equivalent to such recorded Roman titles as *Comes Brittaniae* (Count of Britain) or *Dux Brittaniarum* (Duke of the Britons), which accorded him paramountcy over the various local British rulers. Nennius gives a list of twelve battles in which victory fell to Arthur, notably Badon, where he avers Arthur discomfited 960 adversaries. ✧

This is not, however, the most interesting thing Nennius has to say regarding Arthurian matters. He also notes the existence of a stone placed on a cairn with

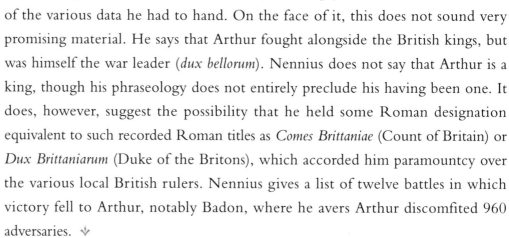

the paw print of Arthur's dog Cabal on it. The print was made, he says, when Arthur was hunting the boar Troynt. One wonders if we have here some version of the story found in *Culhwch and Olwen* in which Arthur gives chase to the obviously mythological boar Twrch Tryth. If so, we can see that, by Nennius's time, the supernatural and mythological had become infused into the Arthurian saga. Nennius also mentions the supposed grave of Arthur's son, Amr. ✣

The *Annales Cambriae* (perhaps tenth century) mention Badon and also Arthur's final battle, Camlann. They inform us that both Arthur and Mordred fell there. ✣

The English historian, William of Malmesbury, writing in the twelfth century, also speaks of Arthur, maintaining that he was the hero of many Welsh fables but that he was deserving of recognition as a veritable leader whose victories engendered hope in the bosoms of his countrymen. He seems, in William's text, to have at one time been subordinate to Ambrosius. However, the twelfth century was also to see publication of a work that shot Arthur to a pinnacle of fame. This was the *Historia Regum Brittaniae* by Geoffrey of Monmouth. ✣

Geoffrey of Monmouth was an ecclesiastic who first produced an edition of Merlin's *Prophecies* and then his famous *Historia* in which those prophecies are contained. This work purports to give the history of Britain from the arrival of Brutus the Trojan until after Arthur's reign, but his account of Arthur's rule is the central portion of the opus. He also made widely known the enigmatic figure of Merlin the magus. He tells how the latter came into prominence in the time of the usurper Vortigern and, when the latter was dethroned by the rightful ruler, Aurelius Ambrosius (called Ambrosius Aurelianus by Gildas), he continued to flourish. Aurelius was succeeded by his brother, Uther, who was Arthur's father. Arthur's reign is described in glowing terms: he not only defeats the Picts and Saxons, but also Lucius, procurator of the Roman Empire. ✣

The question that has occupied scholars is whether Geoffrey invented all this or whether he based his *Historia* on genuine tradition. Geoffrey claims he derived his information from a book in the British tongue (Welsh or Breton) which he obtained from Walter the Archdeacon. This Walter, who died in 1151, is well known to history, but the general consensus formerly was that most of the *Historia* sprang from Geoffrey's imagination. Modern critics tend to be more charitable to him. They are chary of accepting the historicity of the book but understand that Geoffrey may have made use of some genuine bodies of tradition, though there is every possibility that he 'improved' his source material. What kind of sources would he have used? ⅴ

There is no doubt that a great body of lore about Arthur had been building up amongst the Welsh. The romance of *Culhwch and Olwen*, dated about 1100, shows that Arthur's name had become associated with a great many characters in legend. The roll of persons at his court even includes borrowings from Irish mythology, like Conor mac Nessa, king of Ulster in the Cuchullain saga. Arthur is referred to in several early Welsh poems. One such, number 21 in *The Black Book of Carmarthen*, is sometimes called *Pa gur*.[2] In this piece (which is couched in obscure language), Arthur has to enumerate his followers. Kay (Cai) and Bedivere (Bedwyr) are there, but so are characters who have been plucked from Celtic mythology – Mabon son of Modron, in origin the god Maponus; Manawydan son of Llyr, also a god, equivalent to the Irish Manannán mac Lir. There is Anwas the Winged, of whom nothing else is known but who may have been some early British aviator. Kay appears to fight lions, hags and especially the monstrous Cath Palug. *Pa gur* also tells of Arthur polishing off (or at least wounding) one Pen Palach (a character in an obscure Welsh legend) whose name, though it makes him sound like somebody's habitual correspondent, possibly signifies Clubhead. In all, it is a catalogue of Arthurian exploits and Arthur's followers. ⅴ

Another Welsh poem is attributed to Taliesin, himself a figure of legend. This is *Preiddeu Annwfn*, the Spoiling of the Otherworld, and the supposed author is among the party depicted as faring thither. Arthur leads the expedition which consists of three ships, with the possible intention of carrying off the cauldron of the otherworldly ruler; only seven of the party return. This poem possibly pre-dates the Norman invasion and indicates that a vast body of tradition had built up about the hero. ⅴ

It seems to be traditions such as these that Geoffrey utilized. To what extent, if any, he embellished or augmented his source material has not been determined. It is even possible that Walter's book is no fiction. Geoffrey's work, written in Latin, revealed Arthur to the eyes of the literate world. Not all scholars, it must be

stated, regarded it as a reliable work, but it was very popular as reading material. ↓

Geoffrey, however, did not stop here. He then produced a poem, the *Vita Merlini*. Geoffrey's authorship of this work was questioned by Milton, simply because the Latin is so good, but it is not seriously doubted today. Geoffrey certainly did not invent Merlin; a number of Welsh poems that precede his work feature the wizard. These poems associate him with the Lowlands of Scotland. Geoffrey has him meeting Taliesin after Arthur's passing and, in the course of their conversation, Merlin regales his companion with the tale of how Arthur, after his last battle, was borne to the Isle of Apples. Here we have a notion, based on genuine tradition, that Arthur was not dead but would, some day, return. ↓

This belief seems to have taken three forms . In one, Arthur went to some island to be healed of his wounds; in another, he and his companions sleep underground, awaiting the time when they must ride forth again. This latter belief exists about a good many heroes and is termed by folklorists, 'the Barbarossa Legend', because Frederick Barbarossa was one such hero. A belief of this nature was probably first held about some Celtic deity. Plutarch (? died AD 120) declares that there was a legend amongst the Britons that the god Cronus slumbered on an island, guarded by Briareus and flanked by attendants. Cronus, of course, is a Greek, not a Celtic, god, but Geoffrey Ashe has ably argued that Bran was the deity concerned and that he was linguistically confused with Cronus. The former notion, that Arthur was healed of his wounds and then slept in a sea-girt Avalon, led medieval romancers to identify it with the kingdom of Faerie, the realm of Oberon. It was certainly generally held that Arthur was in an otherworldly Elysium, though his Avalon is also identified with Glastonbury whose Tor may have been regarded as the entrance to such a place. Arthur's remains were purportedly excavated at Glastonbury in 1191 but this did not scotch the belief in Arthur's return which found yet a third form in the idea that Arthur had been reincarnated as a bird – a raven, a chough or a puffin. ↓

Geoffrey's works made Arthur and Merlin widely known in the educated stratum of society. No longer were the tales of Arthur confined to the small huts

LEFT *The Court at Dinner, from* Lancelot du Lac *(French, early fourteenth century). Much of our image of courtly and chivalrous behaviour is based on ideas of what life at Arthur's Court must have been like.*

~

of the Welsh but were read with gusto throughout Western Christendom. By now, of course, the Saxon conquerors of the Britons had themselves been conquered by the Normans. ✧

Not everyone believed what Geoffrey had written. Giraldus Cambrensis[3] tells an amusing story of a man plagued by evil spirits. When the Gospel of John was placed on him, the spirits fled, but, when a copy of Geoffrey's *Historia* replaced it,

they returned in great numbers! If Geoffrey's works established Arthur in the Latin language of the learned, there was also a body of translators keen to turn his work into the vernacular. Geoffrey Gaimar and Robert Wace[4] both produced Norman-French versions of the *Historia*. The former's has disappeared; the latter's was completed in 1155. Wace, a native of Jersey, is the first to mention the Round Table. Layamon produced an Anglo-Saxon version. But we must not search for the origins of the Arthurian romances in these. The origins must be sought in the body of oral Arthurian tradition that was already in circulation before Geoffrey put pen to paper. ✧

The Britons, or rather their descendants, preserved tales about Arthur. The descendants of these Britons, together with their culture, survived not only in Wales and Cornwall but also in Brittany. It is from the Bretons that a knowledge of Arthur's exploits reached the French poets and it is the Bretons who seemed to have changed the name Modron to that of Morgan. Modron was the Welsh form of Matrona, the name of an ancient British and Gaulish goddess; but the Bretons believed in a fairy named Morgan whose name possibly signifies 'seaborn'. The two may have been identical or perhaps the one was identified with the other; it is in the form of Morgan that she is known, not only to the French romancers but even to Geoffrey in the *Vita Merlini* and the Welsh writer, Giraldus Cambrensis. We can assume, therefore, that a great deal of Arthurian lore was preserved among the Bretons. ✧

The Bretons passed the stories on to the French. The first French writer of Arthurian romance was Chrétien de Troyes, a poet who lived in the latter half of the twelfth century, and whose works included *Lancelot*, *Perceval*, *Erec et Enide*, *Yvain* and *Cligés*. Lancelot's originally Celtic character has been doubted but there are elements in the tales about him that sit well in a Celtic context and his name, though Germanic, may well have a Celtic equivalent, as is argued in the section devoted to him in the main body of this book. *Erec et Enide* must certainly be of Breton origin for no tradition of Erec existed amongst the Welsh – who, when they produced their own version of the story, replaced Erec with a hero known to them, Geraint. Yvain is a North Briton hero, who ruled the kingdom of Rheged; the Welsh form of his name was Owain. *Cligés* may have been composed entirely by Chrétien and has no traditional basis. In his *Perceval*, Chrétien introduces the Grail theme which has undoubted Celtic antecedents but which enjoys no place in the chronicle of Geoffrey.

In speaking of the Grail, it becomes clear that Chrétien had access to a body of Celtic tradition, inherent in the mythology of the insular Britons, which must have been preserved in the oral traditions of their continental descendants. The basic story of the Grail may be outlined as follows. The land has become barren and, at the same time, the king has been wounded in the thigh (or genitals). The aridity of the first has been caused by the injury of the second. The hero of the romance, Perceval – the name invented as an equivalent of the Celtic Peredur – visits the king in his castle and fails to ask the question ('What is the Grail and whom does it serve?') which would set things right. There is little doubt that behind this tale lies a myth of fertility.

In early times, the health of the king was bound up with the productivity of his realm. If the king were hale and hearty, the crops shot upward and the land was well watered and green. Should the king become infirm, the land would dry up and the crops would fail. This led to rules preventing a man with injury or blemish from inheriting the crown. A mythological instance of this occurs in the case of Nuada, the king of the Tuatha Dé Danaan, the Irish gods, who, when he lost his arm, had to surrender his kingship. It is clearly this sort of notion that lies behind the Grail saga. This myth is not confined to the Celts. I understand that even today in the Sudan there exists a people whose king is murdered by one of his wives before he grows too old, in order to make way for a successor. The Grail King's wound is said to be in the thigh, but this may be a euphemism for castration, indicating that he is as infertile as the Waste Land he rules.

At what stage did the Grail become associated with Arthur and his knights? An early version of the Grail Quest may be found in the account of Bran's expedition to Ireland. This occurs in the romance, *Branwen Daughter of Llyr*, found in the *Mabinogion*. Bran the Blessed (Bendigeidfran) is king of the Island of the Mighty (Britain), and his sister Branwen married the king of Ireland. 'Ireland' here is quite possibly a rationalization of the Otherworld. Bran gives the Irish king, Matholhwch, his cauldron, which conveniently restores life to any corpse placed within it. This seems to be the original Grail. Branwen is maltreated in Ireland and, hearing of this, Bran leads an expedition to rescue her. The expedition is successful, but only seven of those who set forth return alive and Bran himself is wounded in the foot by a poisoned spear. This wound resembles that of the Grail King. Bran dies from it and is buried at the White Hill in London. ⩔

The poem *Preiddeu Annwfn* tells a similar tale about Arthur. He leads an expedition to the Otherworld, perhaps to obtain a cauldron (the language of the poem is obscure). Again, only seven of those who take part return. In what is perhaps another version of the same tale, we are told in *Culhwch and Olwen* of Arthur's expedition to Ireland to procure the cauldron of Diwrnach who is a supervisor employed by the Irish King, Odgar son of Aedd. It is probable that here also Ireland is a substitution for the Otherworld and, if so, the name of Odgar's father is of particular interest. In the myths of the Irish Celts, Aed ('fire') is the name of an important deity, the sun god, possibly to be identified with the Dagda. This sun god may have been the Creator in Celtic mythology. There is evidence that he was also known amongst the Britons, for they had a tradition that Britain took its name from Prydein, son of Aedd. In any event, if Arthur is not depicted as being wounded on the expedition, he is certainly the leader; it would seem that Arthur has replaced Bran in these accounts. Arthur has other points of association with Bran: he seems to have replaced him as the sleeping hero and, in Cornish folklore, after his death he became a raven, while the name Bran signifies 'raven'. Susan Cooper must have had this in mind when she gave Arthur a son named Bran in her *Dark is Rising* pentalogy of children's fantasy novels. In the original story, then, Arthur was the Grail Quester but, before the Grail stories reached their final form, he must have been stripped of such a rôle. Bran, whose name is spelled Bron, now turns up as the Rich Fisher, Arthur has been replaced by Perceval or Galahad or, in the German *Diu Crône*, by Gawain. If Bran was our original quester, however, his wound would indicate he was also the Maimed King. Though Arthur did not succeed him in this capacity in the Middle Ages, it is interesting to note that he does so in the film *Excalibur* (directed by John Boorman). In this, Perceval discovers that Arthur himself is the one whom the Grail serves when, at last, he asks the fateful question, 'Whom does the Grail serve?'. ✧

THE GRAIL

At what stage was Arthur replaced as Grail quester? We cannot answer this. When and how did the Grail assume its Christian character? Robert de Boron is the first to describe it as a Christian object, but it does not necessarily follow that it was he who first christianized a pagan story. It is not, of course, impossible that there actually was some Christian vessel or other artefact whose story became combined with that of the Otherworld cauldron. The Welsh story, *Peredur*, also features a vengeance motif and, although it is difficult to say how much this was part of the original tale, its pagan element seems clear in the involvement of the hags of Gloucester. ✧

ABOVE *Tristan with his black shield.*

Another sage entwined with the tale of Arthur is that of Tristan. This story would seem to have been Pictish in origin but to have picked up many strands in the course of its development. In the final version, Tristan's exploits are set in Cornwall and Brittany though it is not, of course, impossible that a story told of a northerly Tristan was later told of a namesake who lived in the south-west of Britain. The Tristan Stone of Cornwall might be invoked as evidence of a Cornish Tristan, but it is fairly nebulous evidence. The build-up of the Tristan saga is tabulated in the section devoted to Tristan later in this book. Were the Tristan and Arthurian sagas originally connected? It is not really possible to say, though the Arthurian element could be severed from the Tristan story without its suffering any essential loss. ✧

Chrétien's romances mark the beginning of a considerable body of Old French literature devoted to Arthur. Amongst the heroes of these romances we learn of

Tyolet who could speak the language of animals. (Welsh romance featured a similar character, Gwrhyr, Interpreter of Tongues.) We also learn of Claris and Laris, a brace of knightly heroes; of Floriant and his love for Florete; and a good many more. Here too we learn of Guinglain, the son of Gawain, a popular character known as 'the Fair Unknown'. A genuine Celtic background lies behind some of these tales. ✧

While Arthurian romance had taken hold in France, a similar process had also occurred in Germany. Ulrich von Zatzikhoven produced his own version of the Lancelot story round about the year 1195. This differs greatly from French romance as there is no mention of his illicit passion for Guinevere. Instead, he has a plurality of wives which has been adduced as evidence for the Celtic origin of the story; loose or polygamous marital ties were a feature of Celtic society. Von Zatzikhoven shares with Chrétien the idea of Lancelot's having been raised by a lake fairy from whom he obtained his title, Lancelot of the Lake. ✧

German Grail stories also appeared. Wolfram von Eschenbach's *Parzival* was produced in the thirteenth century. He went to great pains to give the impression he had not used Chrétien as a source, but few doubt that he did. His knowledge of French was at times imperfect: for example, Morgan Le Fay becomes the mountain Feimurgan and he mistakes the place name *Terre de la Joie* for a personal name, making it the fairy Terdelaschoye. In the same century Heinrich von dem Türlin's *Diu Crône* (The Crown) saw the light, the only Grail romance in which Gawain is the successful quester. The stories of Erec and Owain (Yvain) were given a German guise by Hartmann von Aue. The Tristan saga entered German in a late twelfth-century version by Eilhart von Oberge and a more celebrated *Tristan* poem followed not long afterwards by Gottfried von Strassburg. ✧

Arthurian romance spread northwards to Scandinavia and southwards to Italy and Spain. Quite a number of variant versions of Arthurian tales appeared in Scandinavia, including Iceland and the Faeroes. Even Geoffrey was represented here, his *Historia* being called *Breta sögur*, thought by some to have been translated at Bergen. Geoffrey's Merlin prophecies were translated and expanded by an Icelander, Gunnlaug (died 1218), under the title *Merlinusspa*. The Tristan saga was also of considerable interest to the Scandinavians. It might be added parenthetically that P.L. Mitchell in 'Scandinavian Literature' in *Arthurian Literature in the Middle Ages* (ed. R.S. Loomis, Clarendon Press, Oxford, 1959) speaks of an independent Scandinavian Arthurian tale called *Samsons Saga Fagra*, but it is in fact doubtful that the 'King Arthur' of this work is the one we are concerned with. ⋎

When we speed southward, crossing the Alps in the process, and find ourselves in Italy, we have reached a land where Arthurian literature exercised a considerable influence. On the Modena Archivolt (underside of an arch in Modena Cathedral) we have what may be the earliest Italian piece of Arthuriana, the sculpture of an Arthurian adventure in relief. It appears to show how Guinevere was carried off by Carados of the Dolorous Tower and how Arthur, Gawain, Galvariun, Kay and Isdernus (? Yder) try to rescue her from Mardoc (? Mordred) to whom Carados has handed her. In literature, Italy produced the comprehensive *Tavola ritonda*, as well as Tristan tales and other works, such as *Pulzella gaia*, an original Italian composition. The Iberian Peninsula was also a place where Arthurian matter was popular, appearing in both Spanish and Catalan; and, as late as the sixteenth century, the Portuguese *Memorial des Proezas da Segunda Tavola Redonda*[5] was produced. ⋎

Dutch, Hebrew, Greek, Irish, Welsh and even Tagalog romances also appeared. In England there were many Arthurian compositions in the vernacular before Malory, the most famous being *Sir Gawain and the Green Knight* (fourteenth century) and Chaucer's *Wife of Bath's Tale*. However, it was in France that the Grail saga was to reach its height as a Christian epic. Undoubtedly, Robert de Boron set the stage for this, but it built up into the *Queste del Saint Graal* (early thirteenth century). In this, the Grail story has reached its classical form and it is here that Galahad becomes a Grail quester for the first time. The author – perhaps a Cistercian – seems to have thought Perceval insufficiently holy to be the real Grail hero, so Galahad has supplanted him. Galahad's more secular approach to knighthood is utterly rejected. The Church may at times have been suspicious of the

BELOW *Sir Dinadan and the sick Tristan.*

~

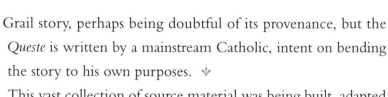

Grail story, perhaps being doubtful of its provenance, but the *Queste* is written by a mainstream Catholic, intent on bending the story to his own purposes. ↓

This vast collection of source material was being built, adapted and re-adapted, told and retold, throughout the Middle Ages; near the close of the Middle Ages there appeared what, for many English-speaking readers, is the standard Arthuriad, that of Thomas Malory. There has been some doubt regarding which, of a number of contemporaries of the same name, is to be identified with our author. There is also doubt as to whether his *Le Morte d'Arthur* was originally written as a single work or as separate tales. The title is a misnomer, given it by Caxton who printed the work. In it there is little trace of Arthur's Celtic origins; he is presented as the rightful king of England, a realm of which no historical Arthur would have heard. This book has proved the basis for innumerable retellings for children and it is in some such form that most of us originally encountered King Arthur. It is full of excitement and vigour, though Malory plays down the supernatural and fantastic. ↓

After Malory, a number of Arthurian works of note were produced in England. The Elizabethan-cum-Jacobean writer Richard Johnston penned two, *Tom a' Lincoln* and *Tom Thumb*.[6] Spenser's *Faerie Queene* may justifiably be classed as Arthurian as it contains a great deal of Arthurian matter and features Arthur himself as a character. Many decry the *Faerie Queene* as boring and slow; but its wealth of detail is something at which the poet aims and there is a general air of ornate colouration about the work which is quite international. After this, however, Arthurian literature seems to have gone distinctly downhill. It might have been saved by Milton who harboured an unfulfilled ambition to write an Arthurian epic. Arthurian works after 1600 are generally held to be inferior. Why is this? ↓

The answer must lie in a profound change of viewpoint in the Western world. In an age when people were becoming, for want of a better word, 'rational' in their outlook, stories of fairies, hags, giants and dragons seemed outmoded, only suitable for the nursery. Moreover, fantasy was inappropriate to a growing industrialization and Protestants may have viewed it as having vaguely 'papist' connotations. With the removal of large sections of the population to the industrial cities, there was much severance of social continuity, and the belief in anything otherworldly – such things forming one of the most compelling aspects of the Arthurian mythology – was regarded as the province of credulous yokels and bumpkins. ✧

Surprisingly, it was in the nineteenth century when industrialization was at its height that, perhaps as a reaction to materialism, an interest began once more to burgeon in Arthurian matters. Tennyson's *Idylls of the Kings* was highly prized by the Victorians. His Arthur, based on Queen Victoria's husband, Prince Albert, was highly idealized, and his work greatly influenced the Pre-Raphaelite painters. This era also saw the publication in 1838–49 of Lady Charlotte Guest's translation of the *Mabinogion*, making the study of Arthurian tales 'scientific' and therefore respectable. Lord Lytton produced a book-length poem *King Arthur* (1848) which, if not of startling quality, does not lack imaginative touches. William Morris, who wrote a number of medieval fantasy novels, also produced an Arthurian poem entitled *The Defence of Guenevere* (1858). This nineteenth-century Arthurian Renaissance did not continue into the hard-bitten and cynical years of the early twentieth century. ✧

If Arthur had died out as a mainstream character in literature with the birth of the rational outlook, he survived in rustic folklore. As faith in the progress of science increased, fewer people were interested in the fireside tales which formed an important source of entertainment in rural households; yet at these firesides many an Arthurian tale was told, shaped or reshaped. Sometimes, a tale which, at first, had no connection with Arthur subsequently came to feature him. To show how this could happen, we shall glance for a moment at the time-honoured belief in the 'Wild Hunt'. ✧

Belief in the Wild Hunt is found, not only in Britain but also on the Continent. Arthur is sometimes regarded as its leader, both in Britain and France, where it is known as *la Chasse Artu*; but investigation reveals that Arthur cannot have been its original leader. ✧

The central theme is that a phantasmal host rides through the clouds, in pursuit of something, but in pursuit of what is generally not clear. In Germany, the hunt was often led by Woden, the Norse Odin. However, Jacob Grimm tells us that, in part of that country, the leader was identified with a Hackelbärend whom he labels as a semi-historical person. Low Saxon lore claims he was, in life, one Hans von Hackelnberg (whom legend has dying in 1521 or 1581). He had slain a boar, it was said, which he mocked and he was then injured in the foot by the beast's tusk and died of tetanus, saying that he did not wish to go to Heaven, but only to hunt. His wish was granted. Grimm points out that *hakolberand* was used as an epithet for Woden in Old Saxon. The leader of a female Wild Hunt in Germany is Frau Gauden, but again Grimm argues that she was Woden in origin, a male *fro* having yielded to a female *frau*. If the Wild Hunt originated in Germany, how did it come to be associated with Arthur and how would Arthur have replaced Woden? When the Anglo-Saxons invaded England they certainly brought their god, Woden, with them and they almost undoubtedly believed in the Wild Hunt. When their descendants intermarried with those descendants of the Britons who had not fled westwards, but had remained to form the bottom stratum of the new society, their offspring may have adapted the Wild Hunt, placing a British leader rather than a German god at its head. So this may be why on Hunting Causeway in Somerset Arthur and his men are said to ride. On Christmas Eve each year Arthur is said to lead his men to Sutton Montis Church, also in Somerset, where the horses are watered at a long-hidden well. The Wild Hunt is also associated with other places: in the 1940s it was said to have gone through West Coker at Hallowe'en, while in 1960 it was reported to have gone through Stogumber. ⌄

BELOW *A knight, bound hand and foot, is wheeled in a cart as Arthur watches from a pavilion, from* Guiron le Courtois *(Flemish, late fifteenth century).*

~

If Arthur persisted in folklore, the early twentieth century was not a time conducive to the development of general Arthurian interest. To establish the reason for this lack of interest, we have to look back to the scientific developments of the previous century. Science was making great strides and began for many to supplant religion. Victorian man began to tell himself, with a smug satisfaction, that *his* science held the answer to everything and that it would sweep the cobwebs of superstition out of the corners of men's minds. These same scientists who regarded themselves as quite open-minded were not prepared to consider anything that did not fit into what they regarded as the boundaries of the possible and they believed the area within those boundaries to be of small extent. So it was that they poured scorn on such ideas as telepathy, now taken seriously by many scientists, because they did not fit into the system. As a result of this outlook, at the beginning of the twentieth century the literate public regarded the credulous Middle Ages with a fine contempt and viewed the outré and fantastical with nothing short of derision. Moreover, this new age was reflected by writers who felt that realism within the Victorian scientific definition was the only area worthy of representation in literature. They further felt that the depiction of heroes resulted in a literature too simplistic and childlike; they turned instead to the anti-hero. To them, character was often far more important than event and no greater taunt could be levelled at a writer than that his characters were wooden. This was no place for the Arthurian romance, where action was everything. ✥

Having said this, how are we to account for the vast interest to be found in Arthurian literature today, an interest embracing both the academic and the common person? ✥

ABOVE *Galahad rides through the forest, from* La Mort Artus *(French, late thirteenth century). Galahad was one of Arthur's twenty-four Knights of the Round Table.*

The answer may lie in the possibility that there is more of interest to the human being than his own rather circumscribed range of personal experience and the limited collective experience of the society in which he finds himself. Man has a sense of wonder and he seeks to look beyond the confines of the everyday. Marvel-filled literature enables him to do this and provides him with the stimulus which his imagination craves. ✥

It must not be supposed that, when realism informed the upper regions of literature, the fantastic was not to be found on the printed page. In the Victorian era the penny dreadful appeared, featuring supernatural characters such as Varney the Vampire who, after causing mayhem amongst maidens in many a thrilling episode, finally put an end to himself by jumping into Vesuvius. The literary offspring of such works in the early twentieth century were a succession of 'popular' tales which neither aspired, nor could claim, to be great literature, but nonetheless slaked the thirst for the marvellous amongst a populace who still looked for it, despite the frowns of the Establishment. Some of these heroes appeared, not in books or magazines but in comic strips, and it is interesting to note that one such strip, *Prince Valiant*, was set in an Arthurian milieu. ✥

So, beneath the rational carapace, there was always an imaginative substratum in literature, but it was a substratum which rarely raised its voice against those who felt themselves in a position to tell people what they ought to like. The base upon which the realistic approach to literature stood lay in a belief that science had swept the mystery from life like dust from a room and that scientific development would contain the medication for all humanity's ills. Then, in the latter part of the nineteenth century, a realization dawned that science was not the universal panacea it had been supposed to be. For, despite the many ills it cured, it seemed to provide others to take their place; the scientists themselves were beginning to sound far less sure about where the boundaries of the possible lay and far less assertive regarding what might lie beyond them. The 'realistic sureties' were found to have shaky foundations. ✧

At this stage people began to discover that it was not evidence of near cretinism to like and respond to reading material by which the imagination was fuelled, by which a set of values was upheld and in which life itself proceeded at a rather gentler pace. The time was ripe for a renewed interest in Arthurian material. ✧

Added to this, there is the knowledge that mankind has always had a spiritual side to its nature. Victorian science tended to deny its existence, 'realistic' intellectuals asserting that spiritual craving was a kind of juvenile thirst which should have been quenched before people 'grew up'. Such ideas later entered mainstream religion and produced such writers as the Anglican theologian, Don Cupitt, who believes God to be no more than a concept or notion, certainly not an actual being. People in the latter half of this century find they still have spiritual yearnings, and the spiritual and mythical aspects of the Arthurian romances have done much to assuage their hunger. ✧

The spiritual messages underlying the Arthurian material have found expression in a number of forms, both Christian and pagan. Many of these have centred on Glastonbury, with its considerable Arthurian associations, where pagan and Christian elements meet and mingle. There was once even a Christian denomination called the 'Catholicate of the West' headed by an ecclesiastic known as the self-styled 'patriarch of Glastonbury', a bicycle salesman in secular life. Many seek spiritual solace in the pagan past of Glastonbury which has been identified by some as the Isle of Avalon. Many people today, unsatisfied with a Christianity which often tends to shy away from the mystical, have looked to the pre-Christian past; some have combined the two, producing a kind of quasi-esoteric hybrid. ✧

But what provoked the apparent shift in consciousness which made the Arthurian literature more acceptable? Undoubtedly, the publication of J.R.R. Tolkien's *Lord of the Rings*[7] had much to do with it. Tolkien was a highly respected academic, not a hack writer, yet his work was deemed to be so contrary to the literary trends of the time that it is rumoured he had to put money towards its publication. Although it appeared in three volumes in 1954–5, it did not attain true fame until the 1960s, when it suddenly gained a cult following on American university campuses. Tolkien chiefly made use of Teutonic sources, but Celtic and even Finnish influences may be discerned in his work; for example it features as a major character the Merlin-like figure of Gandalf the wizard. ✧

Suddenly, the medieval kind of romance became acceptable. Ballantine Books, who published the authorized paperback edition of *The Lord of the Rings* in America, brought out an adult fantasy series which included Arthurian romances such as H. Warner Munn's *Merlin's Ring* and *Merlin's Godson*, both reprints, and a completely new Arthurian novel, Sanders Anne Laubenthal's *Excalibur* (1973). Many new Arthurian novels proceeded from a variety of pens. However, a further stimulus for Arthurian interest lay in the non-fiction works of Geoffrey Ashe whose books on the legends of Arthur were aimed not at grey-haired professors but at the general public. He received the occasional sneer from the groves of Academe but his works can hardly be labelled eccentric and they convey very effectively all the mystique of the Arthurian legends in a lucid and readable style. Those who were more spiritually inclined turned towards less mainstream writers like Anthony Roberts. ✧

The Arthurian saga provided a myth which twentieth-century readers could use (and humanity has always needed its myths), but it also provided something more. When Arthur comes to power, it is in an uncertain world, his society divided into factions and faced with Saxon attack from outside. It is a world where everything could crumble into chaos at a moment's notice. It seems very like our own world where we find speed, stress, violence, noise and danger at every turn, a world

REFERENCE NOTES

1. K. Jackson, ed., *Gododdin*,Edinburgh,1969.
2. This poem is referred to a number of times in this work. It is written in obscure Welsh and is incomplete. The text, with a translation, is to be found in Sir John Rhys's introduction to the Everyman edition of Malory's *Morte d'Arthur*, London, 1906.
3. Giraldus Cambrensis (died *c.* 1223), was a Cambro – Welsh writer. His comment about Geoffrey occurs in his *Journey through Wales*; see L. Thorpe, trans., *The Journey through Wales* and *The Description of Wales*, Harmondsworth, 1978.
4. Wace and Layamon, *Arthurian Chronicles*, London, 1962.
5. This work was published in Coimbra in 1567.
6. The text of *Tom a' Lincoln* is to be found in W. J. Thoms, ed., *A Collection of Early English Prose Romances* (1858). The text of *Thom Thumb* is to be found in I. and P. Opie, *The Classic Fairy Tales*, London, 1973.
7. J.R.R. Tolken, *The Lord of the Rings*, London, 1954.
8. G.H. Williamson, *The Secret Places of the Lion*, London, 1951.
9. R.M.T., *A Book in Preparation for the Coming Light*, London, 1951.
10. J. Michell, *New Light on the Ancient Mystery of Glastonbury*, Glastonbury, 1990. This title was published in a limited edition of 999 copies. The author's arguments do not preclude the existence of an historical Arthur.

which we often feel might fall in upon our heads at any moment. We often try to make sense of the world around us and find it impossible to shape. Yet Arthur shapes his world, imposes law and order within his realm and defeats his external enemies. He does what so many of us aspire to do – he imposes order upon a bewildering chaos. ⩔

Modern interest in things Arthurian has produced some unexpected results. There is, in the West Country, a group of people who regard themselves as reincarnations of Arthurian characters. The lady who believes that she is the reincarnation of Arthur himself, says that in her previous life, she fathered fifteen children! Various accounts of her appear in volumes on folklore published by Bossiney Books of Cornwall, but her identity has been kept a secret. With regard to claimed Arthurian reincarnations, one might note that the writer George Hunt Williamson[8] asserted that the wizard Merlin was reincarnated as Joseph Smith who founded the Mormon Church. A book by a writer called R.M.T.[9] contains what he avers to be messages conveyed by automatic writing from Saint Andrew, Saint John, Saint Christopher and, among others, King Arthur. If this is so, King Arthur's grammar needs some attention. There are others who claim the spirit of Merlin is in touch with them. In all this there is a lesson for the self-styled rationalists: if you try to stamp out the mythic, the imaginative, the spiritual, they will not disappear but, having lingered beneath the surface, will later return. Even in Russia at the time of writing, Boris Yeltsin, President of the Russian Federal Republic, has spoken of the need to bring the spiritual back into Russian life. ⩔

One of the purposes of a book like this is to stimulate readers to open up new areas of investigation into the legend which forms its subject. There are many starting points in the text from which readers can develop new ideas and theories. If I may suggest one area worthy of probing, it is the alternative story of Arthur's death found in the section on Cath Palug, the one in which he falls into the hands, or rather the paws, of a supernatural cat. This Cath Palug, or clawing cat, features in Welsh tradition but somewhere along the line it seems to have been forgotten that *palug* means 'clawing'. It was thought to be a personal name, a Palug having a number of sons who raised the cat on Anglesey. The beast is mentioned in *Pa gur*, in which we learn that Kay was prepared to fight it but, as the poem is incomplete, we do not discover whether he actually did so. Geoffrey Ashe has suggested that the creature could have been a leopard, as it is described as speckled, but it seems to have had a supernatural character. Continental romance says that Arthur fought with Chapalu near Lake Bourget in the French Alps and, in one romance, it kills Arthur and invades and conquers England. ✧

Bearing in mind the Celtic origins of the Cath Palug, it seems likely that Arthur's fatal combat with it also springs from a Celtic source. Is there any evidence in legend for a 'cat that conquered Britain' story? In his book *The Black Horseman* (1971), S.G. Wildman makes reference to the Red Cat of Brimstage, a sculpture, and points out the existence of a number of 'red cat' place names, suggesting there was in England a legendary Red Cat whose story has been lost. Is this the felid which slew Arthur? It would be interesting to investigate this. ✧

The encyclopaedia could also be used by the novelist, the playwright and the poet seeking Arthurian source material. Many of the sections deal with obscure characters and themes which are not easily accessible to the general reader; there are also many starting points for literary works, awaiting development. It could also be used by the scholar who, well versed in his own area of Arthurian studies, needs to check references to characters and events from other areas. Finally, and perhaps chiefly, it should appeal to the ordinary reader who wishes to expand his knowledge of the Arthurian legend or to clarify references made in other works. ✧

New theories regarding Arthur continue to appear. In September 1990 a book by John Michell[10] was published in which the author identifies the Arthur of legend with the star Arcturus and claims that the journey of the Great Bear around the Pole Star is the original of the Round Table. ✧

And so, to use Professor Tolkien's phrase, the road goes ever onward; not only do new Arthurian theories keep surfacing, but yet more Arthurian novels continue to be turned out yearly by a bevy of authors for the delectation of a voracious public. The legends, it seems, will always be a perennial topic of fascination. Whether as exotic fantasies or as profound archetypes of the unconscious mind, the Arthurian characters continue to excite and inspire us, for they have a magical appeal that is timeless. ✧

BELOW *ARTHUR AND MORDRED IN MUTUALLY FATAL COMBAT, Arthur Rackham (1867-1939). Tradition maintained that Arthur would return. His reincarnated form has variously been claimed to be a bird, either a raven, a puffin or a chough.*
~

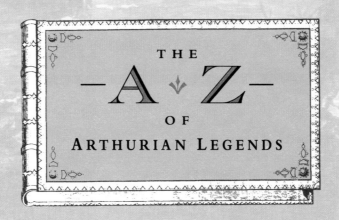

THE
A · Z
OF
ARTHURIAN LEGENDS

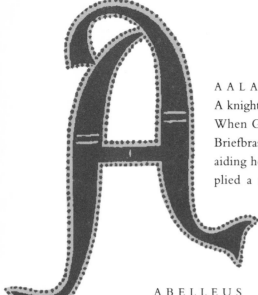

AALARDIN

A knight with magical knowledge. When Guignier, wife of Caradoc Briefbras, lost her breast when aiding her husband, Aalardin supplied a magic shield boss which provided a golden breast. He married Arthur's grand-niece, Guigenor.[6]

ABELLEUS

A knight slain by Tor.

ABLAMOR OF THE MARSH

A knight who possessed a white hart which was killed by Gawain and Gaheris. In retaliation, Ablamor killed two of their greyhounds. This led to combat with Gawain who was on the point of killing him when his lady threw herself between them and Gawain killed her instead. Horror-stricken by this, Gawain did not kill Ablamor.

ACCOLON

A Gaulish knight, of whom Morgan was enamoured. He was hunting with Urien and Arthur when they were separated from their companions. They came upon a vessel where they settled down for the night. To his astonishment, Accolon awoke in a field where he was given Excalibur and told he would have to use it in a fight. His opponent turned out to be Arthur. Neither recognized the other. Arthur had been given a fake Excalibur and at first it looked as though Arthur would lose the contest, but the Lady of the Lake appeared and magically caused Excalibur to fall to the ground. Arthur then seized it and defeated Accolon but, when the King discovered that Morgan had set up the whole affair, he assured

RIGHT *ACCOLON, Aubrey Beardsley (1872-98), from* Le Morte d'Arthur *(1909). Morgan staged an elaborate contest between King Arthur and Accolon in which Accolon received a fatal wound.*

~

Chapter r.

Accolon he would not be punished. However, Accolon had sustained a mortal wound in the fight.[19]

ACHEFLOUR

In *Sir Perceval of Galles*, Acheflour is Arthur's sister and Perceval's mother. Thinking her son had been killed she went mad and lived in the woods. Perceval found her. She recovered her sanity and went to live with him and Lufamour. ▣

ADDANC *see* AFANC ▣

ADDANZ

An ancestor of Perceval.[34] ▣

ADDAON

The son of Taliesen, he was noted for his wisdom; he was slain by Llongad Grwrm Fargod Eidyn.[17] ▣

ADELUF

The name of a number of persons mentioned in Rauf de Boun's *Petit Brut*. The first two were kings before Arthur's time. The third was a son of Arthur.[83] ▣

ADRAGAIN

A Knight of the Round Table who eventually became a hermit. ▣

ADVENTUROUS BED

A bed in the castle of Carbonek where Galahad slept and was wounded by a fiery lance. ▣

AEDD

The father of Prydein from whom Britain took its name in Welsh tradition. (There are also a number of Aedds referred to in Irish mythology.) ▣

AEGIDIUS

Roman count, ruler of Gaul AD 461–4. Jacques de Guise (fourteenth century) claims Arthur flourished when Aegidius ruled Gaul. Philippe de Vignelles (sixteenth century) suggests that Aegidius was in frequent contact with Arthur.[43] ▣

AELLE

Saxon King of Sussex who, with his sons Cymen, Wlencing and Cissa, defeated the Britons at Cymenes ora (AD 477). He fought against them once more near Mearc raedesburna (AD 485) and captured Anderida (modern Pevensey) about the year AD 491. According to Bede, he held the title Bretwalda ('Britain-ruler'), indicating a primacy among the Saxon kings. S.G. Wildman[163] suggests he led the Saxons at Badon; he was certainly flourishing at a time when he might have been a leading adversary of an historical Arthur. ▣

AENEAS

In Greek mythology, the son of Anchises by the goddess Aphrodite (Roman Venus). He was a member of the Trojan royal family and, according to Virgil, made his way to Italy after the fall of Troy, becoming an ancestor of the Emperor Augustus. Geoffrey of Monmouth asserts that he was an ancestor of the ancient British kings and Dryden specifically says that he was an ancestor of Arthur himself. ▣

AESC

An early ruler of Kent. He reigned from 488–512 in the Arthurian period. He may have been the son of Hengist. ▣

AFANC

A legendary Welsh monster which was overcome by Peredur (Perceval) who had been given a stone by the Empress of Constantinople which rendered him invisible to it.[17] Arthur himself killed an afanc at Llyn Barfog.[161] Another story tells how Hu Gadarn slew such a creature, but this tale is a late concoction as Hu Gadarn may have been invented by Iolo Morgannwg (1747–1826), who

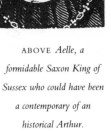

ABOVE *Aelle, a formidable Saxon King of Sussex who could have been a contemporary of an historical Arthur.*

~

ABOVE *Agravain approaches a pavilion, beside the bier sit a damsel and knight, from* Arthurian Legends, Lancelot Cycle *(French, c.1300). Agravain was the ill-fated brother of the Knight Gawain. His discovery of the adulterous relationship between Guinevere and Lancelot cost him his life.*

~

claimed that Hu Gadarn had led the Britons to Britain from Sri Lanka. As to the nature of the afanc, it seems to have had manipulative skills, as the one encountered by Peredur could throw spears. In modern Welsh *afanc* means a beaver; the mythical creature certainly had watery connections. The cognate Irish word *abhac* (dwarf) is derived from *ab*, modern *abha*, a river; J. Vendryes[152] claims it originally signified a spirit inhabiting waters. ▣

AGLOVALE
A brother of Perceval, killed when Lancelot carried off Guinevere. He was the father of Moraien.[19] ▣

AGNED, MOUNT
The site of one of Arthur's battles, mentioned by Nennius. Some manuscripts give the name Breguoin instead. *See* CASTLE OF MAIDENS. ▣

AGRAVADAIN
Husband of the mother of Ector de Maris. She gave birth to Ector after an adulterous affair with King Ban. ▣

AGRAVAIN
A son of Lot and Morgause, brother of Gawain. He married Laurel, the niece of Lionors and Lynette. He knew of the adultery of Lancelot and Guinevere and arranged for them to be found in compromising circumstances. He was slain by Lancelot, either when the pair were discovered or when Lancelot rescued Guinevere after she had been condemned to death.[19] ▣

AGRESTES
The ruler of Camelot in the time of Joseph of Arimathea. ▣

AGRESTIZIA
The name of Perceval's sister in *Tavola ritonda*. *See* DINDRANE. ▣

AGRICOLA
King of Dyfed (South Wales) around the year AD 500, in the traditional time of Arthur. Gildas thought him a good king. He may have liberated Dyfed from the Irish dynasty of the Uí Liatháin which had previously ruled there.[125] He may have been one of Arthur's commanders. *See* DEMETIA. ▣

AGUISANT
A nephew of Arthur. His mother was Arthur's sister, but we are not told her name. His father was called Karadan.[31] ▣

AGUYSANS *see* KING WITH A HUNDRED KNIGHTS. ▣

AHES *see* MORGAN. ▣

AILLEANN
In the Irish romance, *Visit of Grey Ham*, a woman of the Otherworld who had a tendency

to turn into a deer. She took Arthur and his men away to marry various Otherworld wives, wedding Arthur herself. In this work, Ailleann is given an interesting family tree as shown below. ▣

> ❋ THE FAMILY TREE OF AILLEAN ❋
>
> *King of Iceland*
> |
> *Ioruaidh*
> |
> *Daire, King of the Picts ~ Rathlean*
> |
> *Ailleann*

ALAN

The son of Brons and Enygeus, who did not marry and was made ruler of his brothers and sisters. In the *Didot Perceval* he was Perceval's father. He was told by the Holy Spirit that he would be the father of the Grail King.[9,31] He is also said to be a son of King Pellinore. ▣

ALANS *see* SARMATIANS. ▣

ALBANACT

The captain of Arthur's guard in Dryden's opera *King Arthur*. His name was presumably taken from Albanact, son of Brutus, in Geoffrey. ▣

ALBANIO

The hero of one of the books written by an obscure poet named Jegon. These form an unpublished continuation of Spenser's *Faerie Queene*. Albanio was knighted by Arthur. ▣

ALCARDO

A squire, brother of Iseult and companion of Tristan. Later known as Lantris, he was killed attempting to rescue his sister from Mark. ▣

ALCHENDIC

A giant who ruled the ancient city of Sarras, according to the *Prophécies de Merlin*. He had attained his eminence by killing the previous ruler. The folk of Sarras would not desert him, even when the city was menaced by Crusaders under King Richard of Jerusalem. He defeated four champions of the Crusaders and after this a truce ensued, followed a month later by Alchendic's baptism. ▣

ALCINA

An enchantress in the Italian romances of Boiardo and Ariosto. She was a sister of Morgan Le Fay.[2] ▣

ALCLUD

The old name for Dumbarton. Hoel, King of Brittany and Arthur's ally, was besieged there by the Picts and Scots until Arthur came to relieve him. ▣

ALDAN

In Welsh tradition, Merlin's mother, daughter of a nobleman of South Wales.[165] ▣

ALDERLEY EDGE

An elevation in Cheshire. According to a folk-tale, a farmer of Mobberley once had his horse purchased by a wizard for the use of a king and his knights who were slumbering beneath the Edge. The story was told by Parson Shrigley

LEFT *According to folk legend, Arthur and his Knights stopped at Alderley Edge in Cheshire.*

~

ABOVE *Floriant*
chivalrously rids Queen
Alemandine's kingdom of a
troublesome wild beast.

~

(died 1776) who maintained the events had occurred about eighty years before his time. In a rhyming version by J. Roscoe the king is identified as Arthur. Alan Garner used the story in his novel *The Weirdstone of Brisingamen* (1960). ▣

ALDROENUS
King of Brittany, he sent his brother Constantine, Arthur's grandfather, to rule the Britons at their request.[11] ▣

ALEMANDINE
A queen whose kingdom was plagued by the depredations of a wild beast until Floriant quelled it. However, Floriant did still not accept an offer of Alemandine's hand in marriage. ▣

ALEXANDER THE GREAT
King of Macedonia 336–323 BC. He conquered the Persian Empire and died at Babylon. Alexander was much celebrated in medieval romance. In *Perceforest* he is an ancestor of Arthur as the result of an affair with Sebille, the Lady of the Lake in his time.[75] ▣

ALEXIUS *see* ALIS. ▣

ALFASEIN
Baptismal name of Kalafes. ▣

ALICE
Called 'the Beautiful Pilgrim', she was the wife of Alisander.[19] ▣

ALIFATIMA
The King of Spain, a follower of Lucius. He was killed fighting against Arthur, during the latter's campaign against the Romans.[11] His name probably originated from Moorish influence in Spain in the Middle Ages. ▣

ALIS
The Byzantine emperor who, in *Cliges*, married Fenice with whom, unfortunately, Cligés, his nephew, was in love. Alis is a form of Alexius, a name borne by a number of Byzantine emperors. ▣

ALISANDER THE ORPHAN
Son of Baldwin, Mark's brother, by his wife Anglides. Mark had murdered his father. He was imprisoned by Morgan Le Fay but Alice the Beautiful Pilgrim helped him to gain his freedom and they subsequently married. Alisander was welcomed at Arthur's court.[19] ▣

ALOIS

King of Northgalis. He went to war with Amoraldo, King of Ireland, who was supported by Lancelot. Tristan supported Alois. In due course, through the interventions of Guinevere and Iseult, the two leaders were reconciled.[85]

ALON

A grand-nephew of Arthur, he became a Knight of the Round Table.

ALVREZ *see* MIROET *and* KAMELIN.

AMANT

A knight of Mark who accused his royal master of treachery. Trial by combat ensued, in which Mark proved the victor.

AMAZONS

The name of a famous race of warrior women in Greek mythology. Medieval legend claimed they were, in origin, Goths who, under Marpesia, formed an army of women and travelled to Africa by way of the Caucasus.[55] It was only to be expected that they would surface from time to time in Arthurian romance. Thus, Tristan the Younger rescued their queen from the king of the Idumeans. They fought with Gawain and their queen was slain by the Crop-eared Dog. The *Morte Arthure* says they were subjects of Arthur's foe, Lucius. In Spenser's poem *The Faerie Queene* their queen, Radigund, was killed by Britomart.

AMBROSIUS AURELIUS

According to Nennius, this was the fatherless child whom Vortigern intended to sacrifice. Geoffrey of Monmouth, however, maintained that Ambrosius the child was identical with Merlin and distinct from Ambrosius Aurelius. Nennius in fact contradicts himself by saying

Ambrosius was a Roman consul's son. His career, as outlined by Geoffrey, is as follows. When his brother, King Constans of Britain, was murdered by Vortigern he was smuggled to Brittany, whence he returned to Britain with his brother, Uther, anxious to seize the throne from the usurper. He laid siege to Vortigern's tower and burnt it down, thereby causing Vortigern's death. He defeated the Saxons and then had their leader, Hengist, killed. Paschent, Vortigern's son, made war against him and had him poisoned by a Saxon, Eopa.

According to the fifteenth-century poet, Rhys Goch Eryri, his head was buried beneath Dinas Emrys.

That Ambrosius was a genuine historical character is not in doubt. Gildas, who calls him Ambrosius Aurelianus (certainly the more correct form of his name) claims he began the fighting that eventually ended the Saxon attacks. It has even been suggested that he is the original of Arthur, though Geoffrey says that he is his nephew.[11,21,45]

AMBROY OYSELET

A knight in Lovelich's *Merlin* whose existence is due to a misunderstanding by the author who thought the French phrase *oiseau au brai* was a personal name.

AMENE

A queen whose kingdom had almost entirely been conquered by Roaz. Arthur sent Wigalois to aid her.[33] *See* LAR.

AMFORTAS

Known as the Grail King/Fisher King in Wolfram. The son of the Grail King Frimutel, he was wounded in the scrotum by an envenomed spear while jousting. He was carried into the presence of the Grail where he awaited the

BELOW An Amazon battle scene, c.460 BC. Originating in Greek mythology, this strong athletic race of warrior women also feature in Arthurian legend.

~

coming of the questioner (Perceval) who would ask the question about the Grail and thus restore him to health. Amfortas is called Anfortas in Wagner's opera *Parzival*. His name may be derived from Latin *infirmitas*.[34] ▣

AMHAR *see* AMR. ▣

AMINABAD
The son of Joshua and an ancestor of Arthur in the pedigree of John of Glastonbury. Father of Castellors. ▣

AMITE
In French romance, the name of Galahad's mother.[158] ▣

AMLAWDD WLEDIG
According to Welsh sources, the father of Igraine (Eigyr), the mother of Arthur. Amlawdd is also credited with being the father of Goleuddydd and Rieingulid who were, respectively, the mothers of Arthur's cousins, Culhwch and Illtyd. Amlawdd's wife was called Gwen. The word *wledig* is a title meaning, roughly, 'chief', perhaps used as a Celtic translation of the Latin title *protector*. ▣

AMOROLDO
In the *Tavola ritonda*, the son of Marhaus. He was made a knight by Tristan. In due course he ascended the throne of Ireland and became involved in a war with King Alois of Northgalis. Tristan supported Amoroldo, Lancelot supported Alois. However, Iseult and Guinevere brought about a rapprochement between the two knights. Amoroldo was eventually slain by Lancelot.

The name Amoroldo is Italian for Marhaus, and the name is used for both father and son in the Italian romance.[85] ▣

ABOVE *Celtic motifs frequently occur in grotesque ornaments such as this.*

~

AMR
According to Nennius, the son of Arthur, probably identical with Amhar, son of Arthur mentioned in the *Mabinogion*. The form Amr is preferable to Anir, which is also found. Nennius says that Arthur killed him at Archenfield and that he was buried under a mound called Licat Anir.[21] ▣

AMREN
The son of Bedivere. ▣

AMUSTANT
The chaplain to Guinevere, he had originally been chaplain to her father. He eventually became an anchorite. ▣

AMYTANS
A wise man who scolded Arthur in *Lancelot of the Laik* (an anonymous fifteenth-century Scottish poem). In the French original he is unnamed. ▣

ANDRED
Resident at Mark's court, he was a cousin of Tristan on whom he spied, eventually betraying him and Iseult to Mark. He hailed originally from Lincoln. ▣

ANDRIVETE
The daughter of King Cador of Northumberland. On her father's death her uncle, Ayglin, tried to get rid of her by marrying her off to someone unsuitable, but she thwarted his designs by escaping and marrying Kay. With Arthur's support she was all set to overthrow her uncle but then the people of Northumberland forced him to surrender before any violence could occur.[157] ▣

ANFORTAS *see* AMFORTAS. ▣

ANGELICA

The mother, by Arthur, of the illegitimate Tom a' Lincoln.[28]

ANGHARHAD GOLDEN-HAND

The lover of Peredur (Perceval) in the *Mabinogion*. At first she refused to be his lover and he vowed that he would never to speak to any Christian until she changed her mind. Lady Guest, in her edition of the *Mabinogion*, suggests that Angharad's epithet indicated generosity.[17]

ANGIS

A squire of Lancelot.

ANGLIDES

Mother of Alisander the Orphan. After her husband's murder by King Mark, Anglides raised her son secretly.[19]

ANGLITORA

The daughter of Prester John, she eloped with Tom a' Lincoln. Their son was the Black Knight. She abandoned Tom and later murdered him, but he was avenged by the Black Knight.[28]

ANGUISEL *see* ANGUISH.

ANGUISH

King of Ireland and father of Iseult. His name seems to be genuinely Irish in origin, a form of Oengus.

Surprisingly, at the time in question, a King Oengus is thought to have been reigning at Cashel, in the south of Ireland. There may be some confusion with the Scottish king Auguselus in Geoffrey; this name is also found in the form Anguisel.[19]

ANJOU

A French province which was conquered by Vortigern and given to Hengist. Kay, Arthur's seneschal, was its first count. In Wolfram, Herzeloyde was its queen.

ANNA

In Geoffrey, the full sister of Arthur. Geoffrey seems confused about whom she married; he says he wed Lot, but also that she married King Budic of Brittany. L.A. Paton quotes a source which says she was also called Ermine and that she married Budic while her sister married Lot.[131] Miss Paton wonders if she is to be identified with Morgan. The possibility that she was derived from the Celtic goddess Anu cannot be ruled out.[11] *See* BEUNO.

ANNOWRE

A sorceress who got Arthur into her power as she wished him to be her lover, but he would not comply.

ANNWFN

The Celtic Otherworld. An early Welsh poem, *Preiddeu Annwfn*, tells how Arther led a raid there, apparently to carry off the cauldron to be found in that region. The narrator of the story is Taliesin, one of those who took part in the expedition. Those involved sailed overseas in the ship *Prydwen* to reach their goal. They reached the fort or city of the Otherworld, called by a number of names (Caer Rigor, Caer Siddi, etc.), but only seven returned. The language of the poem is obscure. The expedition of Arthur to Ireland in *Culhwch* may be another version of this story, Ireland being substituted for the Otherworld. It is not impossible that the original story told how Arthur obtained Excalibur from the Otherworld.[23]

ABOVE *THE LADY OF THE LAKE WITH ANNOWRE'S HEAD*, William Russell Flint, from Malory's Le Morte d'Arthur. *The evil witch Annowre was slain by Lancelot.*

~

ANTHEMIUS

A Roman emperor who ruled AD 467–72. *See* RIOTHAMUS.

ANTIKONIE

Lover of Gawain and sister of King Vergulaht of Ascalun in Wolfram.[34]

ANTONY

An Irish bishop, secretary to Merlin in Continental romance.[85]

ANTOR

Arthur's foster-father in French sources, his name possibly being a variant of Ector.

APOLLO *see* LIONES.

AQUITAIN *see* MELOT.

ARAVIUS, MOUNT

The home of the giant Rience (Ritho), also called Mount Aravia, nowadays known as Snowdonia.

ARAWN

The name Arawn is used to translate Auguselus, the brother of Urien, in a Welsh version of Geoffrey. The *Triads*, also makes mention of an Arawn, son of Kynvarch. In Welsh tradition Arawn was the name of the king of Annwfn, but it may also have been the name of Urien's brother in Welsh legend before Geoffrey wrote his *Historia*.[29]

ARCHENFIELD

The burial place of Amr, son of Arthur. *See* LICAT ANIR.[21]

ARCILE

A companion of Morgan according to *Li jus Aden* (a French thirteenth-century manuscript).

ARDAN

In French romance, an uncle of Arthur.

ARDERYDD *see* ARTHURET.

ARES

The father of Do and the grandfather of Griflet and Lorete.

ARGAN

A personage with whose wife Uther was in love. Uther defeated him and forced him to build a castle.

ARGANTE

The Queen of Avalon, an elf, to whom, according to Layamon, Arthur went after his last battle. It has been suggested that she was a form of the British goddess Arianrhod.

ARGISTES

When Merlin was a boy (according to Italian romance), he prophesied that this man would be hanged, drowned and burned. Argistes set fire to Merlin's house. The fire spread to his own, so he rushed to the well, but the chain entwined itself about his neck. As he was in the well, people threw in burning rafters. Thus he died in the way Merlin had foretold.[85] ▣

ARGUS

In *Y Saint Greal*, the Welsh version of the Grail story, another son of Elaine, the mother of Galahad.[35] ▣

ARGUTH

An ancestor of Lot.[14] ▣

ARIANHROD *see* ARGANTE. ▣

ARIES

In Malory, a cowherd who raised Tor, son of King Pellinore, whom he believed to be his own child. In French romance, he was a king and the real father of Tor.[11] ▣

ARNIVE

In Wolfram, Arthur's mother who was rescued by Gawain from the clutches of Klingsor.[34] ▣

ARON

One of the Twenty-four Knights of Arthur's Court.[29] ▣

ART AOINFHEAR

In the Irish romance entitled *Caithrĕim Conghail Clăiringnigh* (edited by P. M. McSweeney and published by the Irish Texts Society), the son of Arthur. In other Irish material, this Art was the son of King Conn of the Hundred Battles, a legendary god, who was thought to have reigned in prehistoric times. ▣

ARTGUALCHAR *see* ARTEGALL. ▣

ARTEGALL

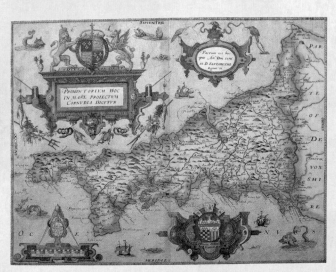

This personage occurs for the first time in Geoffrey where, as Artgualchar, he is described as an earl or count of Guarensis (Warwick). Richard Grafton, in his Chronicle at Large (1569), says he was a Knight of the Round Table and first Earl of Warwick. Spenser says he was the son of King Cador of Cornwall and bore the arms of Achilles. Spenser further tells us that he married Britomart, the warrior maiden, daughter of King Rience.

RTHUR

Legendary King of Britain, the traditions and literary compositions about whom form the subject matter of this work. ▣

1. **NAME**. The name Arthur may be (and according to K. H. Jackson[109] certainly is) a form of Artorius, a Roman *gens* name, but, according to J. D. Bruce,[64] it is possibly of Celtic origin, coming from *artos viros* (bear man) – *see* Welsh *arth gwyr* (T. R. Davies).[73] Bruce also suggests the possibility of a connection with Irish *art* (stone). ▣

2. **LIFE**. Arthur is not mentioned by any contemporary and his historicity cannot be regarded as certain. Milton (*History of England*) reckoned him a fiction, but Gibbon (*Decline and Fall of the Roman Empire*) felt there might be substance behind the legend. Modern opinion tends to echo Gibbon. The earliest mention of Arthur is in the *Gododdin* (sixth century) of Aneirin, but it is possible that the line alluding to Arthur may not have formed part of the original. Nennius (early ninth century) links Arthur's name with a succession of battles but does not describe him as a king, saying that he came to the aid of various British rulers.

An outline of the hero's life is given by Geoffrey of Monmouth (twelfth century) in his *Historia Regum Brittaniae*. Just how much of this life was Geoffrey's invention and how much was culled from traditional material is uncertain. He tells us that King Arthur was the son of Uther and defeated the barbarians in a dozen battles. Subsequently, he conquered a wide empire and eventually went to war with the Romans. He returned home on learning that his nephew Mordred had raised the standard of rebellion and taken Guinevere, the queen. After landing, his final battle took place.

MERLIN TAKETH THE CHILD ARTHVR INTO HIS KEEPING

RIGHT *MERLIN TAKETH THE CHILD ARTHUR INTO HIS KEEPING, Aubrey Beardsley (1872-98), from Le Morte d'Arthur (1909). According to Malory's fifteenth-century account Arthur was the son of Uther and Igraine.*

~

The saga built up over the centuries and Celtic traditions of Arthur reached the Continent via Brittany. Malory (fifteenth century) produced a huge Arthuriad that many would regard as the standard 'history' of Arthur. In this, we are told of Arthur's conception when Uther approached Igraine who was made, by Merlin's sorcery, to resemble her husband. The child was given to Ector to be raised in secret. After Uther's death there was no king ruling all England. Merlin had placed a sword in a stone, saying that whoever drew it out would be king. Arthur did so and Merlin had him crowned. This led to a rebellion by eleven rulers which Arthur put down. He married Guinevere whose father gave him the Round Table as a dowry; it became the place where his knights sat, to avoid quarrels over precedence. A magnificent reign followed, Arthur's court becoming the focus for many heroes. In the war against the Romans, Arthur defeated the Emperor Lucius and became emperor himself. However, his most illustrious knight, Lancelot, became enamoured of Guinevere and an affair between them followed. The quest for the Holy Grail took place and Lancelot's intrigue with the queen came to light. Lancelot fled and Guinevere was sentenced to death. Lancelot rescued her and took her to his Continental realm; this led to Arthur crossing the Channel to make war on his former knight. While away from Britain he left his natural son Mordred in charge. (Mordred was also his nephew, the result of an unwittingly incestuous affair between Arthur and his sister Morgause. Arthur had been unaware of the incestuous nature of the intrigue because he was ignorant of his own parentage.) Mordred rebelled and Arthur returned to quell him. This led to Arthur's last battle on Salisbury Plain, where he slew Mordred but was himself gravely wounded. (In Welsh accounts, the site of this battle is called Camlann.) Arthur was then carried off in a barge, saying he was heading for the vale of

ABOVE *The enthroned Arthur, from* Lancelot du Lac *(French, early fourteenth century).*

~

LEFT THE MARRIAGE OF KING ARTHUR TO GUINEVERE, *John H. Bacon. On their marriage Arthur received the Round Table as Guinevere's dowry.*

~

Avilion (Avalon). Some said he never died, but would one day return. However, his grave was supposedly discovered at Glastonbury in the reign of Henry II (1154–89).

One of the most mysterious aspects of Arthur's reign involves his relationship with Morgan Le Fay. In Malory she is his sister but, when Geoffrey mentions her in the *Vita Merlini*, he seems to know nothing of the kinship, nor does he mention any enmity between them. This seems to be a later development. It has been suggested that Arthur was originally her lover and only latterly her brother, but such a suggestion is unsupported by evidence. Whether Morgan is in origin identical with Arthur's sister (Anna in Geoffrey) cannot be decided with certainty. In *The Mists of Avalon* by Marion Zimmer Bradley (1982), Morgan is the sister with whom Arthur unknowingly commits incest – this is not implausible. Morgan's enmity towards Arthur is generally taken to spring from the fact that Arthur's father, Uther, killed her father, Gorlois. (See Boorman's film *Excalibur* (1981).)

The actual status or title of Arthur is also uncertain. He is usually styled a king, sometimes an emperor and, in Rosemary Sutcliffe's novel *Sword at Sunset* (1963), he is represented as turning Britain into the last vestige of the Western Roman Empire. It is certainly not impossible that he did so. Nennius does not speak of him as a king but as *dux bellorum* (leader of wars), a title which suggests he held a Roman-invented designation such as *Dux Brittaniarum* (leader or 'duke' of the Britons). Apart from his title, the question of where Arthur functioned also arises. Various persons have favoured the view that he was a leader in the north, in the south-west, in Wales or throughout Britain, but the truth of the matter is that we cannot be certain.

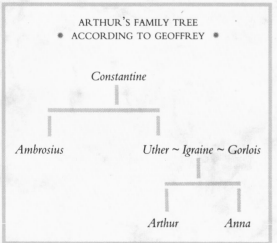

ARTHUR'S FAMILY TREE
✳ ACCORDING TO GEOFFREY ✳

Constantine

Ambrosius   *Uther ~ Igraine ~ Gorlois*

Arthur   *Anna*

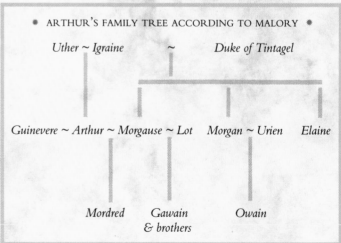

✳ ARTHUR'S FAMILY TREE ACCORDING TO MALORY ✳

Uther ~ Igraine   *~*   *Duke of Tintagel*

Guinevere ~ Arthur ~ Morgause ~ Lot   *Morgan ~ Urien*   *Elaine*

Mordred   *Gawain*   *Owain*
              & brothers

Nennius's list of battles does not really help, as some or even all of them may not have been originally associated with Arthur. ▣

3. **DATE**. The date of Arthur's death is given by Geoffrey as AD 542. Malory places his life in the fifth century. Geoffrey Ashe puts forward the argument that Arthur is, at least to some extent, to be identified with the historical Celtic king Riothamus. If this is so, he would have flourished in the fifth century. It is not impossible that the legendary Arthur is a composite of a number of persons so called, living at different times. ▣

4. **FAMILY**. Arthur is given as having various ancestors, descendants and kinsfolk. His family tree given by Geoffrey is shown at the foot of page 42. A later family tree, found in Malory is also shown.

The *Morte Arthure* calls Igraine's first husband Hoel and their daughters Blasine, Belisent and Hermesent.

As to Arthur's ancestry, his grandfather, Constantine, is given the pedigree, shown right, by the priest Gallet.

The ancestry of Igraine, Arthur's mother, is given thus by John of Glastonbury:

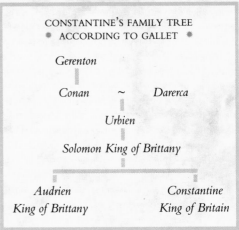

CONSTANTINE'S FAMILY TREE ✴ ACCORDING TO GALLET ✴

Gerenton

Conan ~ Darerca

Urbien

Solomon *King of Brittany*

Audrien *King of Brittany* Constantine *King of Britain*

In the maternal pedigree of Arthur which was provided by Gruffudd Hiraethog (sixteenth century), the anonymous son is replaced by Amlawdd who was the father of Igraine in Welsh tradition. This pedigree differs from the one above and is as follows:

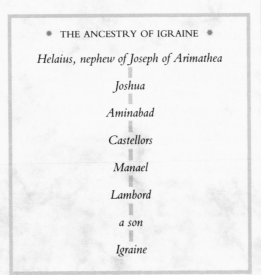

✴ THE ANCESTRY OF IGRAINE ✴

Helaius, nephew of Joseph of Arimathea

Joshua

Aminabad

Castellors

Manael

Lambord

a son

Igraine

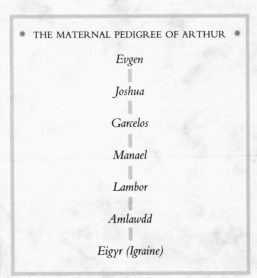

✴ THE MATERNAL PEDIGREE OF ARTHUR ✴

Evgen

Joshua

Garcelos

Manael

Lambor

Amlawdd

Eigyr (Igraine)

IN *BONEDD Y ARWYR* THE
FOLLOWING MATERNAL
❋ PEDIGREE OF ARTHUR IS FOUND ❋

Llyr

Bran

Kradoc

Evdaf

Kynan

Kadien

Gwrvawr

Ffrwdwr

Kynwal

Amlawdd

Eigyr (Igraine)

Arthur

THE SAME WORK CONTAINS TWO PATERNAL PEDIGREES
OF ARTHUR AND A FURTHER PATERNAL
❋ PEDIGREE IS FOUND IN MOSTYN MS 117. THESE ARE AS FOLLOWS: ❋

MOSTYN MS 117	*BONEDD YR ARWR-1*	*BONEDD YR ARWR-2*
Llyr	Llyr	Llyr
Bran	Bran	Bran
Karadawc	Karadoc	Karadoc
Kynan	Turmwr Morvawr	Evdaf
Kadwr	Tutwal	Kynan
Eudaf	Kynor	Kadienn
Moruawr	Kustennin	Morvawr
Tutwal	Uther	Tudwal
Kynuawr	Arthur	Kynnvor
Kustenhin		Kustenin
Uther		Uther
Arthur		Arthur

The ancestors of Arthur seem to be taken from the royal line of the kingdom of Dumnonia (Devon and Cornwall) and it has been argued that Geoffrey was the first to connect him with this line.

In *Brut y Brenhinedd*, a medieval Welsh history, an alternative maternal pedigree is given thus:

Cunedda
|
Gwen
|
Eigyr (Igraine)
|
Arthur

Another pedigree of Arthur is supplied by Wolfram:

Mazadan ~ Terdeleschoye
|
Brickus
|
Uther
|
Arthur

Arthur is given the following children by various sources: sons – Loholt, Llacheu, Borre, Arthur the Little, Mordred, Rowland, Gwydre, Amr, Adeluf, Morgan the Black, Ilinot, Patrick the Red; daughters – Melora, Ellen, Gyneth.

5. SURVIVAL. Arthur's survival after death was believed in by many Britons who awaited his return. He was thought to have journeyed to Avalon (a Celtic paradise) or to be lying asleep in a cave somewhere, awaiting arousal. The finding of his possible grave at Glastonbury did not extinguish these beliefs.

ABOVE *ARTHUR'S TOMB (1854), Dante Gabriel Rossetti (1828-82). Such was the power of the legend of Arthur that many believed in his survival after death.*

LEFT *Damsel comes to the Court of Arthur who is seated at table, from Guiron le Courtois (Flemish, late fifteenth century). This painting illustrates the popular view of the lavish richness and pageantry of Arthur's Court.*

~

6. ATTRACTION OF THE LEGEND OF ARTHUR. We must consider the allure of Arthur's saga and why he is so widely known when compared with other national heroes, such as the Russian Ilya Muromets, the Serbian Prince Marco, etc. To some extent the lines of transmission assisted the legend. It was originally adopted from the Bretons by their neighbours, the Normans, who travelled far and wide and took it with them. But another factor is the magical echoes of the legend that convey a sense of the mysterious, the otherworldly, the intangible that is absent elsewhere and which renders them unique.

See ACCOLON, ACHEFLOUR, AEGIDIUS, AENEAS, CADOC, FFYNNON CEGIN ARTHUR, GIANT OF MONT ST MICHEL, GREAT SPIRITS SPRING, GWYDDBWYLL, PARIS, SEVEN KINGS OF CORNWALL, TY-NEWYDD STANDING STONES.

ARTHUR OF BRITTANY

A descendant of Lancelot, the hero of a romance in which he seeks the hand of Florence, daughter of the king of Sorlois; this place is found in what is now modern Iraq.[75]

ARTHUR OF DALRIADA

The son of Aedan mac Gabrain, King of Dalriada. Although he lived somewhat later than the traditional dates of Arthur, R. Barber has argued in favour of his being the Arthur of legend.[49]

ARTHUR THE LITTLE

In the *Prose Tristan* he is an illegitimate son of Arthur whose mother had been raped by Arthur. He supported Arthur against his Cornish and Saxon foes and went on the Grail Quest.[158]

ARTHUR'S BATTLES

Nennius gives us a series of battles in which Arthur led the British side. There is no certainty that any of the battles were originally associated with Arthur. They are listed as follows:

1. At the mouth of the River Glein. There are two English rivers called Glen, either of which might be the site.

2–5. The River Douglas in Linnuis (K.H. Jackson[109] thinks Linnuis might be Lindsey).

6. On the River Bassus (location unknown).

7. At Cat Coit Celidon in the north, the region called Silva Caledoniae (Wood of Scotland) in Latin.

8. At Guinnion (location unknown).

9. At the City of the Legions, identified as Chester (called *Urbs Legionis* in Latin).

10. At the River Tribuit (possibly in Scotland).

11. At Mount Agned (K.H. Jackson[109] suggests High Rochester for this). In one tenth-century manuscript it is called Breguoin, but there may be confusion here with a victory ascribed elsewhere to Urien of Rheged.

12. Badon.[46,109]

ARTHUR'S CAVE

A cave on Anglesey where Arthur was thought to have taken shelter during his strife with the Irish. His treasure may have been hidden in a cromlech, surrounded by stones, which once stood there. The treasure was said to be guarded by supernatural creatures.

ARTHUR'S INSIGNIA

Nennius tells us that, at the battle of Guinnion, Arthur had an image of the Virgin Mary on his shoulders. The *Annales Cambriae* claim that Arthur carried the cross on his shoulders at Badon. At Stow in Scotland the Church of St

Mary at Wedale once had what were believed to be fragments of the image of the Virgin Mary that Arthur wore.[1,21] ▣

ARTHUR'S O'ON

A Roman temple (second century AD) near Falkirk, Scotland. It was pulled down in 1743, but the dovecote at Penicuick House, close at hand, was built as a replica of it. N.L. Goodrich[87] argues that the temple was used by Arthur and was the original of the Round Table. Interestingly, a suburb of Falkirk is called Camelon. ▣

ARTHUR'S OVEN

Some French priests were shown this in 1113. While it cannot be identified with certainty, it undoubtedly lay west of Exeter. King's Oven on Dartmoor has been suggested as its site. ▣

ARTHUR'S SEAT

Mountain at Edinburgh. The sleeping Arthur is said to lie in a cavern inside it, with his knights about him. The name 'Arthur's Seat' is also borne by a number of other elevations. ▣

ARTHURS, SUCCESSION OF

B. Le Poer Trench in his book, *Men among Mankind* (1962), argues that there was a series of Arthurs, hereditary priests of the Great Goddess, and that the last was identical with Arviragus. He accepts the identification of Arthur with Arviragus which J. Whitehead[162] proposed. ▣

ARTHUR'S STONE

1. A stone in Gower, Wales. It is said that, on his way to his final battle, Arthur removed this stone from inside his shoe and flung it into the distance. The stone landed at Cefn-y-Bryn. ▣

2. A stone at Dorstone (Herefordshire) from which Arthur was said to have drawn Excalibur. There is a confusion here; Excalibur was not the original sword in the stone. It is also said that Arthur is buried beneath the stone or that it marks the burial place of a king overcome by Arthur. ▣

ARTHUR'S TOR

A Country Durham earthwork, said to contain treasures guarded by the ghosts of Arthurian warriors.[164]

ARTHURET

(In Welsh: Arderydd) The scene of a battle fought about the year AD 575 in which Rhydderch Hael defeated Gwenddolau. Merlin is said to have taken part in the battle – traditions vary as to the side he was on – and to have lost his sanity because of a vision he saw in the sky there.[12]

ARVIRAGUS

A personage who became known to history because of an obscure reference by the Roman writer Juvenal, made between the years AD 80 and 90, in which Arviragus appears as a British opponent of the Romans. Geoffrey makes him a king of Britain who succeeded his brother Guiderius who had been killed in Claudius's invasion of Britain (AD 43). Peace was established between Claudius and Arviragus, the latter marrying Claudius's daughter, Genvissa.

Later, Arviragus revolted, but peace was restored through Genvissa's good offices. Elsewhere Arviragus was thought to have given Joseph of Arimathea the famous twelve hides of land in the Glastonbury locality. G. Ashe thinks Arviragus may have been a local prince in the Somerset area who maintained his independence after the Claudian conquest.[42] I.H. Elder identifies him with Caratacus, while E. Ratcliffe[132] and J. Whitehead[162] all argue that Arviragus, Caratacus and Arthur were different names for the same person.[11]

See ARTHURS, SUCCESSION OF *and* MARIUS.

ASCALUN *see* VERGULAHT.

ASSURNE

A river. *See* SURLUSE.

ASSYSLA

In the *Breta sogur* (the Scandinavian version of Geoffrey of Monmouth's works), an island on which Arthur died.

ASTLABOR

Alternative form of Esclabor.

ASTOLAT

Dwelling place of Elaine the White who died of love for Lancelot. The name may come from Alclud, the old name for Dumbarton, through an intermediary Asclut. In Malory it is Guildford (Surrey).[19] *See* SHALOTT.

ATHRWYS

In the shady area of early Welsh history, he may have been King of Gwent when his father, Meurig, was King of Glenvissig. He is identified by Blackett and Wilson[52,53] with the Arthur of legend, but he probably lived in the seventh century.

ATLANTIS
In the writings of Plato, the name of an island which sank beneath the Atlantic Ocean. Some have argued that Plato was recounting a genuine legend, while a different body of opinion has contended that the story is a moral fable. According to G. Knight[101] some occultists maintain that Merlin originally came from Atlantis. The same is said of Igraine.[117]

AUDRIEN *see* ALDROENUS.

AUGUSELUS
In Geoffrey, he is designated the King of Scotland. He was Urien's brother, possibly called Arawn in Welsh tradition. He supported Arthur in his Roman campaign but, on his

ABOVE *Sea horse. Both Merlin and Igraine may have come from the sea-covered city of Atlantis.*

~

return, fell by the hand of Mordred.[11]
See ANGUISH.

AURELIUS AMBROSIUS
see AMBROSIUS AURELIUS.

AURELIUS CONAN
According to Geoffrey, the king who ruled Britain after Constantine, Arthur's successor. Gildas, a contemporary, makes Aurelius Conan and Constantine local kings, calling the former Aurelius *Caninus* and saying that he enjoyed war and plunder.[11]

AVAL
An island off the coast of Brittany where Arthur is supposed to be buried.

LEFT *ARTHUR IN AVALON*, Edward Burne-Jones (1833-98). *In this Pre-Raphaelite version of the death of Arthur, the composition, colour and imagery all make reference to Italian Renaissance religious paintings, creating a sombre and reverential tone.*

~

AVALLOC

William of Malmesbury maintains that Avalloc lived in Avalon with his daughters. Avalloc is also found in Welsh pedigrees in which he is the father of the goddess Modron; he was evidently a god himself in origin. He is found in Arthurian romance as Evelake.

AVALON

The island to which Arthur was taken after his last battle, to be healed of his wound. Geoffrey calls it Avallo in the *Historia* and insula pomorum (island of apples) in the *Vita Merlini*. It is often seen as having a connection with apples because of the similarity of its name to various Celtic words denoting that fruit: Old Irish *aball* Middle Welsh *afall*, Middle Breton *avallenn*, Celtic *avallo*. It has also been connected with Avalloc, evidently originally a god who, according to William of Malmesbury, lived there with his daughters. The present form of the name may have been influenced by the Burgundian place name Avallon. One school of thought suggests that it comes from Irish *oileán* (island). It was perhaps originally a Celtic paradise. It was said to produce crops without cultivation, to be ruled by Guingamuer, Morgan's lover, or by a king named Bangon. In *Perlesvaus*, Guinevere and Loholt died before Arthur and were buried there. Avalon was then identified with Glastonbury, probably because Arthur's grave was supposedly found at Glastonbury in the reign of Henry II and, as tradition had had him borne away to Avalon, the two were considered the same. However, because of the first syllable in Glastonbury's name, some may have thought it identical with Caer Wydyr, the Fort of Glass, another name for Annwfn. Another tradition claims that a man named Glast or Glasteing found his eight-footed pigs here under an apple tree, and called it Insula Avalloniae.

Not all tales suggested that Avalon was identical with Glastonbury. According to *Ogier le danois* (a medieval French romance with some Arthurian content), it lay near the Earthly Paradise. In the Spanish medieval poem *La Faula* it seems to be considered an oriental isle, for the narrator tells how he was carried to the East on the back of a whale and arrived at an island where Arthur and Morgan were still alive.

That Avalon seems to have had a connection with the pagan Celtic religion is supported by the fact that, in the *Vita Merlini*, Morgan is described as the chief of nine sisters living on the island – just like the nine Celtic priestesses able to turn into animals, heal the incurable and prophesy the future who lived on the Gaulish isle of Sena, according to the Roman writer Pomponius Mela. It is also noteworthy that, in Irish mythology, the name of the island over the seas belonging to the sea-god Manannán was Emhain Abhlach. [12,22,42,51,137]

AVENABLE *see* GRISANDOLE.

AVILION

An alternative name for Avalon, used by Malory and in modern times by Tennyson, who calls it 'the island-valley of Avilion'. The idea that it was a valley is found in both Malory and Ralph Higden's *Polychronicon* (fourteenth century).

AYGLIN

The uncle of Andrivete, she flouted his wishes by marrying Kay.

OVERLEAF

AVALON

Amanda Cameron

~

BABYLON
see THOLOMER.

BACH BYCHAN
The page of Tristan in the Welsh romance *Trystan*. His name means 'little small one'.

BADON
A battle in which Arthur was said to have totally defeated the Saxons. Gildas is the first to refer to it, but he does not mention Arthur by name. The date of the encounter is uncertain, but it is generally placed between AD 490 and 516, sometimes more specifically about AD 500. In *De excidio*, Gildas is ambiguous: his statement could be variously interpreted as meaning that the battle occurred in the year he was born, forty-four years before he wrote, forty-four years after the coming of the Saxons or forty-four years after the resurgence of the Britons under Ambrosius. As regards the first of these possibilities, it is worth noting that T.D. O'Sullivan in a recent study opines that Gildas wrote *De excidio* as a young man. Although Gildas does not name the British commander, both Nennius and the *Annales Cambriae* identify him as Arthur. So does Geoffrey, who regards Badon as identical with Bath. A recent linguistic argument, against this identification, by N.L. Goodrich[87] betrays insufficient knowledge of the Welsh language.

Other locational suggestions have been variously Liddington Castle near Swindon and Badbury Rings (Dorset). The battle is described as a siege, though it is not clear who was beleaguered by whom.[11,21,46,87]
See GREENAN CASTLE.

BAGDEMAGUS
King of Gore, a Knight of the Round Table and a cousin of Arthur. He seems to have been a benign character, but he took umbrage when Tor was made a Knight of the Round Table before him. His son was Meleagaunce and, when this character carried off Guinevere, Bagdemagus prevented him from raping her. At the time of the Grail Quest he took a special shield with a red cross on it, intended for Galahad, and for his pains he was wounded by a white knight. He was eventually killed by Gawain.[19,31]

BALAN
The younger brother of Balin. After killing a certain knight, he had to assume a guardian's rôle, fighting all comers in place of the knight whom he had slain. In this capacity he fought with Balin, neither recognizing the other. Each received a fatal wound.[19]

BALDULF
Brother of Colgrin, the Saxon leader. He was on his way to help his brother during the siege of York when his force was attacked by Cador and defeated. After this, he sneaked into York disguised as a minstrel. He was eventually slain at Badon.[11]

BALDWIN *see* BEDWIN.

BALIN
A famous knight, who was born in Northumberland. He had incurred Arthur's displeasure by killing a Lady of the Lake. However, he and his brother Balan captured Rience and became supporters of Arthur. When Pellam tried to kill him for slaying his brother Garlon, Balin struck Pellam with the Lance of Longinus. This was the Dolorous

Stroke. Balin was also known as the Knight of the Two Swords. He and his brother unwittingly killed each other.[19] Balin's name may be a variant of Brulen/Varlan who, elsewhere and long before Arthur's time, was thought to have struck the Dolorous Stroke.

See COLOMBE. ▨

BALOR

A one-eyed giant in Irish mythology who seems to be related to Yspadadden in *Culhwch*.[70] ▨

BAN

King of Gomeret or Benwick. He supported Arthur in the battle with the rebel leaders at the outset of Arthur's reign. His realm was on the Continent and, in return for his assistance, Arthur was to aid him against his foe, King Claudas. When Claudas destroyed Ban's castle at Trebes, he died of a broken heart. Ban's wife is usually called Elaine but, in the French medieval romance *Roman des fils du roi Constant*, she is named Sabe. In that romance, he has a daughter called Liban. His son Lancelot became Arthur's chief knight. Ban also had an illegitimate son, called Ector de Maris, whose mother was the wife of Agravadain. Ban's sword was called Courechouse. He was the brother of King Bors of Gaul. It has been suggested that he was, in origin, the god Bran and that the name Ban de Benoic (Ban of Benwick) was a corruption of Bran le Benoit (Bran the Blessed; see the *Mabinogion*, where Bran is called Bendigeidfran, Bran the Blessed). Ban's name has also been connected with Irish *bán* (white).[19,126] ▨

BANIN

King Ban's godson, a Knight of the Round Table. ▨

LEFT *King Ban asks Merlin to interpret the Queen's dream, from Lestoire de Merlin (Bologna, early fourteenth century). Ban was the King of Benwick and Gomeret.*

~

BARATON

The name of the King of Russia in Arthurian romance. ▨

BARUC

The ruler of Baghdad, with whom Gahmuret took service in Wolfram's *Parzifal*. In actual fact, the potentate denoted was the Caliph of Baghdad, head of Islam in the Middle Ages, an anachronism since the Arthurian period predated Mohammed. The title Baruc seems to come from the Hebrew personal name Baruch. In the *Livre d'Artus*, Baruc is the name of a knight.[34] ▨

BASSUS

The site of one of Arthur's battles was the River Bassus.[21] It has not been identified. ▨

BATRADZ *see* SARMATIANS. ▨

BAUDWIN

A knight whom Arthur made constable of his realm at the time of his accession. He was one of the governors of Britain while Arthur went to war with Rome. He later became a hermit and physician.[19] ▨

BEAROSCHE

The scene of a siege in Wolfram's *Parzifal*. Its lord, Duke Lyppaut, defended it against his sovereign, King Meljanz of Liz, who had gone to war because he had been piqued when he was rejected by the duke's daughter, Obie. Gawain fought on the side of the defenders, Perceval on that of the attackers. Peace was made in due course, Obie's little sister Obilot playing an important role.[34]

BEATRICE

The wife of Carduino, rescued by him from an enchantment.[85]

BEAUTÉ

Guinevere's maid who fell in love with Gliglois, Gawain's squire.

BEDEGRAINE

A forest, the site of a major battle between Arthur and rebel forces at the beginning of his reign. Malory identifies it as Sherwood or a part thereof. There was within it a castle of Bedegraine, loyal to Arthur, to which the rebels had laid siege before the battle.[19] *See* BRASTIAS.

BEDIVERE

(In Welsh: Bedwyr) He is one of Arthur's prominent followers in the earliest Welsh traditions. He helped Arthur to fight the Giant of Mont St Michel. In Geoffrey, he was made Duke of Neustria and perished in the Roman campaign. In Malory, he was present at Arthur's last battle. He and Arthur alone survived and he was charged with flinging Excalibur into the lake. He had only one hand. His son was called Amren, his daughter Eneuavc and his father Pedrawd. His grandfather was also called Bedivere and founded the city of Bayeux.[11,17,19]

BEDWIN

A bishop who appears in a number of Arthurian sources. In *The Triads* he is described as the chief bishop of Kelliwig.

Bedwin is identical with Bishop Baldwin, a companion of Gawain in *Sir Gawain and the Carl of Carlisle*. He is also mentioned by this name in *Sir Gawain and the Green Knight*. *See* ALISANDER THE ORPHAN.

BEDWYR *see* BEDIVERE.

BEK, ANTHONY

According to the historian G.M. Cowling,[164] it was said that, in 1283, Anthony Bek, bishop-elect of Durham, met Merlin while hunting in the forest.[164]

BELAGOG

According to one tradition, a giant who guarded Arthur's castle which was nothing more than a grotto.[164]

BELAYE

A princess of Lizaborye, she was Lohengrin's second wife.

BELCANE

The Queen of Zazamanc. She was the mother, by Gahmuret, of Feirefiz.[34]

BELI

A legendary early Briton, thought originally to have been a god. His daughter or sister was Penardun who, by Llyr, was the mother of Bran who was thought to have been Arthur's ancestor in both the male and female lines. According to Henry of Huntingdon, Beli was the brother of the historical British king Cunobelinus or Cymbeline (first century).[17] *See* BELINANT.

BELIDE

Daughter of King Pharamond of France, she became enamoured of Tristan but, as he did not requite her love, she died of lovesickness. ▣

BELINANT

The father of Dodinel. He may be, in origin, the Celtic god Beli. ▣

BELISENT

In *Arthour and Merlin* (a thirteenth-century English poem), a sister of Arthur who married Lot. *See* BLASINE *and* HERMESENT. ▣

BELLANGERE

The Earl of Laundes, he was the son of Alisander the Orphan and the killer of King Mark of Cornwall.[19] ▣

BELLEUS

A knight wounded by Lancelot in unfortunate circumstances. Chancing on Belleus's pavilion, Lancelot went to bed there. Then Belleus came to the bed and climbed in, mistaking the slumbering Lancelot for his lover. He embraced him and the shocked Lancelot arose and wounded him but, to atone for the harm he had done, he made him a Knight of the Round Table.[19] ▣

BELLICIES

In Italian romance, daughter of King Pharamond of Gaul; she fell in love with Tristan and, when her passion was unrequited, killed herself.[85] ▣

BENWICK

The Kingdom of Ban. *Lestoire de Merlin* (part of *Vulgate Version*) states that the town of Benwick was Bourges. Malory points out that Benwick is variously identified with Bayonne and Beaune. Saumur has also been suggested.[19] ▣

ABOVE *The giant Belagog.*
~

BERNARD OF ASTOLAT

Father of Elaine the White and Lavaine.[19] ▣

BERRANT LE APRES

see KING WITH A HUNDRED KNIGHTS. ▣

BERTHOLAI

Champion of the False Guinevere.[31] ▣

BERTILAK

The name of the Green Knight.[26] ▣

BETHIDES

The son of Perceforest, he made an unfortunate marriage to Circe. ▣

BETIS *see* PERCEFOREST. ▣

BEUNO

An important saint in North Wales. He was said to be the grandson of Arthur's sister Anna through her daughter Perferren. Beuno's popularity survived the Reformation.[50,80] ▣

BIAUSDOUS

Son of Gawain. He managed to unsheath the sword Honoree and thereby marry Biautei, daughter of the King of the Isles.[157] ▣

BIAUTEI *see* BIASDOUS. ▣

BISHOP OF THE BUTTERFLY
see PETER DES ROCHES. ▣

BLACK HORSE

S.G. Wildman[163] has propounded a theory that the black horse was the symbol of the Arthurian Britons, and that it is possible to find out where Arthurian influence prevailed by discovering the whereabouts of inns called the Black Horse. ▣

SIR BORS   SIR ECTOR   SIR TRISTRAM   SIR PALAMIDES   SIR LUCAN

RIGHT *The arms of the Knights of the Round Table.*

~

BLACK KNIGHT

1. A knight with whose wife Perceval had innocently exchanged a ring. The Black Knight, furious, tied her to a tree but Perceval overcame him and explained the situation, so that they were reconciled.

2. Arthur's grandson, the son of Tom a' Lincoln and Anglitora.

3. A warrior who guarded a horn and a wimple on an ivory lion. Fergus killed him.

4. Sir Percard, who was killed by Gareth.

5. One of Arthur's knights who was defeated by the Knight of the Lantern. He was the son of the King of the Carlachs.

BLAES

One of the twenty-four Knights of Arthur's Court, possibly identical with Blaise, the master of Merlin.[29]

BLAISE

A hermit, to whom Merlin's mother went when she was enceinte (pregnant). When Merlin was two, he dedicated to Blaise the story of the Grail. Blaise also wrote an account of Arthur's battles. He hailed originally from Vercelli

RIGHT *Lancelot wounded by the Black Knight (who wears blue), from* Lancelot du Lac *(French, early fourteenth century). In one legend the Black Knight is said to be Arthur's grandson.*

~

(Italy). He may be identical with the Blaes of *The Triads* in which he is called the son of the Earl of Llychlyn.[19,29,85]

BLAMORE DE GANIS

A Knight of the Round Table. On one occasion he accused King Anguish of Ireland of murder but he was defeated in trial by combat by Tristan. Afterwards, they became friends. When Lancelot quarrelled with Arthur, Blamore and his brother Bleoberis supported their father, Lancelot, and Blamore became Duke of Limousin. After Arthur died, Blamore became a hermit.[19]

BLANCHARD

The fairy steed of Lanval, given him by his lover Tryamour.[20]

BLANCHE-FLEUR

1. The mistress of Perceval. Besieged by King Clamadeus, who desired her, she would have killed herself but Perceval defeated him in single combat.[6]

BELOW LEFT *The Knight Bors, with the aid of magic, was tricked into relinquishing his virginity to the daughter of King Brandegoris.*

~

2. In Gottfried, the sister of King Mark; she eloped with Rivalin of Parmenie. Their son was Tristan. When she heard of her husband's death, she died of grief.[13] ▣

BLASINE
A sister of Arthur. She married Nentres of Garlot. Their son was Galachin, who became the Duke of Clarence.
See BELISENT *and* HERMESENT. ▣

BLENZIBLY
Tristan's mother in the Icelandic *Saga of Tristan and Isodd.* Her lover, Plegrus, was killed jousting with Kalegras who thereafter became her lover and Tristan's father.[99] ▣

BLEOBERIS
A Knight of the Round Table, brother of Blamore. He was defeated by Tristan when he abducted Segwarides's wife from Mark's court. He supported Lancelot, who was his relation, when the latter quarrelled with Arthur. He became Duke of Poitiers and eventually a Crusader.[19] ▣

BLIOCADRAN
Name given to Perceval's father in French romance. ▣

BLOIE
The name of the Lady of Malehaut. ▣

BLONDE ESMERÉE
Daughter of the King of Wales, turned into a serpent by the magicians Mabon and Evrain. She was eventually freed by Guinglain who kissed her. ▣

BORRE
The illegitimate son of Arthur by Lionors. When he grew up, he became a Knight of the Round Table. He is usually identified with Loholt.[11] ▣

BORS
1. The King of Gaul or Gannes and Arthur's ally in the battle against the rebel kings at Bedegraine. He married Evaine and they were the parents of the younger Bors.[19] *See* BAN.
2. Knight of the Round Table and son of the elder Bors, whom he succeeded as King of Gannes. He was a chaste knight, but the daughter of King Brandegoris fell in love with him. Her nurse forced Bors to make love to her with the aid of a magic ring. As a result, Bors became the father of Elyan the White, later Emperor of Constantinople. Bors was one of the three successful knights on the Grail Quest but, unlike Galahad and Perceval, he returned to Arthur's court and eventually died on crusade.

It has been suggested that, in origin, Bors may have been a character who figures in Welsh legend as Gwri.[19]
See TWENTY-FOUR KNIGHTS. ▣

BOSO

Ruler of Oxford, one of Arthur's vassals, who accompanied the king on his Roman campaign.[11]

BOUDIN

The father of Alisander the Orphan and brother of Mark of Cornwall who murdered him.[19]

BRABANT

A territory sited partially in the Netherlands and partially in Belgium. *See* LOHENGRIN.

BRADMANTE

According to Ariosto, this female warrior of the Carolingian era was told that the House of Este would descend from her.[2]

BRAN THE BLESSED

A hero of Welsh legend, originally a god, who was demoted after the advent of Christianity. Some of the information we have about him suggests that part of his legend went into the formation of the Arthurian tales. For example, he had a cauldron of plenty and was wounded in the foot by a poisoned spear, suggesting connections with the Grail and the Fisher King. Tradition states that his head was buried under the White Hill in London to protect the country but Arthur dug it up, as he wanted to be the sole guardian of Britain.

Bran had a son called Caratacus who was identified with the British leader of that name who opposed the Romans at the time of the Claudian invasion (AD 43). Bran himself – though not, perhaps, in an early tradition – was thought to have introduced Christianity to Britain. His father was Llyr and his mother Penardun. In *Bonedd yr Arwyr*, Bran is made both a paternal and maternal ancestor of Arthur. *See* BAN *and* THIRTEEN TREASURES.

ABOVE *The Welsh hero Bran, was wounded by a poisoned spear.*

~

DOUBLE DESCENT ✴ OF ARTHUR FROM BRAN ✴

Bran
|
Caradoc
|
Eudaf
|
Conan
|
Kadien
|
Morvawr★

Tudwal	Ffrwdwr
Kynnvor	Kynwal
Constantine	Amlawdd
Uther	Igraine

Arthur

★Morvawr, son of Kadien in the paternal pedigree, may be identical with Gwrvawr, son of Kadien in the maternal pedigree.[10,17,143]

BRANDEGORIS

King of Stranggore. One of the kings who rebelled against Arthur at the outset of his reign. It has been argued that his name means 'Bran of Gore' and that he was originally identical with the god Bran.[11] *See* ELYAN.

BRANDILES

Knight of the Round Table. His father was Sir Gilbert. He is mentioned in the Second Continuation of Chrétien's *Perceval* and the *Gest of Sir Gawain* in which he fought with Gawain, who had defeated his father and two brothers, as well as seducing his sister. In the

Gest, this fight was stopped to be resumed later, but the two never met again. In the Second Continuation, there was a second fight between the two which was haunted by Brandiles's sister who had Guinglain, her son by Gawain, with her. *See* BRIAN DES ILLES.

BRANGIEN
The maidservant of Iseult who, according to Gottfried, was very good-looking. When Iseult was on her way to Mark, Iseult's mother gave Brangien and Gouvernail a love potion to administer to the couple. Unfortunately, owing to a mistake, Tristan and Iseult drank it, thus precipitating their affair. On the night of her wedding Iseult substituted Brangien for herself so Mark would not guess she had already lain with Tristan. Subsequently, Iseult tried to have Brangien murdered to ensure her silence, but the attempt was unsuccessful and Iseult repented of it. Brangien later had an affair with Kaherdin, son of King Hoel of Brittany.[4,13]

BRAS-DE-FER
Chamberlain of Antichrist. The poet Huon de Mery in his work *Le tornoiement de l'Antechrist* tells how he went to the enchanted spring in Broceliande and Bras-de-Fer rode up. The poet and the chamberlain went to a battle where the forces of Heaven fought against the forces of Hell. Arthur and his knights fought on the side of Heaven.[67]

BRASTIAS
One of Arthur's Knights who was made a warden in the north of England and who fought at Bedegraine. He had originally been in the service of the Duke of Tintagel.[19]

BREDBEDDLE
A knight who assisted Arthur in the story of *King Arthur and the King of Cornwall*. When Arthur, Tristan, Gawain and Bredbeddle went to visit the King of Cornwall's abode, Bredbeddle, with the aid of a holy book, controlled a friend whom the king had sent to observe them.

BREGUION *see* AGNED.

BRENT KNOLL
This Somerset hill was the site of a battle between Yder and three giants who lived there. Accompanying Arthur, who sent him on ahead, Yder encountered the giants alone on the hill and, when Arthur and his followers arrived, the giants were dead, but unfortunately, so was Yder.

BREUNIS SAUNCE PYTÉ
One of Arthur's enemies, whom Gareth slew. P.A. Karr's *King Arthur Companion* comments on his ubiquitousness. He had originally been knighted by Arthur.[19]

ABOVE *Lancelot, Mad and Asleep, Enchanted by Brisen, William Russell Flint, from Malory's* Le Morte d'Arthur. *Another example of a recurring theme in the Arthurian Legends, that of mistaken or concealed identity between sexual partners.*

~

RIGHT *An early map showing Britain under the Romans.*

~

BREUNOR

Called the Black, Breunor arrived at Arthur's court wearing a coat that fitted him badly. He was given the nickname 'La Cote Male Tailée' (the badly-cut coat) by Kay. He would not take off the coat until he had avenged his father. He rendered assistance to the damsel Maladisant who at first hurled abuse at him, but eventually married him. He became lord of Pendragon Castle.[19] *See* DANIEL *and* DINADAN. ▣

BRIAN DES ILLES

In *Perlesvaus* we are told that, aided by Kay who had slain Arthur's son Loholt, he attacked Arthur's realm. He laid siege to Carduel but was eventually driven off by Lancelot. He was subsequently defeated by Arthur and then became his seneschal. He is perhaps identical with Brandiles in origin. It has been suggested that Brian is based on a historical person, Brian de Insula, illegitimate son of Alan Fergeant (eleventh century).[22] ▣

BRIANT OF THE RED ISLE, KING

The father of Tristouse. ▣

BRICKUS

In Wolfram, son of Mazadan and grandfather of Arthur.[34] ▣

BRISEN

When King Pelles wanted Lancelot to sleep with his daughter Elaine so that Galahad would be conceived, Brisen was the one who arranged this on two occasions. (Lancelot was under the misapprehension that Elaine was Guinevere.) ▣

BRITOMART

In Spenser's *Faerie Queene*, a warrior maiden who was the daughter of Arthur's foe, Rience. She married Artegall. Spenser took her name from that of the Cretan goddess Britomartis. The idea of a female knight may have been suggested to Spenser by Marfisa in Ariosto's *Orlando Furioso*.[27] *See* RADIGUND. ▣

BRITTANY

A territory which, in the Arthurian period, was largely inhabited by an immigrant population from Britain. In Geoffrey, the Breton royal family was closely related to the British. He tells us that the Breton kingdom was founded when the Roman emperor Maximianus (properly called Maximus, reigned AD 383–8) bestowed the crown on Conan Meriadoc, a nephew of Octavius, elsewhere called Eudaf, King of Britain. When the British wanted a king, Conan's successor, Aldroenus, gave them Constantine, his brother. Constantine was Arthur's grandfather. In the Arthurian legend, King Hoel of Brittany was said to be Arthur's relation and ally. Traditionally, this Hoel reigned from about AD 510–45. *See* SOLOMON. ▣

BROCELIANDE

A forest which is the setting for a number of Arthurian adventures. Situated in Brittany, it is now called the Forest of Paimpont.
See BRAS-DE-FER *and* ESCLADOS. ▣

BRONS

Also called Hebron, he was the husband of Enygeus, the sister of Joseph of Arimathea. They had twelve sons. He was given the Grail by Joseph. According to the *Didot Perceval*, Brons became the Rich Fisher. When he was cured, he was carried off by angels. This source also says he was Perceval's grandfather. He may be, in origin the god Bran.[9,31] *See* FISHER KING. ▣

BRITAIN

The realm ruled by Arthur. The island derives its name from the Priteni, the term the Picts used for themselves. The Roman province of Britain did not include Scotland (except for the Lowlands) though, in legend, Arthur, seen as the Romans' successor, ruled the entire island.

Legendary historians claimed the country was first ruled by Albion, a giant. The career of Albion was delineated in Holinshed's Chronicles (1577). Geoffrey does not mention him, but says the giants pre-dated men there. Subsequently, he says, the island was colonized by Brutus, a descendant of Aeneas, and remained independent until Roman times. Another tradition is found in the White Book of Rhydderch (fourteenth century). This says the country was first called Myrddin's (Merlin's) Precinct, then the Isle of Honey and finally named Prydein (Britain) after its conquest by Prydein, son of Aedd. Geoffrey does not mention this tradition, but it may predate him. Aedd may be identical with the Irish sun god, Aedh. It was also said that Prydein came from Cornwall and conquered Britain after the death of Porrex, one of the successors of Brutus in Geoffrey. Geoffrey may have known of traditions concerning Prydein, but may have felt they contradicted his story about Britain deriving its name from Brutus. Irish tradition said that Britain derived its name from Britain, son of Nemedius, who settled there.

Ordinary history tells us little about Britain before Roman times. Archaeology informs us that, before 2800 BC, the inhabitants were Neolithic hill farmers referred to as the Windmill Hill People. Then came the Beaker People who used copper and gold. These people may have been Celts. At some stage Celts able to use iron became the foremost people of the island, but it is difficult to say when they were actually established. The problem is discussed by M. Dillon and N.K. Chadwick.[74] Julius Caesar landed on the island a couple of times but the Roman conquest actually took place in the reign of Claudius. Britain was eventually abandoned by the Romans and left to fend for herself against Picts from the north, Irish from the west and Angles, Saxons and Jutes from beyond the North Sea. The period of the historical Arthur would have been after this.

ABOVE *Bwrdd Arthur,*
near Bryn Rhyd-yr-Arian,
Llansannan, Clwyd.
It is suggested this is a
symbolic representation of
Arthur's Knights.

~

BRULAN *see* VARLAN.

BRUMART
A nephew of King Claudas who sat on the siege Perilous and was finally destroyed for his temerity.

BRUNISSEN
The wife of Jaufré.

BRUNOR
One of the best knights of the Old Table.[85]

BRUTO
The hero of an Italian romance, *Bruto di Brettagna*, in which he obtains a hawk, a scroll and two brachets (small hounds) at Arthur's court to give to his lover.[85]

BRYCHAN
An early legendary king, thought to be the father of a great many saints, even as many as sixty-three.[80]
See GWLADYS, SAINT *and* KYNVARCH.

BRUYANT
Called the Faithless, he killed Estonne, who was Lord of the Scottish Wilderness and was killed in turn by Passaleon, Estonne's son, an ancestor of Merlin[75]. (Estonne is a minor character in the romance of Perceforest).

BUDICIUS
The name of two kings of Brittany, according to Geoffrey. One brought up the exiled Ambrosius and Uther. The other married Arthur's sister, Anna, and was the father of Arthur's supporter, Hoel.

There may be a confused memory here of King Budic I of Cornouaille (in Brittany) who traditionally reigned before AD 530.

BUGI
The husband of Arthur's niece Perferren.[50]

BULGARIA
Arthurian tradition gave this country kings named Netor and Madan. Actually, Bulgaria had not come into existence during the Arthurian period.

BURLETTE
DELLA DISERTA
Abductor of Pulzella Gaia, the daughter of Morgan. Lancelot rescued her from him.[85]

BURY WALLS
Place in Shropshire where, according to local legend, Arthur held court.

BWLCH Y SAETHU
According to Welsh legend, Arthur was killed with arrows at this pass in Snowdonia whither he had pursued his enemies after a battle at Tregalen. When he fell, his men went to a cave called Ogof Lanciau Eryri where they had intended to wait until he came back. A shepherd was once thought to have gained entrance to the cave and seen them there. He found them armed with guns![135]

BWRDD ARTHUR
Arthur's table and the name of two features in Clwyd. One is a circle of twenty-four indentations in rock, the other is a barrow at Llanfair Dyffryn Ceiriog.

BYANOR
The recipient of a sword that formerly belonged to Arthur in Samuel Sheppard's unpublished poem *The Faerie King* (seventeenth century).

BYZANTIUM *see* CONSTANTINOPLE.

CABAL
The hound of Arthur. According to Nennius, when Arthur was pursuing the boar Troynt, Cabal's footprint was left on a stone and Arthur erected a cairn over it. Another story makes Cabal take part in the hunt for the boar Ysgithyrwyn.

CADBURY *see* CAMELOT

CADO
In the *Life of St Carannog* (a medieval saint's life), he ruled with Arthur in the West Country. He may be identical with Cadwy, son of Gereint.

CADOC, SAINT
This Welsh saint was supposed to be the son of King Gwynnlym of Glamorgan and Gwladys of Brecon. In the *Life* of the saint, Arthur demanded that Cadoc hand over to him a man named Ligessac who had killed some of his followers and who had been in sanctuary with Cadoc for ten years. When the matter was adjudicated upon, Arthur was offered a hundred kine (cattle) as compensation. He demanded that they be red before and white behind. With God's aid, they were produced, but they turned to bundles of fern when Arthur's men seized them.

CADOG
One of the Twenty-four Knights of Arthur's Court.[29]

CADOR
The ruler of Cornwall, variously described as a king or duke. He was a supporter of Arthur and helped him against the Saxons, defeating Baldulf and Cheldric. A Cador, son of the King of Cornwall, friend of Caradoc Briefbras and brother of Guignier, may be the same character. In origin, Cador may be Cadwy, son of Gereint.[11] Cador is also the name of a King of Northumberland who became Kay's father-in-law.

CADWALLON
(Catwallaun) According to Geoffrey,[11] the King of the Vendoti, a people who lived in North Wales.

CADWY
The son of Gereint and, according to the *Dream of Rhonabwy* (part of the *Mabinogion*), a contemporary of Arthur. *See* CADO *and* CADOR.

CAELIA
The fairy queen, lover of Arthur's son, Tom a' Lincoln, to whom she bore a son, the Faerie Knight. She eventually drowned herself.[28]

CAER GAI
A place in Merioneth where, according to bardic tradition, Arthur was raised.

CAERLEON
A city on the River Usk, one of the most important cities of Arthur's realm, according to Geoffrey who calls it the City of the Legion. Geoffrey claims it was founded by King Belinus, perhaps the Beli of the genealogies. Geoffrey says that Dubricius was its archbishop.[11]

CAI *see* KAY.

CALADBOLG *see* EXCALIBUR.

CALADVWLCH
see EXCALIBUR.

CAM
A river in Somerset, near Cadbury Castle. In a nearby field, Westwoods, a large number of skeletons bear grim testimony to a battle and it has been suggested that this was the site of Camlann.

CAMAALIS *see* CAMELOT.

CAMAL
A suitor of Hermondine, killed by Meliador.

CAMBRIDGE
The site of one of England's major universities, which, according to Prior Nicholas Cantelupe (died 1441), received its charter from Arthur.[123] An even less likely tradition, current in Elizabethan times, was that the university had been founded by the Spanish Prince Cantaber in Anno Mundi 3588.*
*Since the creation of the world.

CAMEL
A river, the possible site of Camlann battle.

CAMELIARD
The kingdom of Leodegrance, who was Guinevere's father. It has been suggested that it was in Scotland or else in south-west England. One of its important cities was Carolhaise.[19]

CAMILLE
Enamoured of Arthur, this sorceress of Saxon ancestry captured him. Lancelot rescued him and Camille killed herself.

CAMLANN
The site of Arthur's final battle. Malory has only Arthur, Bedivere and, for a very brief period, Lucan survive this battle. Arthur was sorely, perhaps mortally, wounded. In *Culhwch*, a number of other survivors are mentioned – Sandav, because he was so beautiful that all mistook him for an angel, and Morvran, because he was so ugly that all supposed him a devil. We are also told in *Culhwch* that the battle was planned by nine people, one of whom was Gwynn Hyvar, the steward of Cornwall and Devon. Others thought to have survived the battle were Saint Derfel and Saint Petroc. Welsh tradition spoke of seven survivors. The date of the battle has caused some debate. The *Annales Cambriae* state it was twenty-one years after Badon, perhaps intending AD 515, 520 or 539. Geoffrey claims it was in 542. The Irish *Annals of Tigernach* place it in 541 and the Spanish *Anales Toledanos* much later, in 580. As to the site, Malory favours Salisbury Plain. Slaughter Bridge on the River Camel (Cornwall) is a traditional site, while Blackett and Wilson identify it with Camlan (Wales).[52] The *Didot Perceval* places it in Ireland. *See* ODBRICT *and* TREGALEN.

CANAN
The father of Lac and grandfather of Erec.

OVERLEAF *CAMELOT, Amanda Cameron.*

rthur's capital. According to the romances, it was named after a pagan king called Camaalis. At the time when Joseph of Arimathea arrived in Britain, it was the chief city of the country. In Joseph's time, King Agrestes ruled it. He seemed to embrace Christianity but, after Joseph's departure, persecuted the Christians until God drove him mad. The city is first mentioned by Chrétien in his Lancelot. Malory tells us the chief church was St Stephen's. Attempts have been made to identify Camelot. In Roman times Colchester was called Camulodunum, which has a not-too-dissimilar sound. In modern times, some have thought it was Cadbury Castle (Somerset) where, as we know from archaeology, there was a leader's fortified dwelling during the Arthurian period. A tradition that Camelot was Cadbury Castle also existed in the sixteenth century. See WINCHESTER.

artis moyepne demain vber fidelem in easdem operahinibus a si b

Elementum Aquae in vegno
erunt mulién
minerali Utriusqi

otafub pediti cherubim mpneul i quo est tdominis Deus noster qui dedie

Soli (q̃;   Lunam   labores

errante   triões

pluuiasq̃   gẽinosq̃;

CANDACES
The son of King Apollo of Liones; in his day Liones and Cornwall were united. ▣

CANOR
A king of Cornwall who was aided by the Irish king Gonosor. ▣

CANTERBURY
This city was called Durovernum by the ancient Romans. The archiepiscopal see was founded in AD 597. In Arthurian romance the Archbishop of Canterbury was one of Arthur's advisers; he survived his final battle but was subsequently murdered by Mark of Cornwall. The inclusion of an archbishop of Canterbury in Arthurian saga is probably an anachronism, rather than an assertion that there was a bishopric of Canterbury in pre-Saxon times. According to the Scandinavian *Breta sogur*, Arthur was buried at Canterbury. ▣

CAPALU
In French romance the name for Cath Palug. ▣

CARADOC
King of Vannes and Nantes, who married the unfaithful Ysaive, niece of Arthur. *See* CARADOC BRIEFBRAS. ▣

CARADOC BRIEFBRAS
His epithet *briefbras* (short arm) is a pseudo-translation into French of Welsh *vreichvras* (strong-armed). In the romances, he was the son of Eliavres the wizard and Ysaive, wife of King Caradoc of Vannes and Nantes. When Caradoc Briefbras confronted Eliavres about his parentage, Eliavres and Ysaive caused a serpent to twine around his arm and it took the combined efforts of his wife, Guignier, and her brother, Cador, to rid him of it. When King

Mangoun of Moraine sent him a horn to expose any infidelity on the part of the wife of him who drank from it, Caradoc's draught showed his wife to be faithful. In Welsh tradition Caradoc's wife was Tegau Eurfon, his father Llyr Marini, his son Meuric and his steed Lluagor. He was the legendary ancestor of the ruling house of Morgannwg and may have founded the kingdom of Gwent in the fifth century.[31]

CARADOS

Also called the King of Carados, he was one of those kings who rebelled against Arthur at the outset of his reign. B. Saklatvala[142] identifies him with the Saxon leader Cerdic.

CARADOS OF THE DOLOROUS TOWER

He had an enchantress for a mother. He captured Gawain and lodged him in a dungeon. Lancelot slew him, striking off his head with the only sword which could kill him, and Gawain and other prisoners were thus freed. Carados was the brother of Sir Turquine.[19]

CARANNOG, SAINT

He was possibly of Welsh origin. Arthur had taken possession of his floating altar, which had gone astray, but he returned it when Carannog drove off a serpent at the king's behest.[46]

CARATACUS

A historical personage, King of the Catuvellani, a tribe of Britons who lived in the vicinity of modern-day St Albans, at the time of the Roman invasion of Britain in AD 43. He led a hard-fought anti-Roman campaign, but was eventually handed over to his foes by Cartimandua, Queen of the Brigantes. He was then pardoned by the Emperor Claudius.

E. Ratcliffe[132] argues that the stories of Caratacus became misplaced in folklore and that he was the original of Arthur. A similar argument is advanced by J. Whitehead.[162] Both Ratcliffe and I.H. Elder regard Caratacus as identical with Arviragus, while E.R. Capt avers that he was Arviragus's cousin.

CARBONEK

This castle contained the Palace Adventurous, wherein was the Grail.

CARDUEIL

One of Arthur's residences, perhaps Carlisle.

CARDUINO

A knight who was brought up secretly after his father, Dondinello, had been poisoned. He went to Arthur's court and then on a quest to succour Beatrice who, with her subjects, had been turned into animals by a wizard. Carduino slew the wizard and restored Beatrice to her former shape by kissing her. They married.[85]

FAR LEFT *Canterbury Cathedral. Both the Cathedral and the Archbishop of Canterbury feature in Arthurian romance.*

BELOW *Caratacus is one of the contenders for the original Arthur.*

~

CARIADO

In Thomas's *Tristan*, a knight in love with Iseult who told her that Tristan had married Iseult of the White Hands. ▣

CARLACHS

A race or nation. In Irish romance, the King's son, the Black Knight, became one of Arthur's knights and was killed by the Knight of the Lantern. ▣

CARL OF CARLISLE

A giant who was host to Gawain, Kay and Bishop Baldwin. He had become a giant because of a spell which was broken when, at his own behest, his head was duly cut off by Gawain. Gawain married his daughter. Arthur knighted him and made him Lord of Carlisle. He became a Knight of the Round Table.[109] ▣

CARNED ARTHUR

In Welsh folk belief Arthur was buried under this cairn in Snowdonia. ▣

CARNWENNAN

Arthur's dagger.[17] ▣

CARRAS

King of Recesse, the brother of King Claudas, he waged war against Arthur, until Gawain persuaded him to stop.[6] ▣

CARVILIA

In the works of Torquato Tasso (1544–95) the Italian poet, one of the many daughters of Morgan Le Fay. ▣

CASTELLORS

Son of Aminabad and ancestor of Arthur according to the pedigree provided by John of Glastonbury.[14] *See* GARCELOS *and* MANAEL. ▣

CASTLE EDEN

A village in Co. Durham, said to be haunted by Arthur's knights in the guise of chickens. Arthur's hall was once thought to have stood there.[164] ▣

CASTLE KEY

An earthwork, modern Caynham Camp (Shropshire) which, according to the medieval *History of Fulk Fitzwarin*, was built by Kay. ▣

CASTLE OF MAIDENS

A castle in Arthurian romance said to contain young women, either as inmates or prisoners. Duke Lianour ruled it, but seven brothers slew him and took it over. They in turn fell at the hands of three of Arthur's knights and, afterwards, the duke's daughter took charge of it. With regard to its origin, Geoffrey said that Ebraucus, King of Britain, founded the Castle of Mount Agned which later became known as the Castle of Maidens. As to its location, it may have been identified with Edinburgh which, in the Middle Ages, was known as Castellum (or Castra) Puellarum, but some of the tales place it in the vicinity of Gloucester.[46]

CASTLE RUSHEN

Beneath this castle on the Isle of Man are said to be giants, buried in caves by Merlin who defeated them.

CAT COIT CELIDON

The site of one of Arthur's battles in the southern reaches of Scotland, in the area once known as Silva Caledoniae (Wood of Scotland).[21]

CATH PALUG

A monstrous member of the cat family which appears in Welsh Arthurian poetry. The adjective *palug* means 'clawing'. In the poem *Pa gur*, we are told that Kay went to Anglesey with a view to killing lions and was especially prepared for an encounter with Cath Palug. The poem is incomplete, but it may have told how Kay slew the beast. Welsh tradition told how the creature was produced by the pig Henwen and thrown into the sea, only to be raised by the sons of Palug on Anglesey. (Geoffrey Ashe suggests that a captive leopard, kept by a Welsh king, may have given rise to the tale.) In Continental tales we learn how Arthur slew a giant cat near Lake Bourget in the French Alps. This combat is commemorated in the local names Col du Chat (cat's neck), Dent du Chat (cat's tooth) and Mont du Chat (cat's mountain). In French the animal was called Capalu. In the *Romanaz de Franceis* (medieval romance) Arthur fought the cat Capalu in a swamp and it killed him. It then invaded England and became king. It has been suggested that we may have here an alternative tradition of Arthur's death. In *Bataille Loquifer* (medieval romance with limited Arthurian content) there is a youth called Kapalu, a servant of Morgan.[29]

BELOW *The cat monster Cath Palug, said to be the progeny of the pig Henwen.*

~

CATIGERN

A son of Vortigern.[11]

CATUVELLANI

A tribe of Britons. *See* CARATACUS.

CATWALLAUN LONGHAND

A North Welsh ruler who is said to have driven the Irish (led by Serigi) out of Anglesey about the year AD 500. He may be identical with Cadwallon who, according to Geoffrey, ruled Gwynedd in Arthur's time.

CAVERSHALL

A castle in Staffordshire where, according to local legend, Arthur held court and succoured a lady. The existing castle dates from the thirteenth century.

CAW

According to Welsh tradition, the father of Gildas, Hueil and Cywyllog. Caw himself was regarded as a saint.[95]

CELIDOINE

Son of the first Nascien who came to Britain and became king of Scotland. He was an ancestor of Galahad. His name seems to have been derived from Caledonia, the Latin term for Scotland.[24,31]

CERDIC

Traditionally, a Saxon leader who fought against the Britons in the Arthurian period. A.G. Brodeur[62] argues that he was entirely fictitious, his name being taken from place names. He says that the West Saxons, of whom he was supposedly the leader, only began their campaign by conquering the Isle of Wight about AD 530. However, many authorities regard him as historical. He was the supposed founder of the kingdom of Wessex. A problem is caused by his name, however, which is Celtic, not Teutonic. This has led J.P. Clancy (*Pendragon*) to suggest he may have been a rebellious British king. Perhaps, speculates S.G. Wilsman,[63] he was a one-time ally of Arthur's who changed sides. However, B. Saklatvala[142] claims he was the King Carados of Arthurian romance. G. Ashe[43] has produced the most interesting surmise of all, that Cerdic was possibly a son of Arthur (whom he identifies as Riothamus) who had gathered a mixed Celto-Germanic following on the Continent. J. Morris maintains that the pedigree which makes him an ancestor of the ruling house of Wessex is a fabrication.[125] Asser's *Life of Alfred the Great* (ninth century unless, as has been contended, it is a forgery) claims that Cerdic and his son Cynric were Jutes.

CERIDWEN

The mother of Taliesin. She was the mother of a hapless son who was called Morfran, but nicknamed Afgaddu. She was preparing a magic cauldron for him, three drops from which would reveal all secrets, past, present and future. When Gwion, the cauldron's attendant, accidentally imbibed the drops, he was swallowed by Ceridwen when he was in the form of a grain of wheat and she in that of a hen. She then gave birth to him as Taliesin. This story seems far older than the period of the historical Taliesin. It is similar to a tale told about the Irish hero, Finn mac Cool, and may enshrine a Celtic divinatory practice involving thumb chewing. This practice was known in early Ireland as Imbas Forosnai and seems to have rested on the notion that chewing the raw flesh of the thumb imparted sagacity.[16]

CERNUNNOS

The name of a Celtic horned god. The name is only known from a single inscription and it is possible the horned god went by a number of names. As Merlin was associated with stags, it is possible he was connected with the Cernunnos cult.

CHASTEL MARTE

In *Perlesvaus*, the king of this castle was Perceval's uncle. He seized the Grail Castle but Perceval besieged him and he killed himself.[22]

CHASTIEFOL

One of Arthur's swords.

CHATEAU DE LA CHARETTE

see QUEEN OF SORESTAN

CHELDRIC

In Geoffrey, a Saxon leader who brought reinforcements from Germany to Colgrin and took part in the battles of Lincoln, Caledon Wood and Bath (Badon), after which he fled. He was finally defeated and killed by Cador.[11]

CHELINDE

The wife of Sador, who was the son of Brons.[158]

CHESTER

This city was named Deva in classical times but it was also known as the City of the Legion, as was Caerleon-upon-Usk. R.B. Stoker, in his *The Legacy of Arthur's Chester* (1965), argues that Chester, rather than Caerleon, was Arthur's chief city. G. Ashe[47] suggests that perhaps Arthur's battle at the City of the Legion was fought there.

LEFT *The Water Tower at Chester. The city of Chester rivals Caerleon as the site of King Arthur's chief city.*

~

CHLODOMER

According to the eccentric R.W. Morgan (*History of Britain*), this King of Orleans (reigned AD 511–24) died fighting against Arthur. Actually, he perished in battle fighting against the Burgundians.

CHRAMM

According to J. Morris,[125] he led a rebellion against Clothair, King of the Francs, who was aided by Cunomorus (*see* MARK). Morris claims both fell in the battle.

CIRCE

A sorceress in classical mythology. She is found in Homer's *Odyssey* and Apollonius Rhodius's *Argonautica*. In *Perceforest* she married Bethides and brought the Romans into Britain.[75]

CISSA

A son of Aelle, he accompanied his father when he defeated the Britons.

CIST ARTHUR *see* MOEL ARTHUR.

CITY OF SOULS

A spirit-haunted, otherworldly city visited by Lancelot in *Perlesvaus*.[22]

CITY OF THE LEGION

The scene of one of Arthur's battles, according to Nennius. K.H. Jackson[109] identifies it unhesitatingly as Chester, called Urbs Legionis in Latin; but there is the possibility that it was Castleford which the Romans called Legiolium. Geoffrey calls Caerleon the City of Legion.[82]

CLAIRE

Sister of Sagremor, who was saved from two giants by Guinglain.

ABOVE *Merlin with Kings Ban, Bors and Arthur, from* Lestoire de Merlin *(Bologna, early fourteenth century). The Kings went to war with Claudas.*

~

CLAMADEUS

A king who laid siege to Blanchefleur's castle but was then slain by Perceval in single combat.[6]

CLARINE

The mother of Lancelot in a German version of his story. She was the wife of King Pant of Gennewis.[30]

CLARIS

A Knight of the Round Table and a hero of the romance *Claris et Laris*. Laris was his companion whom he rescued from Tallas, King of Denmark. He married Laris's sister, Lidoine.[64]

CLARISSANT

A daughter of Lot and Morgause who married Guiromelant. She was the mother of Guigenor.[22]

CLARISSE

Sister of Gawain.

CLAUDAS

King of the Desert Land, the opponent of King Bors, whose kingdom he seized on the latter's death. After Bors's death, his sons fell into the hands of Pharien whose wife was Claudas's lover. Claudas had them brought to him but they escaped in the guise of greyhounds, killing his son, Dorin. A war took place between Britain and Claudas when the latter imprisoned Guinevere, after insulting one of her damsels. Claudas was supported by the Romans but they were defeated. The realm of Claudas was identified with Berry, as in Old French *berrie* signifies a desert. Clovis I, King of the Franks AD 481–511, is a possible prototype of Claudas.[19,31]

See BRUMART *and* PHARIANCE.

ABOVE *Lot and his sons leave the dead bodies of the Sesnes, from* Arthurian Legends, Lancelot Cycle *(Bologna, c.1270). His daughters were Soredamor and Clarissant.*

~

CLERIADUS

The husband of Meliadice, one of Arthur's descendants. He succeeded Philippon, Meliadice's father, as King of England.[75]

CLIGÉS

Son of Alexander, son of the Emperor of Constantinople and his wife Soredamor, daughter of Lot. When Cligés's uncle Alis (Alexius) was emperor he married Fenice with whom Cligés fell in love. Unable to court her in the circumstances, he went to Arthur's court. In due course, Alis died and Cligés married Fenice. His story is told in Chrétien's romance *Cligés*. There is a knight named Cligés, perhaps a different person, in *Yder*.[64]

CLITON

A sister of Morgan.[12]

CLODION

A son of Pharamond, killed in combat by Tristan.[2]

CLOTHAIR

King of Soissons, later King of all the Franks. J. Morris[125] claims that Cunomorus (*see* MARK) fell in a rebellion against him in AD 560.

CLYDNO

One of Arthur's warriors, father of Cynon in Welsh tradition.

CLYDNO EIDDYN

The cauldron of Clydno Eiddyn was one of the Thirteen Treasures of Britain.[29]

COEL

According to a sixteenth-century manuscript, an ancestor of Arthur through his mother. Stuart-Knill[148] also claims he was one of Arthur's ancestors. He was possibly a historical figure who flourished in the North Country in the early fifth century. Tradition gives him a wife named Stradwawl (road-well) and a daughter called Gwawl (wall), which tends to reinforce this. Gwawl may have been the wife of Cunedda. J. Morris suggests that he was the last Dux Brittaniarum.[125] A great body of legend grew up about him. He was thought to have been the founder and ruler – king (Henry of Huntingdon), duke (Geoffrey of Monmouth) – of Colchester, tradition pushing him back some centuries. His city, according to legend, was besieged by the Roman emperor Constantius Chlorus (ruled AD 305–6) for three years, after which Constantine married Helena, Coel's daughter. Their son was Constantine the Great (born AD 265). A four-teenth-century manuscript says Coel became king of all Britain and died in AD 267. The adjective *hen* (old) was applied to him. There can be little doubt he was the Old King Cole of nursery rhyme.

COLCHESTER

This was Camulodunum in Roman times. *See* CAMELOT.

COLGREVANCE

A Knight of the Round Table who hailed from Gore. There are differing accounts of his death. In one version he was killed by Lionel, in another story, he was one of those who accidentally surprised Lancelot and Guinevere together and was therefore slain by the escaping Lancelot.[19]

COLGRIN

According to Geoffrey, he became leader of the Saxons when Uther died. Arthur defeated him at the River Douglas, so he fled to York where he was besieged by Arthur. His brother Baldulf joined him there. Reinforced by Cheldric, who brought Saxons with him from overseas, they fought Arthur unsuccessfully at Lincoln and Caledon Wood. They left for Germany but came back and landed in Britain again.

Colgrin and his allies were eventually defeated by Arthur at Bath (Badon) where Colgrin fell.[11]

COLOMBE

The lover of Lanceor, the son of the King of Ireland. When Lanceor was slain by Balin, she killed herself.[19]

CONAN

Conan Meriadoc became the first ruler of Brittany, according to Geoffrey.[11] Gallet claims that Conan is one of Arthur's original ancestors.[50]

CONDWIRAMURS

In Wolfram, the wife of Perceval and Queen of Brobarz.[34]

CONON

In Dryden's *King Arthur*, the father of Arthur's beloved Emmeline.

CONRAD

A bishop who unsuccessfully charged Merlin with heresy.[85]

CONSTANCE

The wife of King Ban and mother of Lancelot in Italian romance.[85]

CONSTANS

In Geoffrey, he was the son of King Constantine of Britain and brother of Aurelius Ambrosius and Uther. This makes him Arthur's uncle. When Constantine died, Vortigern persuaded Constans to become king. He had first to leave the monastery in which he had immured himself. He was only a puppet king and eventually Vortigern brought about his assassination by Picts. In French romance he is called Moine but this word merely signifies a monk. *See* IVOINE.

CONSTANTINE

1. Arthur's grandfather. The brother of Aldroenus, King of Brittany, he was made King of Britain and had three sons, Constans, Aurelius Ambrosius and Uther. He was stabbed to death by a Pict. In Welsh genealogies Constantine is given a father called Kynnvor while, according to Gallet, his father was King Solomon of Brittany. It has been suggested that the original of Constantine was the Roman emperor Constantine III (ruled AD 407–11). He was an ordinary soldier who was made emperor by the Roman troops in Britain, despite the fact that there was a Roman Emperor of the West, called Honorius, ruling at the time. Constantine landed in Gaul and established himself at Arles, his son Constans leaving a monastery to join him, just as, according to Geoffrey, Constans, son of Constantine, left his monastery to become King of Britain. One of Constantine's subordinates, Gerontius, then rebelled and threw off Constantine's rule. Gerontius defeated and killed Constans. Constantine eventually surrendered with another of his sons to Honorius's troops, but both were killed when in custody. If he indeed died in AD 542, this Constantine lived too early to be the grandfather of the historical

Arthur; but, if he lived earlier, the relationship is not impossible.[11]

2. Historically, a sixth-century King of Dumnonia. In Arthurian romance, he was Arthur's cousin, son of Cador of Cornwall who succeeded him as King of Britain. The sons of Mordred rebelled against him, but Constantine defeated them. He killed them separately, each before an altar where he was seeking sanctuary.[11] *See* ALDROENUS.

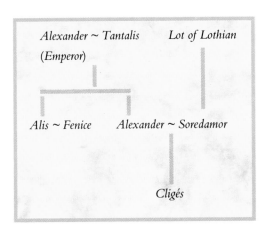

Alexander ~ Tantalis (Emperor)		Lot of Lothian
Alis ~ Fenice	Alexander ~ Soredamor	
	Cligés	

CONSTANTINOPLE

Formerly called Byzantium, this city was renamed after Constantine the Great. At the time when the Roman Empire was divided into two, Constantinople became the capital of the Eastern or Byzantine Empire.

Emperors who ruled there in the traditional Arthurian period were Marcian (AD 450–57), Leo I (AD 457–74), Leo II (AD 474), Zeno (AD 474–5 and again 476–91), Basiliscus (AD 475–6), Anastasius I (AD 491–518), Justus I (AD 518–27) and Justinian I (AD 527–67). Geoffrey says that the Byzantine emperor contemporary with Arthur was Leo, and G. Ashe identifies him with Leo I. In *Cligés*, the imperial family of Constantinople is given the tree shown above, illustrating its kinship with Lot of Lothian.

ABOVE *Map of Constantinople (1422), known as Byzantium in the traditional Arthurian period.*

~

In *Peredur* (*see Mabinogion*) the Empress of Constantinople was the paramour of Peredur (Perceval) with whom she was said to have dwelt for fourteen years. She had previously aided him by giving him a stone which rendered him invisible to the afanc. In *Floriant et Florete* the Emperor of Constantinople is Filimenis.[16,17,18]

CORBON

Son of Renoart and Morgan (consequently Arthur's nephew) in *Bataille Loquifer* (an obscure medieval romance which also contains a few Arthurian references). ▣

CORNWALL

The realm of King Mark. Actually, in Arthurian times, part of the kingdom of Dumnonia, though it is not impossible that perhaps someone called Mark ruled territory within this kingdom. ▣

COUDEL

An early king of Northgalis who fell fighting against the Christians. His death is described in the *Estoire*. ▣

COURECHOUSE

The sword of King Ban. ▣

CRADELMENT

A king of Northgalis, one of those who rebelled against Arthur at the outset of his reign. ▣

CREIDDYLED

A maiden over whom Gwyn, son of Nudd, and his followers fought the followers of Gwythr, the son of Greidawl, at each May Kalends (or May Day) and were fated to do so until Doomsday. The episode is taken from Celtic mythology and the protagonists were probably originally divine figures. It has been suggested that, in Creiddyledd, we have the original of Shakespeare's Cordelia.[17] ▣

RIGHT *Craig-y-Dinas, Pontneddfechan, Mid Glamorgan, where King Arthur and his warriors are said to lie sleeping in a cave*

BELOW *Cornwall, the wild and rugged coastline of King Marl's realm.*

~

CRAIG-Y-DINAS

rock in Wales which featured in a story told by Iolo Morgannwg. Iolo Morgannwg was the bardic name of Edward Williams (1747–1826). He collected a great deal of early Welsh lore but, as a bard, felt he could augment it. Consequently he is not regarded as a reliable source. In Iolo's story a Welshman, led by a magician, found Arthur and warriors sleeping in a cave there, guarding treasure. A similar tale, narrated by J. Rhys, has a Monmouthshire farmer as its protagonist. For tales of a similar nature set in England, see ALDERLEY EDGE *and* THOMPSON. *A cave called Ogo'r Dinas near to Llandebie was also thought to house the sleeping Arthur.*[135]

CROP-EARED DOG

This earless, tailless creature who, despite his dogginess, was fully able to converse in human speech, was one of the heroes of the Irish romance *Eachtra an Mhadra Mhaoil*. He was an enchanted prince named Alexander, son of the King of India. His step-mother, Libearn, had turned him and his brothers into dogs to ensure that her son, the Knight of the Lantern, would obtain a handsome inheritance. When this knight humiliated Arthur and his court, the Crop-eared Dog and Gawain went to track him down. When their quarry had at length been captured, he changed Alexander back to his own shape. Alexander eventually became ruler of India.

CULHWCH

A cousin of Arthur. The table below shows how they were related. After the death of Culhwch's mother, his father remarried. His step-mother put him under obligation to marry Olwen. Arthur agreed to help him and they interviewed Olwen's father, the chief giant Yspadaddan. The latter said he would surrender his daughter only on performance of a set of tasks. With the aid of Arthur's men, Culhwch performed some of these and married Olwen. The question arises as to why Culhwch did not perform all the tasks on the list. Commentators are not sure whether this was due to carelessness on the part of the composer or whether a portion of the story became lost in transmission.[17] *See* WRNACH.

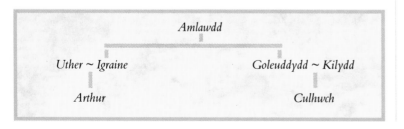

CUNDRIE

The name of two women in Wolfram:

1. A Grail damsel learned in star lore. She told Perceval that his wife and sons had been summoned to the Grail Castle and that the Grail Question would now free Anfortas and his family.

2. Daughter of Arthur's sister Sangive and Lot. She married Lischois.[34]

CUNEDDA

A ruler of the Votadini in North Britain who migrated with a number of his subjects to Wales round about AD 430. He rid a large part of Wales of Irish settlers. His pedigree suggests that his was a Roman family in origin, running as follows:

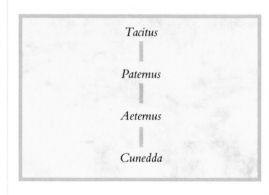

According to *Brut y Brenhinedd*, a medieval Welsh history, Cunedda's daughter, Gwen, was the mother of Eigyr (Igraine), Arthur's mother, thus making Cunedda Arthur's great-grandfather.[10] Cunedda may have married Gwawl, daughter of Coel.

CUNOBELINUS

King of the Catuvellani who, in the first century, made himself ruler of a considerable part of south Britain. He is the king called Cymbeline by Shakespeare. In Welsh tradition he is a relation of Arthur.

RIGHT *Arthur and his Knights return to Camelot, from* Guiron le Courtois *(Flemish, late fifteenth century). There were twenty-four Knights in Arthur's lavish Court at Camelot.*

~

CURETANA
The sword of Holger. *See* OGIER.

CYLEDYR THE WILD
One of the followers of Arthur in *Culhwch*, he obtained the shears from between the ears of the boar Twrch Trwyth.[17]

CYMBELINE *see* CUNOBELINUS

CYMEN
A son of Aelle, he accompanied his father when he defeated the Britons.

CYNFARCH
The father of Urien.[29]

CYNON
The lover of Morfudd, Owain's twin sister, in Welsh tradition.

CYNRIC
Son of Cerdic.

CYON
One of the Twenty-four Knights of Arthur's Court.[29]

CYWYLLOG
Daughter of Caw and wife of Mordred in Welsh tradition which relates that after her husband's death, she became a nun and founded the church of Llangwyllog, Anglesey.[50]

DAGONET

Arthur's fool, whom Arthur himself made a knight.[19] ▣

DAHUT *see* MORGAN. ▣

DAIRE

A Pictish king, father of the Otherworld woman Ailleann. ▣

DAMAS

A proud knight who used to trap other knights and make his brother, Sir Ontzlake, fight them. Arthur put a stop to this practice.[19] ▣

DAMART

A magician killed by Betis. After this feat, Betis's name was changed to Perceforest. ▣

DANAIN THE RED

The Lord of Malehaut. ▣

DANIEL

In the *Tavola ritonda*, a knight, brother of Dinadan, leader of the knights who discovered Lancelot and Guinevere together in compromising circumstances. Daniel was also the name of an Arthurian knight in a thirteenth-century German poem by Der Stricker.[85]
See BREUNOR. ▣

BELOW St. David is an example of an interesting mixture of religious history and legend. The sixth-century bishop is believed to have founded ten monasteries including Menevia and Glastonbury.

~

DARERCA

The sister of St Patrick in Jocelyn's *Life of St Patrick*. She was said to have been Patrick's youngest sister and to have had seventeen sons. Gallet makes her an ancestor of Arthur in the illustration below.

Gallet makes Darerca's sister Tigridia marry Grallo, Conan's grandson, thus connecting her with Arthur.[50] ▣

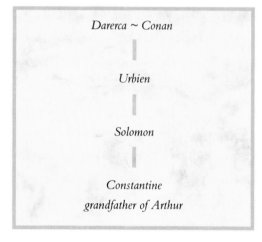

Darerca ~ Conan

|

Urbien

|

Solomon

|

Constantine
grandfather of Arthur

DAUGHTER OF THE KING OF LOGRES

In the romance of *Tyolet*, it was she who required a knight to cut off the white foot of a stag. This challenge was taken up successfully by Tyolet, who became the husband of the unnamed daughter of the king. ▣

DAVID, SAINT

The patron of Wales. He may have inherited the monastery of Henllan from his father and is credited with founding the monastery of Menevia. Various sources link him with Arthur: according to Geoffrey he was Arthur's uncle; a Welsh manuscript makes him Arthur's grand-nephew; and in *Brut y Brenhinedd*, a medieval Welsh history, he is Arthur's second cousin. The date of David's death is uncertain. ▣

DAVID'S SWORD

A sword belonging to the biblical King David. It was used by King Varlan to kill King Lambor in one version of the Dolorous Stroke.

DEMETIA

(In Welsh: Dyfed) A kingdom in south Wales. Geoffrey of Monmouth states that it was ruled in Arthur's time by Stater. Ordinary history knows nothing of this ruler and tells us of a king named Agricola who ruled there in about AD 500, and of another ruler, Vortipor, who was an old man in AD 540. Before Agricola's time an Irish dynasty, the Uí Liatháin, ruled there.[11,125]

DEMETRUS

According to Heywood, Merlin's maternal grandfather. The name seems to be a corruption of the place name Demetia from where Merlin's mother came.

DEMOGORGON

In classical mythology, the being who was thought to have resolved primeval chaos into order. According to Conrad Celtis (1459–1508), Renaissance historian, he was the father of a nation in the Arctic northlands, the Germans. In Erasmo de Valvasone's *La Caccia*, Arthur entered the cave of Demogorgon on his route through a mountain to Morgan's palace.[85]

DENMARK

Various references are made to this country's rulers in Arthurian tales. It is not possible to say who was actually in power in Denmark in the Arthurian period: the first definitely historical king of all Denmark was Gorm the Old who commenced his reign about the year AD 900. Danish traditional lists go much further back, claiming there were various smaller kingdoms in Denmark before unification under Gorm, notably that of Lethra which had a list of kings going back to Skioldr, son of Odin. In Anderson's *Royal Genealogies*, kings of Denmark in the traditionally Arthurian period were Harald IV (AD 481–527) and also Eschyllus (AD 527–43). Geoffrey says that Aschil, King of Denmark, supported Arthur in his last battle, but the *Morte Arthure* says Mordred made the Danes his allies. In *Claris et Laris* it was ruled by Heldins, then by Tallas, who was defeated by Arthur and succeeded by Laris. Geoffrey Gaimar (a twelfth-century Welsh writer) says in Arthurian times it was ruled by King Gunter. Another Arthurian tale features a king of Denmark named Tryffin. The King of Denmark is called Jozefant in *Durmart* and Aminaduc (described as a Saxon) in the *Livre d'Artus*.

BELOW *The arms and costume of Danish warriors*

~

DINADAN

 A *Knight of the Round Table who saw no purpose in fighting for fighting's sake. He was the brother of Breunor the Black. He was killed by Mordred and Agravain.* [19]

RIGHT *DINADAN, Aubrey Beardsley (1872-98), from Le Morte d'Arthur (1909).*

~

DENW

In Welsh tradition a daughter of Anna, Arthur's sister, and Lot. She married Owain.

DERFEL

A saint, founder of Llanderfel in Gwynedd. In Welsh tradition it was said he had taken part in, and survived, the battle of Camlann.[80]

DETORS

A King of Northumberland.

DEWI, SANT *see* DAVID, SAINT.

DIANA

In Roman mythology, she was the goddess of the moon, the hunt and childbirth among several other things. She was said to be the godmother of Nimue, and to have officiated at a marriage between Nimue and Merlin, after which Nimue kept Merlin in a magic castle.

DIANE

The goddess of the wood, mother of Dyonas and grandmother of Vivienne in the *Vulgate Version. See* DIONES.

DILLUS

An enemy of Arthur. One of the tasks set Culhwch by Yspadadden was to obtain this man's beard to make a leash. To do this, Kay flung him into a pit and yanked out the hairs of his beard with tweezers.[17]

DINABUTIUS

The boy who taunted the young Merlin for not knowing the name of his father. This drew the attention of one of Vortigern's counsellors to Merlin as Vortigern was seeking a fatherless child.

DINAS

The seneschal of Mark and a Knight of the Round Table. He sympathized with Tristan, whom he felt had been mistreated, and became his companion. When Lancelot ran off with Guinevere, Dinas went with him and became Duke of Anjou. According to the *Tavola ritonda*, after Mark's death Dinas became the King of Cornwall.[19,85]

DINAS EMRYS

The mountainous place in Snowdonia where Merlin had his confrontation with Vortigern. Merlin claimed that the tower which Vortigern could not make stay up was falling over because of a subterranean pool containing dragons. Excavation has revealed the pool. As to how the dragons became confined there, the story of *Llud and Llefelys* in the *Mabinogion* gives details. When Llud ruled Britain, a scream, whose origin could not be determined, was heard each May Eve. Llefelys, King of France, furnished the information that it was caused by battling dragons. The scream would be uttered by the dragon of the British nation when it was about to be defeated. The dragons were captured and buried at Dinas Emrys.

BELOW *Dinas Emrys, near Beddgelert, Gwynedd, site of an underground pool full of dragons. Today, only the pool remains.*

~

DINDRANE

The sister of Perceval, she went on the Grail Quest. The questers came to a castle where it was the custom to demand the blood of passing women to cure the leprous chatelaine. Hearing of this, Dindrane voluntarily donated her blood and died in so doing. In Italian romance, Perceval's sister is called Agrestizia.[22,34]

LEFT *PERCEVAL'S SISTER CUTS HER HAIR TO MAKE A GIRDLE, William Russell Flint, from Malory's* Le Morte d'Arthur.

DIONES

The father of Nimue. His godmother was said to be the goddess Diana.

DIONETA

The name of two persons mentioned in the fourteenth-century Welsh *Birth of Arthur*:
1. A daughter of Gorlois and Igraine, half-sister to Arthur.
2. A daughter of Gwyar and Lleu (Lot), sister to Mordred and Gwalchmai.

DIONISE

An enchanted chatelaine, liberated by Gawain, who refused to marry her.

DIRAC

The brother of Lac and uncle of Erec.

DIWRNACH

An Irishman who refused to give Arthur his cauldron for Culhwch. Arthur led an expedition to Ireland, Diwrnach was slain and the cauldron appropriated.[17] *See* THIRTEEN TREASURES.

DO

A forester of Uther and the father of Griflet and Lorete. His own father was called Ares.

DODINEL

A Knight of the Round Table, called 'the Savage', perhaps originally identical with Perceval. He used to hunt game in wild forests, hence his sobriquet. He was the son of Belinant and Eglante.[19] Another version of the story made the Lady of Malehaut his mother.

DOGSHEADS

Opponents of Arthur, fought by Arthur or Kay in *Pa gur*. They are not necessarily monsters. H. Butler[65] has advanced the theory that they were related to the Conchind (Dog-heads), a legendary people who ruled Ireland. There may be some connection with the Cunesioi, a tribe whom Herodotus places beyond the Celts in the Iberian Peninsula, and the Concani who, according to Horace, lived in Spain. ▣

DOLLALLOLLA

The wife of Arthur in Henry Fielding's *Tragedy of Tragedies* (1730). This was a parody and consequently Arthur's queen had a ridiculous name. ▣

DONDINELLO

The father of Carduino, he was killed by poisoning. ▣

DORIN

The son of Claudas who was killed in a fight with Lionel and Bors. ▣

DORNAR

A son of King Pellinore and a Knight of the Round Table. ▣

DOUGLAS

The name of a river in Linnuis (?Lindsay) where four of Arthur's battles were fought.[21] ▣

DRIANT

A son of King Pellinore and a Knight of the Round Table who received his death wound from Gawain. ▣

RIGHT *BALIN SLAYS PELLAM WITH THE DOLORES STROKE, William Russell Flint, from Malory's* Le Morte d'Arthur.

DOLOROUS STROKE

The stroke which caused the Waste Land to be rendered barren, making the Grail Quest necessary. In Malory it occurred when Balin stabbed Pellam with the Lance of Longinus, destroying three countries as a result. Another version in the Estoire places it earlier when King Varlan (or Brulens) killed King Lambor with David's Sword.[19,31] ▣

DRUDWAS

The son of King Tryffin of Denmark. While he is listed as a follower of Arthur, one story[64] tells how he was to meet Arthur in single combat. He craftily told his three pet griffins to go ahead and kill the first man who came to the field, expecting it to be Arthur. However, Drudwas's sister was Arthur's mistress and she delayed her lover. Drud himself arrived first and the griffins, not recognizing him, killed him. *See* TWENTY-FOUR KNIGHTS.

DRUIDAN

A dwarf on whom Gawain bestowed his mistress Ydain who had tried to leave him.[6]

DUBRICIUS, SAINT

(Also Dubric; in Welsh: Dyfrig) An important Celtic saint, who died about the year AD 550. He was a bishop and possibly also abbot of Caldey. According to Geoffrey, he was Archbishop of Caerleon and crowned Arthur. In her recent book *Merlin* (1988) N.L. Goodrich has sought to identify the saint with Merlin.

DUMNONIA

A considerable British kingdom in post-Roman times. It covered Devon, Cornwall and other areas of the south-west of England. Constantine, whom legend makes Arthur's successor, was King of Dumnonia.

DUN STALLION

A horse of Arthur's said to haunt the Co. Durham village of Castle Eden.[164]

DYFED *see* DEMETIA.

DYFRIG *see* DUBRICIUS.

DYONAS

The father of Vivienne, according to the *Vulgate Version.*

DYWEL

Brother of Gereint.[17]

BELOW *Dun Stallion, King Arthur's horse is said to haunt Castle Eden.*

~

EAGLE OF GWERNABWY

The world's oldest creature which assisted Culhwch and his companions to find Mabon by introducing them to the Salmon of Llyn Llw.[17]

EBRAUCUS

Founder of the Castle of Mount Agned, later known as the Castle of Maidens.[11]

ECTOR

Arthur's foster-father and the father of Kay. Ector is the Welsh form of the name Hector.[19]

ECTOR DE MARIS

Son of Ban whom he succeeded as King of Benwick. The brother of Lancelot, he loved Perse whom he rescued from Zelotes to whom she had been promised by her father.[19]

OVERLEAF ELAINE, *Amanda Cameron.*

BELOW An early engraving of Edinburgh seen from St Anthony's Chapel.

~

EDA ELYN MAWR

The British Museum Harleian MS 4181 (entry 42) gives this as the name of Arthur's killer.

EDEN

A river. *See* UTHER.

EDDAS

The name given to two Norse compositions, the *Poetic Edda* and the *Prose Edda*. An eccentric writer, L.A. Waddell, maintained that the former was not an epic of the Norse gods, as is generally supposed, but a recording of the doings of an early Sumerian hero whose exploits formed the basis of the Arthurian saga. This contention has not met with approbation from mainstream scholars.[154]

EDINBURGH

This city was known in the Middle Ages as Castellum Puellarum. *See* CASTLE OF MAIDENS.

EDOR

An ancestor of Lot.[14]

EFFLAM, SAINT

An Irish saint mentioned by Le Grand, a hagiologist whose work is not deemed wholly dependable as he may have altered some of his source material. Efflam came to Brittany to find himself facing an unfriendly dragon. Arthur, equipped with a club and lionskin shield, came to his aid but could not prevail against the monster. Efflam, after blessing Arthur, put the dragon to flight.

Hic canet errante lunam, solisq; labores
treturuq; pluuiasq; hyad. gēinosq; triōes
cherubin ste m humana depictus effigieter hab

ts naturam corrigens in vegno minerali · Utriusque Cosm Hominius actibus
istonā · Benedichus dominius Deus nester qui dedit nobis an minom tutela
ginum. Cum eorundem in easdem operantenibus et effect intrens limen sup
egatiſhous liquris depicit. Homo natus de muliere brevi ipa ith, cudiō. an

las que fer artus moyepne demain veber fidelis
Inm a redmm si beber Rotasub peditz cherubm lep
habens mows septem Elementum Aquae et Terrae

tes scilicet · Fortvois mi Cherubin iste m humana depurtus effigueter ha
mißio comprehsum extradas que fer artus moyepne demain veber fidelis
is qqueu affrttatur. Tinma redmm si beber Rotasub peditz cherubm le
naut celos decem ad habens mows septem Elementum Aquae et Terrae.

ELAINE

 his name, a form of Helen, is borne by a number of people in Arthurian romance.

1. The daughter of Pelles. He tricked Lancelot into sleeping with her and, on another occasion, Lancelot slept with her thinking that she was Guinevere. She and Lancelot were the parents of Galahad.

2. The daughter of Bernard of Astolat, she was Elaine the White and fell in love with Lancelot who wore her sleeve as a token during a joust. She died of love for him and was brought by boat up the Thames to Arthur's court with a letter saying why she had died. She is, of course, the famous Lady of Shalott.

3. Daughter of Pellinore. She killed herself after the death of her lover, Sir Miles of the Laundes.

4. Daughter of Igraine, sister of Morgan and Morgause, half-sister of Arthur. She married King Nentres of Garlot.

5. Lancelot's mother, wife of King Ban.

6. A niece of Arthur, variously described as a daughter of Lot or Nentres. She fell in love with Perceval. ✥

ABOVE ELAINE,
Charles Edwin Fripp
(1854-1906).
~

EFRAWG

Father of Perceval in *Peredur* (*see* MABINOGION). This seems to be a title ('York') rather than a name, indicating that this was the place he ruled.[17] ▪

EFRDDF

The twin sister of Urien of Rheged.[29] ▪

EGLANTE

The mother of Dodinel the Savage. ▪

EHANGWEN

Arthur's hall, built by Gwlyddyn the carpenter.[17]

EIDDILIG

According to the Welsh *Pedwar Marchog ar Hugan Llys Arthur*, he was one of the Twenty-four Knights of Arthur's Court.[29]

EIGYR *see* IGRAINE.

ELERGIA

In the *Tavola ritonda*, a witch who imprisoned Arthur. Tristan rescued him.[85]

ELIABELLA

In Italian romance, Tristan's mother and a cousin of Arthur, presumably identical with Malory's Elizabeth (Eliabel). Arthur had been at war with King Meliodas of Liones and Eliabella married Meliodas to cement peace between the two. *See* MARK.

ELIAVRES

A knight with magical powers. He fell in love with Ysaive, a niece of Arthur. She was the wife of King Caradoc of Vannes and Nantes. He bewitched Caradoc into sleeping with a bitch, a sow and a mare, while he himself slept with Ysaive on whom he begot Caradoc Briefbras. The latter, discovering what had happened, informed King Caradoc of the truth. The enraged cuckold made Eliavres copulate with a bitch (by which he became the father of Guinalot), a sow (by which he became the father of Tortain) and a mare (by which he became the father of Lorigal).[16]

ELIAZAR

A son of Pelles and an uncle of Galahad.

ABOVE *Elergia, a witch who kept Arthur a prisoner.*

~

ELIDUS

A King of Ireland.

ELIEZER

The son of Evelake.

ELIS

The son of a duke who was Arthur's uncle. Readers of some editions of Malory may think that Elis was the duke's name also, but this is due to a misprint in Caxton's original edition.[19]

ELIVRI

Arthur's head groom.[17]

ELIWLOD

Arthur's nephew, the son of Madog, son of Uther. After his death he appeared to Arthur in the guise of an eagle in the early Welsh poem *Ymddiddan Arthur a'r Eryr*. It has been suggested that he was the original of Lancelot. *See* TWENTY-FOUR KNIGHTS.

ELIZABETH

The wife of Meliodas. When heavily pregnant she went into the woods to look for her husband and gave birth to Tristan, but died in doing so. She was the sister of Mark of Cornwall.[19]

ELLEN

The daughter of Arthur in the Scots ballad of *Childe Rowland*. She is referred to in the ballad as Burd Ellen, *burd* signifying 'lady'.

ELMET

A Celtic kingdom, centred on Leeds, which was in existence in the Arthurian period. Its exact extent cannot be determined.

ELPHIN

The son of Gwyddno Garanhir, he rescued Taliesin when Ceridwen had placed him in a leather bag in the sea. Taliesin repaid Elphin's kindness by rescuing him when he was a prisoner of Maelgwyn.[16]

ELSA

Daughter of the Duke of Brabant, she was championed by Lohengrin against Telramund. Lohengrin then married her but cautioned her not to ask his name. She bore him two children but, at length, she asked the forbidden question, so he left her.

ELVES

Creatures in Teutonic mythology. Layamon says that, at Arthur's birth, elves bestowed gifts upon him. They arranged for him to be rich, valiant and long-lived. Elves do not figure in Celtic mythology but Layamon may have equated Celtic spirits with them.[32]

ELYAN

The son of Sir Bors by the daughter of King Brandegoris. He later became Emperor of Constantinople.[19]

ELYZABEL

Cousin of Guinevere, she was imprisoned by Claudas for suspected espionage. He refused to release her and this led to war with Arthur.

EMMELINE

In Dryden's *King Arthur*, a blind girl, daughter of Duke Conon of Cornwall, was promised to Arthur but was carried off by Oswald, the Saxon King of Kent. Merlin restored her sight when she was still a prisoner and Arthur eventually defeated Oswald and rescued her.

ENDELIENTA, SAINT

A saint who, according to tradition, had a cow which was killed by the lord of Trenteny. Arthur was her godfather and either killed the wrongdoer himself or had him killed. Endelienta revived the dead man.

ENEUAVC

The daughter of Bedivere.

ENGRES

In the Icelandic *Saga of Tristram* a king, brother of Iseult. He offered Iseult's hand to whomsoever would kill a dragon.[99]

ENID

The heroine of Chrétien's *Erec et Enide* and the Welsh *Gereint and Enid*. In each of these tales she is the wife of the hero. According to *Erec*, her father was Liconaus, whereas in *Gereint* he was named Ynwyl. *Erec* tells us that her mother was called Tarsenesyde. The origin of Enid's name is uncertain and it was perhaps at first a territorial designation.[5,17]

ENYGEUS

Sister of Joseph of Arimathea, wife of Brons and mother of Alan.

EOPA

The Saxon who, at the instigation of Paschent, son of Vortigern, poisoned Ambrosius Aurelius. He subsequently fell in a battle against Uther.[11]

ERBIN

The father or, according to the *Life of St Cyby*, the son of Gereint.

EREC

The husband of Enid who succeeded his father as King of Nantes. He first encountered Enid when he gave chase to someone who had insulted Guinevere. After he married Enid she scolded him for giving up knightly adventures so he undertook some more. C. Luttrell holds that the romance of *Erec* was entirely the invention of Chrétien.[110] Erec is usually regarded as the son of Lac, but the Norse *Erex Saga* calls his father Ilax.[5,99] The *Erex Saga* is a Norse version of the story of Erec.

ERIES

A son of Lot who became one of Arthur's knights. He may have been the same as Gaheris and became a separate character due to manuscript miscopying.

ERLAN

An ancestor of Lot.[14]

ERMALEUS

In *Beaudous*, Gawain's cousin whom Biausdous defeated and sent as a captive to Arthur. He was the son of the King of Orkney.

ERMID

Brother of Gereint.[17]

ESCANOR

The name of a number of knights in Arthurian romance. In *L'Atre Perilleux* Escanor was a knight whose strength grew at noon, then lessened. He abducted Arthur's female cupbearer but was eventually killed by Gawain. The romance *Escanor* features two persons of that name: Escanor Le Beau who fought a duel with Gawain, though they became friends; and Escanor Le Grand who was the son of a giant and a witch and the uncle of Escanor Le Beau. He made Griflet a prisoner.[64]

ESCLABOR

The father of Palamedes. He was a nobleman of Babylon who was sent to Rome as part of a tribute. While there, he saved the emperor's life. In due course he came to Logres where he saved the life of King Pellinore and then hied himself to Camelot.[64]

ESCLADOS

A knight who defended a wondrous fountain in the Forest of Broceliande. Owain slew him and then subsequently married his widow, Laudine.[5] By marrying the widow of his victim Owain may well have enshrined a pagan custom whereby whoever defeated a king was ritually married to his territory.

ESCLARIMONDE

A fairy, lover of Escanor Le Beau and Brian des Illes.

ESCLARMONDE

The wife of Huon. In *Le Chanson d'Esclarmonde* (a sequel to *Huon de Bordeaux*), Huon discovered that, as he was married to Esclarmonde, a mortal, his right to inherit the kingdom of Faerie was disputed by Arthur who had resorted thither after his reign in Britain. The fairies refused to obey Huon, but Morgan took Esclarmonde to the Terrestrial Paradise, where she was bathed in the Fountain of Youth and changed by Jesus into a fairy.

ESCOL

A follower of Arthur. His father was King Aelens of Iceland.[32]

ESCORDUCARLA

The lady of Vallone, she planned to make Merlin, of whom she was enamoured, a prisoner; but he made her a prisoner instead.

ESTONNE

The Lord of the Scottish Wilderness, father of Passaleon. He was killed by Bruyant the Faithless.[75]

ESTORAUSE

The pagan king of Sarras who imprisoned Galahad, Perceval and Bors, but who, when he was dying, asked their forgiveness which was granted.[19]

ESTRANGOT *see* ILLE ESTRANGE.

ETTARD

She was loved by Pelleas but did not reciprocate his feelings. Nimue made her fall in love with Pelleas by magic but also made Pelleas transfer his affections to her (Nimue). Ettard, now hated by Pelleas, died of love.[19]

EUDAF

A variant form of the name Evdaf found in Mostyn MS 117.

RIGHT Merlin (disguised as a minstrel) seated at a feast with Arthur and Ban, from Lestoire de Merlin *(Bologna, early fourteenth century). Merlin outwitted Escorducarla's plans and she became his captive.*

EUGENIUS

According to Boece in his *Scotorum Historiae*, a King of Scotland, ally of Mordred. He captured Guinevere who remained a prisoner of the Picts.[83]

EURIC

King of the Visigoths, AD 466–84. He was opposed by the Emperor Anthemius who counted Riothamus amongst his allies.

EUSTACE

The Duke of Cambenet who took part in the rebellion against Arthur.[19]

EVADEAM

He was transformed into a dwarf by magic. Gawain had been told he would assume the shape of the next man he met. He met Evadeam and became a dwarf, while Evadeam regained his original shape. Gawain later resumed his true form and Evadeam became a Knight of the Round Table.[31]

EVAINE

The wife of the elder Bors. She was the mother of Lionel and the younger Bors. After her husband's death, she left her children to the care of Pharien and became a nun. She was the sister of Elaine, wife of Ban.[31]

EVANDER

A king. *See* SYRIA.

EVDAF

Son of Kradoc and father of Kynan in the Welsh maternal pedigree of Arthur found in *Bonedd yr arwr*. Geoffrey calls him Octavius, Duke of Gwent; he subsequently became King of Britain. He was the uncle of Conan Meriadoc.

EVELAKE

A king born in France in early times. He was sent to Rome as part of a tribute and afterwards went to Syria. He slew the governor's son and fled to Babylon where he aided King Tholomer and was rewarded with land. He became King of Sarras, and Joseph of Arimathea helped him to fight against Tholomer. Joseph then baptized him, giving him the name Mordrain. He remained alive with unhealed wounds, living only on the Sacred Host, until the knight who would obtain the Grail should come. He had two sons, Eliezer and Grimal. Evelake in origin may be Avalloch, father of Modron, mentioned in the *Triads*. Avalloch may have been a god with some association with apples.[19,24,31]

ABOVE SIR PERCEVAL
AND THE SICK KING
EVELAKE, William Russell
Flint, from Malory's
Le Morte d'Arthur.
Evelake is shown receiving
the Sacred Host.

~

BELOW *HOW ARTHUR
DREW THE SWORD,*
H.J. Ford, from Tales of
King Arthur and the
Round Table, *(1906).*

~

EVGEN
In the maternal pedigree of Arthur provided by Gruffudd Hiraethog (sixteenth century), he is numbered amongst Arthur's ancestors.

EVRAIN
One of the wizards who changed Blonde Esmerée into a serpent.

EXCALIBUR
The sword given to Arthur by the Lady of the Lake. Some sources suggest that Arthur gave it to Gawain. After Arthur's last battle he made Bedivere return it to the water where it was grasped by a hand and drawn under. Its scabbard prevented the wearer from losing blood. When Gawain fought the magician Mabon over the fairy Marsique, she obtained the scabbard for him but it subsequently disappeared. The Welsh name for Excalibur was Caladvwlch, equating linguistically with Irish Caladbolg, the name of a sword borne by heroes in Irish legend, derived from *calad* (hard) and *bolg* (lightning).[19,128]

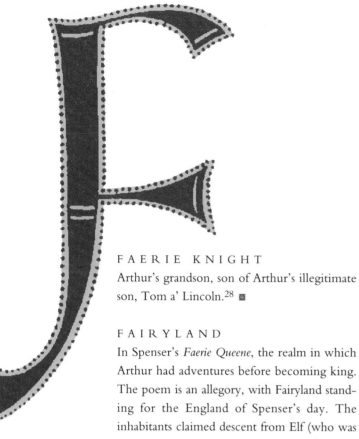

FAERIE KNIGHT
Arthur's grandson, son of Arthur's illegitimate son, Tom a' Lincoln.[28]

FAIRYLAND
In Spenser's *Faerie Queene*, the realm in which Arthur had adventures before becoming king. The poem is an allegory, with Fairyland standing for the England of Spenser's day. The inhabitants claimed descent from Elf (who was created by Prometheus) and a fay from the gardens of Adonis. Early kings included Elfin, son of Elf, who ruled England and America; Elfinan, who founded the city of Cleopolis; Elfiline, who built a golden wall around it; Elfinell, who defeated the Goblins in battle; Elfant; Elfar, who killed two giants, one with two heads, the other with three; and Elfinor, who built a brazen bridge upon the sea. The immediate family of Gloriana, queen of Fairyland, of whom Arthur became enamoured, was as follows:

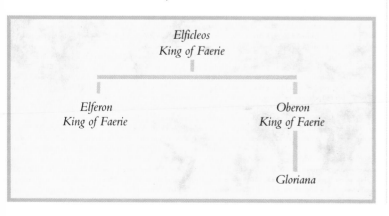

Elficleos
King of Faerie

Elferon
King of Faerie

Oberon
King of Faerie

Gloriana

FARAMOND *see* PHARAMOND.

FAUSTUS
A son of Vortigern.

FEIMURGAN
see MORGAN (LE FAY).

FEIREFIZ
In Wolfram's *Parzifal*[27], son of Gahmuret and Belcane. He and Perceval, his half-brother, went to Arthur's court after they met. He fell in love with the Grail Damsel, Repanse de Schoie. He became a Christian and they went to India where they became the parents of Prester John.[34] Because his parents were of different colours, Feirefiz was piebald.

FELIX
Tristan's grandfather, father of Meliodas and Mark, according to *Tristano Riccardiano*. In the *Tavola ritonda*, Felix was King of Cornwall and Liones. In Malory, Meliodas and Mark were brothers-in-law.[85]

FENICE
Wife of Alis, who was Emperor of Constantinople. *See* CLIGÉS.

FENICE
Queen of Ireland in *Durmart le Gallois*.

FERGUS
A ploughboy who aspired to knighthood, having seen Arthur and his knights. After various adventures he married Galiene, the Lady of Lothian. His horse was called Arondiel. A Knight of the Round Table of Cornish provenance, a follower of Tristan, was also called Fergus, but this is probably a different character.[64] *See* BLACK KNIGHT.

FERRAGUNZE

A knight who made various assertions to Arthur and Meliodas, among them that he was never jealous of his beauteous wife, Verseria. They tested him in this but, although they arranged for him to find Verseria in the embraces of Gawain, he did not become jealous.[85]

FFYNNON CEGIN ARTHUR

A well in Caernarvon with oily-looking water which was said to have acquired this appearance from animal fat in Arthur's kitchen.

FFRWDWR

An ancestor of Arthur in the maternal pedigree in *Bonedd yr arwr.*

FILIMENIS *see* CONSTANTINOPLE.

FINBEUS

A knight who lent Guinevere a stone which he had obtained from his fairy mistress. Guinevere coveted the stone which made the wearer beautiful, wise and invincible. When she had returned it, she sent Gawain to retrieve it which he did by fighting Finbeus.

FISHER KING

A king encountered during the Grail Quest. He is sometimes, but not always, identified with the Maimed King. He is called Pelles in the *Vulgate Version*, in which the Maimed King is named Parlan or Pellam. In Manessier's Continuation we are told he was wounded by fragments of a sword which had killed his brother, Goon Desert. By Chrétien we are told he could not ride as a result of his infirmity, so he took to fishing as a pastime. Robert de Boron gives his name as Bron and tells us he earned his title by providing fish for Joseph of Arimathea. In *Sone de Nausay* he is identified with Joseph of Arimathea himself.[64] By Wolfram he is called Anfortas.

FISH-KNIGHT

A strange fish monster which looked like a mounted knight. Arthur fought it in order to release a fairy called the Lady of the Fair Hair.[15]

FLORENCE

A son of Gawain who was amongst the party that surprised Lancelot and Guinevere together. Florence was among those killed by the escaping Lancelot.[19] ▣

FLORETE

Wife of Floriant and daughter of the Emperor of Constantinople. ▣

FLORIANT

The hero of the romance *Floriant et Florete*. He was the son of Elyadus, King of Sicily, and the fosterling of Morgan le Fay.

Floriant was a member of Arthur's court and Arthur supported him against the Emperor of Constantinople who made war on him. Floriant fell in love with Florete, the Emperor's daughter, and married her.[64]

See WHITE STAG. ▣

FLORIE

1. The niece of King Joram whom Gawain married and who bore him Wigalois. Elsewhere she is called Floree, daughter of the King of Escavalon.[33]

2. The Queen of Kanadic who raised Arthur's son Ilinot, but later caused his death from lovesickness by sending him away.[34] ▣

FLORISDELFA

An enchantress who learned her arts from Merlin. She sent him a herd of magic horses and a crystal tower on a chariot drawn by fire-breathing elephants. She eventually killed herself when she perceived the beauty of Iseult.[85] ▣

FLURENT

The mother of Iseult in the Icelandic *Saga of Tristan*.[99] ▣

FLYING HORSE

This was made by Merlin and is found in the French romance *The Fair Magalona and Peter, Son of the Count of Provence*.[58] ▣

FORT OF GLASS *see* AVALON ▣

FORTUNE

In the *Morte Arthure*, Arthur dreamt that he beheld Fortune spinning her wheel on which he was placed. The wheel was then twirled about until he was smashed to fragments. He was told that this presaged his downfall. ▣

FOUNTAIN OF THE TRUTH OF LOVE

This was created by Merlin according to *Astrée*, a seventeenth-century novel begun by Honoré d'Urfé (1567–1625) and concluded by his secretary, Baro. It is in the section by Baro that the fountain is mentioned. It was guarded by lions which would not eat a pure and honest person.[75] ▣

FOUNTAIN OF YOUTH

The fountain in which Esclarmonde bathed in the Terrestrial Paradise. ▣

ABOVE *Merlin created a flying horse, a magical creature which occurs often in mythological literature.*

~

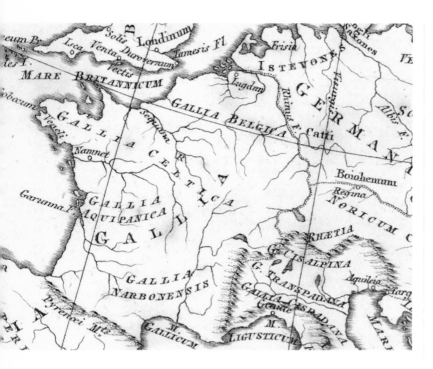

ABOVE *France used to be known as Gaul or Gallia.*

FRANCE

In Arthurian romance, this country is sometimes called by the older name of Gaul. In the Arthurian period the Franks, from whom its present name derived, had established themselves there by about AD 457. Childeric I ruled them until about AD 481 when he was succeeded by Clovis I, possibly the King Claudas of Arthurian tales. From AD 511 Clovis's sons divided the kingdom. Pharamond, who perhaps comes originally from Frankish tradition, is the King of France in some Arthurian sources. *Culhwch* mentions two French kings, Paris and Iona, at Arthur's court. ▣

FRANCHISE TRISTAN

A country, formerly called Servage, conquered by Tristan. ▣

FRIMUTEL

In Wolfram, the father of the Grail King Amfortas.[34] ▣

FRISIANS

A Germanic people who gave their name to islands off the coast of the Netherlands and Germany. The Byzantine historian Procopius, who was writing in the traditional Arthurian period, numbers the Frisians among the barbarian invaders of Britain. Layamon says that King Calin of Friesland (the land of the Frisians) was subject to Arthur. In the *Alliterative Morte Arthure*, King Frederick of Friesland was an ally of Mordred. ▣

FROCIN

A dwarf who betrayed King Mark's secret that he had horse's ears. Mark had his head cut off.[4] ▣

FROLLO

A Roman tribune who ruled Gaul for the Emperor Leo. When Arthur invaded Gaul, he defeated Frollo in battle. Frollo retreated to Paris, outside which city he was slain by Arthur in single combat. The Vulgate *Lancelot* makes him an ally of King Claudas and a claimant to the throne of Gaul. Elsewhere he is said to have been a German who became King of Gaul. In the *Prose Tristan* he had a son called Samaliel who eventually became a knight of great renown.[31] ▣

FULGENTIUS

Geoffrey lists him as an early King of Britain, and John of Fordun (a Scottish historian) claims he was an ancestor of Lot. ▣

GABAN

In the *Polistoire del Eglise de Christ de Caunterbyre*, we are told that he made the sword later wielded by Gawain, back in the days when Christ was fourteen years old. Gaban may represent a survival of the ancient Celtic smith god Gobniu/Gofannon.[83]

GADDIFER

The King of Scotland. He was made king when his brother Betis became King of England in the time of Alexander the Great.[75]
See PERCEFOREST.

GAHERIS

One of the sons of Lot and Morgause. At first he was the squire of his brother Gawain. He surprised Lamorak and Morgause in bed together and killed Morgause, for which Arthur banished him. With another brother, Agravain, he killed Lamorak. Gaheris was married to Lynette. He was killed by Lancelot during the rescue of Guinevere. Both he and another Gaheris were Knights of the Round Table.[19]
See ERIES.

GAHMURET

In Wolfram, the father of Perceval. He went to the Orient and took service with the Baruc of Baghdad. He rescued the dark-skinned Belacane, Queen of Zazamanc, from a Scottish army and married her. He returned to Europe and married Herzeloyde, Queen of Wales and Northgalis. He returned to aid the Baruc and was killed. His sons were Perceval by Herzeloyde and the pie-bald Feirefiz by Belacane.[34]

GAILHOM *see* GORE.

GALAGANDREIZ

One of Lancelot's fathers-in-law.[30]

GALEGANTIS

The name of Lancelot's maternal grandfather; also the name of one of Arthur's knights.

GALEHAUT

Called 'the high prince', he was the ruler of the District Isles, Surluse and other kingdoms. His father was called Brunor and his mother was a giantess called Bagota. He invaded Britain but became a firm friend of Lancelot and, through him, a friend of Arthur. He was made a Knight of the Round Table. When he thought Lancelot was dead, he himself died from sickness and fasting.[19]

RIGHT *Sir Galehaut in search of the Knight of the Litter meets a Lady on the horse Palfrey, before the Castle of the Four Ways, from* Guiron le Courtois *(Flemish, late fifteenth century).*

~

GALAHAD

1. The natural son of Lancelot. His name may be of Welsh origin or come from the place name Gilead in Palestine. His mother is variously called Elaine, Amite and Perevida. He was placed as a child in a nunnery, the abbess there being his paternal great-aunt, and he was later knighted there by Lancelot. One day a sword in a stone was seen in a river by Arthur's knights. It was said in an inscription that only the world's best knight could pull out the sword. Galahad was led into Arthur's court where he sat in the Siege Perilous and then drew the sword out. When the Grail appeared in a vision at Arthur's court, Galahad was one of the knights sent on the Grail Quest. He was given a white shield, made by Evelake, with a red cross which Joseph of Arimathea had drawn in blood. In the course of the quest he joined up with Perceval, Bors and Perceval's sister. On board Solomon's ship, Galahad obtained the sword of David. After the death of Perceval's sister, the remaining trio split up and, for a while, Galahad travelled with his father, Lancelot. He visited Evelake who then died. When he rejoined Bors and Perceval, they came to Carbonek and achieved the Grail. Galahad mended the broken sword, which the other two had failed to do, and Joseph of Arimathea appeared and celebrated Mass. Jesus appeared to the questers and told Galahad he would see the Grail more openly in Sarras. Galahad used the blood from the Grail Spear to anoint the Maimed King, so he was cured. With his companions he left and came to a ship with the Grail on board. On this they sailed to Sarras where the pagan king, Estorause, had them cast into prison where they were fed by the Grail. They forgave Estorause before they died, and Galahad became the next King of Sarras. A year later he came upon Joseph of Arimathea saying Mass. He then beheld the Grail and requested that he should now die and this he was allowed to do. Galahad may quite possibly have been the creation of the author of the *Queste,* as it is there he first appears, but he may be taken from a Welsh character, Gwalhafed, mentioned in *Culhwch.* The historical Saint Illtyd has also been suggested as his prototype. ▣

2. A son of Joseph of Arimathea, born in Britain. He became King of Wales, then called Hocelice. He was an ancestor of Urien.[19,24] ▣

3. Galahad was the original name of Lancelot himself. *See* TWENTY-FOUR KNIGHTS. ▣

✸ DESCENT OF GALAHAD ✸

Nascien

Celidoine

Narpus

Nascien

Eian

Isaiah

Jonaan

Lancelot

Ban

Lancelot

Galahad

BELOW *SIR GALAHAD,*
James Jebusa Shannan (1862-1923).

GALENTIVET

The brother of Griflet, Galentivet was once involved in an attack on Escanor, which was regarded as treacherous and for which Gawain received the blame.[157]

GALERON

A Scottish knight of Galway (Galloway) whose lands were confiscated by Arthur. However, he went on to become a Knight of the Round Table.[19]

GALES LI CAUS

According to the writer Gerbert, the father of Perceval, a Knight of the Round Table and the husband of Philosophine.

GALESCHIN

The son of Arthur's sister Belisent and King Nentres of Garlot. He aided Arthur while the latter was fighting the Saxons who were attacking the city of Clarence.

When they were beaten, Galeschin was made Duke of Clarence. This is an anachronism: the duchy of Clarence was created in 1362 and the place name to which it related was Clare (Suffolk).[31]

GALIAN

A son of Owain in the Faeroese ballad *Gallians tattur* which was written down in the eighteenth century.[102]

GALIENE

The Lady of Lothian, she married Fergus.

GALIHODIN

A cousin of Galehaut, a sub-king in Surluse. A Knight of the Round Table, when Lancelot fled Arthur's court he joined him and became Duke of Sentoge.[19]

ABOVE *Galahad and Perceval, in a chapel, pray for Bohart, from* Lancelot du Lac *(French, early fourteenth century). Perceval was the son of Gales li Caus and Philosophine.*

~

GALVARIUN

A knight of Arthur depicted on the Modena Archivolt (underside of an arch in Modena Cathedral).[85]

GANDIN

According to Wolfram, the name of Perceval's grandfather.[34]

GANIEDA

The twin sister of Merlin, she is found in both the *Vita Merlini* and the Welsh poems where she is called Gwendydd. In the *Vita* she is the wife of Rhydderch and her adultery is spotted by Merlin. The idea of her being an adulteress may have stemmed from Jocelyn's *Life of St Kentigern* in which Rhydderch's wife, Languoreth, becomes enamoured of a soldier. The Welsh poems do not say definitely that Ganieda was married to Rhydderch.[12]

GANNES

The realm ruled by King Bors I.

GARANWYN

A son of Kay in Welsh tradition.

GARCELOS

An ancestor of Arthur in a maternal pedigree by Gruffudd Hiraethog, a Welsh writer of the sixteenth century. The name Garcelos may be a corruption of Castellors, found in the pedigree provided by John of Glastonbury.

GAREL

An Arthurian knight who conquered the land of Kanedic whose king, Ecunaver, had announced his intention of attacking Arthur. Garel married Queen Laudame of Anfere. His exploits are recounted in the romance *Garel von dem blüenden Tal* by Der Pleier.

GARETH

Son of Lot, King of Lothian and Orkney, by Arthur's sister, Morgause. He came to Arthur's court in disguise and was put to work in the kitchens where Kay gave him the contemptuous nickname 'Beaumains' ('Fair Hands' – indicating that they were unsullied by work). When Lynette came to Arthur looking for someone to help her sister Lyonors against the Red Knight of the Red Lands, Gareth went with her, accompanied by a dwarf who knew his identity. On the way he overcame Black, Green and Red Knights and finally the Red Knight of the Red Lands – despite the fact that he had to put up with Lynette's caustic tongue for she had no wish for her cause to be championed by a scullion, or kitchen drudge. Gareth eventually married Lyonors. His story, told by Malory, may have been based on a lost French romance. During Arthur's war against the Roman Emperor Thereus, Gareth killed King Datis of Tuscany. He himself was killed by Lancelot while the latter was rescuing Guinevere.[19]

GARGANTUA

A giant, the son of Grandgousier who was made by Merlin from a bull whale's bones and a phial of Lancelot's blood, and Gargamelle whom Merlin made from the bones of a cow whale and ten pounds of Guinevere's nail clippings. Gargantua served Arthur who supplied him with a sixty-foot club. The giant once had an encounter with Tom Thumb who placed him under an enchantment.[112]

GARLON

An evil and invisible knight, brother of King Pellam. He was killed by Balin.[19]

GARLOT

A kingdom ruled by Nentres who married a sister of Arthur. It was also said to be the kingdom of Urien and may have been identical with Galloway.[19]

GARWEN

One of Arthur's three mistresses, according to *Triad* 57. She was the daughter of Henin the Old.[29]

GASCONY

This region in the south-west of France was ruled by King Ladon in *Claris et Laris*. In the Irish Arthurian tale, *The Visit of Grey Ham*, the Hunting Knight is the son of the King of Gascony.

In Welsh tradition Gascony is the kingdom of the elder Bors.

GASOZEIN

This character appeared in *Diu Crône* and claimed that Guinevere was his wife and that she should leave Arthur and go with him. The choice being left with Guinevere, she refused, but her brother Gotegrim believed her refusal to be wrong so, in anger, he carried her off, intending to kill her.

Guinevere was eventually rescued by Gasozein himself who then fought Gawain over her but eventually admitted that his claim had been false.

GASTE FOREST

A realm ruled by Pellinore, possibly identical with the Waste Land.

GAURIEL

A warrior who married the ruler of Fluratrone, who abandoned him, but said she would return to him if he would capture three knights of Arthur for her. He did so. Afterwards, he spent a year with Arthur. Gauriel had a pet ram which he had trained to fight.

The romance featuring him was German, written by Konrad von Stoffeln.

GAWAIN

1. The eldest son of King Lot and Morgause and one of Arthur's most prominent knights.

In Welsh tradition his father is sometimes given as Gwyar, but sometimes Gwyar is said to be his mother. In French he is called variously Gauvain, Gauwain, Gayain, etc. In Latin he is Walganus, in Dutch Walewein and in Irish Balbhuaidh. In Welsh his name is Gwalchmai (hawk of May or hawk of the plain). R.S. Loomis[105] argues that Gawain and Gwalchmai were originally different characters and that the Welsh identified their hero Gwalchmai with the Continental Gawain. He suggests that Gawain is in origin the *Mabinogion* character Gwrvan Gwallt-avwy and that his name may have arisen from Welsh *gwallt-avwyn* (hair like rain) or *gwallt-advwyn* (fair hair). R. Bromwich[29] disagrees and argues that Gawain and Gwalchmai were always identical.

The father of Gawain was King Lot who, in his early days, was a page to Arthur's sister, Morgause, on whom he fathered Gawain, who was baptized and set adrift in a cask. (In *De Ortu Waluuanii* his mother is called Anna rather than Morgause.) He was rescued by fishermen and eventually found his way to Rome where he was knighted by Pope Sulpicius. Arriving at Arthur's court, he became one of the king's most important knights. In early romance he is depicted as a mighty champion, though in later stories, for example French tales and Malory whom they influenced, he is less likeable. He married in various tales Ragnell, Amurfine, the daughter of the Carl of Carlisle and

the daughter of the king of Sorcha. In *Walwein* he became the husband or lover of Ysabele, while in Italian romance he was said to be the lover of Morgan's daughter, Pulzella Gaia. He had sons called Florence, Lovel and Guinglain. After Arthur's rift with Lancelot, he became violently opposed to that knight. He was killed with a club when Arthur was landing in Britain to oppose Mordred. Gawain had a peculiar gift that he grew stronger towards noon and this has led to speculation about his being a solar hero in origin. Surprisingly, the same gift is attributed to Escanor, one of his opponents. Gawain's death did not mark his last appearance in the Arthurian saga for his ghost subsequently appeared to the king. According to Breton tradition, he survived Arthur's last battle and Arthur abdicated in his favour.

Gawain's horse was called Gringalet. William of Malmesbury says his grave was discovered at Ros, a place which cannot be identified with certainty, in the reign of King William II (1087–1100). His skull was supposed to be in Dover Castle.

The story of the beheading contest which features in the tales of Gawain and the Green Knight (*see* GREEN KNIGHT), the Carl of Carlisle (*see* CARL OF CARLISLE) and Gawain and the Turk (*see* GROMER) has a parallel in Irish mythology where Cu Roi, King of Munster, proclaimed Cuchullain champion of Ireland. The decision was rejected by two other champions, so Cu Roi arrived in the guise of a giant at Emhain Macha (modern Navan Fort) where the King of Ulster had his court, and challenged each of the three to behead him, on condition that he could afterwards do the same to them. Each of Cuchullain's rivals tried but, when the head was sliced off, Cu Roi replaced it and neither of them would let him have his turn. When Cuchullain cut off Cu Roi's head and once again the latter replaced it on his shoulders, Cuchullain was prepared to let him strike him as agreed, whereupon Cu Roi disclosed who he was and declared Cuchullain unrivalled champion. The similarity of these tales may indicate a common source, or even that Gawain is identical in origin with Cuchullain as the tales about him may be indigenous to the north of England; in ancient times, the north-west of England contained a tribe called the Setantii, while the original name of Cuchullain was Setanta. It may well have been that Cuchullain was a Setantii hero with a reputation on both sides of the Irish Sea, whose memory was kept alive under the name of Gawain by the medieval descendants of the Setantii in England.

J. Matthews[119] points out that the story of Gawain's birth and his being set adrift in a cask parallels that of his brother Mordred and suggests that originally Gawain was Arthur's son, who fathered him incestuously on his sister who, in the original story was Morgan. The adult Gawain became Morgan's knight and his story is predated by the mythical tale of the Celtic god Mabon whose mother, Modron (earlier Matrona), is the prototype of Morgan. He also suggests that Galahad replaced Gawain as a Grail quester because of Gawain's pagan associations. That Perceval similarly replaced Gawain was suggested earlier by J.L. Weston.[160]

2. A knight, called 'the Brown', who had the baby Gawain baptized.[119,160]

See GREEN KNIGHT *and* UALLABH.

ABOVE *Gawain and two ladies at the Castle of Nohant, from* Lancelot du Lac *(French, early fourteenth century).*

TOP LEFT *Gawain rescues his mother Morgause from the Sesnes, from Arthurian Legends, Lancelot Cycle (Bologna, c.1270).*

BELOW LEFT *Gawain riding in pursuit of the Holy Quest, from the Quest of the Grail (French, late thirteenth century).*

~

GEREINT

The King of Dumnonia who married Enid and whose adventures are recounted in the Welsh romance of *Gereint and Enid*. In French romance the hero of this tale is Erec but, as Erec was not generally known amongst the Welsh, they substituted Gereint, one of their own heroes, for him. Gereint may be a historical figure, a cousin of Arthur, though J. Gantz[18] denies his historicity. Although he is listed as Arthur's contemporary, he may have belonged to an older generation, as the *Dream of Rhonabwy* says his son Cadwy was Arthur's contemporary. Gereint's father's name is given as Erbin but, in the *Life of St Cyby*, Erbin is called his son. *Culhwch* supplies the names of two of his brothers, Ermid and Dywel.[17]

GERENTON

An ancestor of Arthur and father of Conan, he was mentioned in Gallet's pedigree.[50]

GERMANY

In Arthurian times, this country was the domain of various tribes, but the romance *Claris et Laris* has it ruled by Emperor Henry, father of Laris.

GENERON

In Heywood's *Life of Merlin*, a castle of Vortigern which takes the place of the tower that keeps falling down in other versions of the story.

GENVISSA

Geoffrey maintains she was a daughter of the Roman Emperor Claudius. She married Arviragus and, when Arviragus revolted against Claudius, Genvissa arranged peace between them.[11]

ABOVE GEREINT
AND ENID, *King and
Queen of Dumnonia.
Arthur A. Dixon,*

~

GERONTIUS

A Roman leader who overthrew the rule of the historical Roman emperor, Constantine III, in Britain.

GIANT OF MONT ST MICHEL

This giant, who resided at Mont St Michel in Brittany, seized Helena, the niece of Hoel, the King of Brittany. Arthur, accompanied by Kay and Bedivere, set off after him. He found that Helena was already dead, but he slew the giant.[11]

GILAN

The Duke of Swales, he was the original owner of the dog Petitcrieu which he later gave to Tristan.

GILANEIER

The name of Arthur's queen in the romance *Jaufré*.

GILDAS JUNIOR

Alternative name for Tremeur, son of Trephina. *See* CUNOMORUS.

GILDAS, SAINT

Saint Gildas was a British writer of the original Arthurian period. His work, *De excidio et conquestu Britanniae*, does not mention Arthur by name, though it does mention the battle of Badon. According to story, he was the son of Caw and, when he was in Ireland, he learned that Arthur, his friend, had killed his brother Hueil, but this did not cause discord between himself and Arthur. The *Dream of Rhonabwy* calls him Arthur's counsellor. T.D. O'Sullivan[129] opines that Gildas wrote *De excidio* as quite a young man.

GILIERCHINS SEE HOEL.

GILLOMANIUS

A King of Ireland who aided Paschent when he invaded Britain.[11]

GILMAURIUS

According to Geoffrey, the King of Ireland who was defeated when Arthur invaded that country. No such king of Ireland is known to history.

GISMIRANTE

One of Arthur's knights who heard a tale of a land where the king's daughter went naked to church every year. Anyone who saw her lost his head. Gismirante went there and ran off with her. She was abducted by a savage man, but Gismirante rescued her. Gismirante's story is found in a cantare by the Italian poet Antonio Pucci (fourteenth century).

GLAIN

In a Cornish poem, a magic snake's egg for which Merlin was searching.[88]

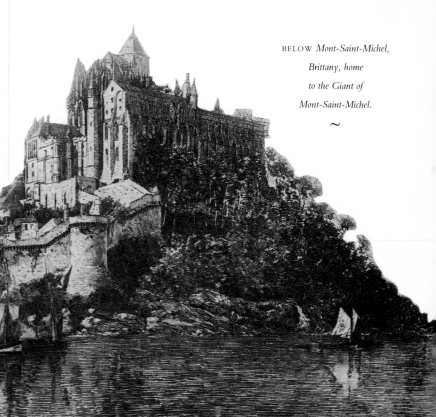

BELOW *Mont-Saint-Michel, Brittany, home to the Giant of Mont-Saint-Michel.*

~

GLASTONBURY

A small town in Somerset, the site of a medieval abbey, which was variously said to have been founded by Deruvian and Phagan, missionaries sent by the Pope to the British king, Lucius, and by Saint Patrick before his mission to the Irish. There is in fact no real evidence for an abbey there before the seventh century. In the romance Perlesvaus, Glastonbury is identified with Avalon. Saint Joseph of Arimathea was thought to have founded the old Church there. In the Middle Ages, bones, which were identified by their discoverers as those of Arthur and Guinevere, were found there. Although most authorities regard the find as a hoax, this is not necessarily the case. According to a story found in the Life of Gildas, Melwas (Meleagaunce) abducted Guinevere and took her to Glastonbury, but Gildas mediated between him and Arthur.[42,44,86,89,103] *See* GILDAS, SAINT.

GLASTONBURY CROSS

A cross unearthed at the excavation of Arthur's supposed grave at Glastonbury in 1191. The inscription on the cross read *Hic iacet sepultus inclitus Rex Arturius in insula avalonia.*

The cross was lost but, in recent times, a pattern-maker named Derek Mahoney claimed to have found it and reburied it. ▣

GLASTONBURY THORN

A thorn which was said to have come from a staff, planted by Joseph of Arimathea on Wearyall Hill, and which became a thorn tree, flowering every year at Christmas. The thorn is first mentioned in the *Lyfe of Joseph of Arimathea* (*c.* 1502). The trunk of the tree was cut down by a Puritan zealot.

The tree has a number of descendants alive today, notably in front of the Church of Saint John the Baptist, Glastonbury. They bloom in late December or early January.[153] ▣

GLASTONBURY ZODIAC

According to a theory which was advanced by K. Maltwood in *A Guide to Glastonbury's Temple of the Stars*, carved in the landscape around Glastonbury are giant figures, delineated by various markings which correspond to the signs of the Zodiac in the sky above them. Maltwood related these figures to episodes in the Grail Quest.

The existence of the Zodiac has not won scholarly recognition, though the idea has a number of adherents.[42,137] ▣

GLEIN

The mouth of a river at which one of Arthur's battles was fought.[21] Either of the English rivers called Glein may be the site. ▣

GLEWLWYD

Arthur's porter in *Culhwch*, to whom the epithet *gafaelfawr* (great grasp) is applied. In the poem *Pa gur*, he figures as the gatekeeper who will not admit Arthur unless he identifies himself and his followers.[17] *See* TWENTY-FOUR KNIGHTS. ▣

GLIGLOIS

Gawain's squire, son of a German noble. Both he and Gawain fell in love with Beauté, Guinevere's maid, but she preferred Gliglois. ▣

GLITEN

A sister of Morgan.[12] ▣

GLITONEA

A sister of Morgan.[12] ▣

GLOIER

The King of Sorelois. ▣

GLORIANA

The queen of Faerie in Spenser. Arthur saw her in a dream and fell in love with her. In Spenser's allegory, she stands for Queen Elizabeth I of England.[27] ▣

GLORIANDE

Wife of King Apollo of Liones. ▣

GLWYDYN

The builder of Ehangwen, the hall used by Arthur for feasting. T.F. O'Rahilly[128] suggests his name may be a form of Gwydion, that of a Celtic god, the son of Nodens.[17] ▣

GOBNIU

An Irish smith god who may have been identical in origin with the Welsh god Gwydion.[70] *See* TREBUCHET. ▣

ABOVE Fairies have always had mythological powers.

LEFT TOP Glastonbury Tor. Archaeologists have excavated traces of a settlement on the Tor dating to the Arthurian period.

LEFT Glastonbury Abbey. Claims have been made that Glastonbury is the site of Arthur and Guinevere's graves.

~

GOG AND MAGOG

In the Middle Ages it was believed that Gog and Magog were nations that had been confined behind mountains by Alexander the Great, who had used 6000 bronze- and ironworkers to build a gate to hold them back. They attacked Arthur but the giant Gargantua helped him to overcome them.[38,112]

GOLEUDDYDD

In Welsh lore, Arthur's aunt, wife of Kilydd, sister of Igraine and mother of Culhwch.

GOLWG HAFDDYDD

The maid of Iseult in the *Ystoria Trystan*. This work is a Welsh version of the Tristan legend.

GONOSOR

A king of Ireland converted by Joseph of Arimathea. Because of the help he gave King Canor of Cornwall, Cornwall afterwards paid tribute to Ireland until Tristan killed Marhaus.[158]

GOON DESERT

The brother of the Fisher King, he was killed by Partinal. The sword broke in the commission of this act and rejoining it was one of the feats involved in achieving the Grail.[64]

GOREU

A cousin of Arthur who, on three occasions, is said to have rescued him from imprisonment. He was the son of Constantine by an unnamed daughter of Amlawdd Wledig. His name, meaning 'best', was earned by him for managing to gain entrance with his followers to Wrnach's stronghold.[17]

See YSPADADDEN.

GORLAGON

Arthur's pet wolf who turned out to be a man enchanted by his faithless wife with the aid of his magic wand. Arthur obtained the wand and turned him back into a human.

Gorlagon's tale is found in the Latin romance *Arthur and Gorlagon* (fourteenth century).[112]

GORE

ABOVE *Lancelot on the Pont Dépeé, the bridge shaped like a sword, from* Lancelot du Lac *(French, early fourteenth century).*

~

A kingdom bordering on Scotland from which it was separated by the River Tember. Its capital city was Gailhom. If one of Arthur's knights entered it, only Lancelot could rescue him. It was accessible only by crossing one of two bridges, one like a sword, the other subaqueous. It is variously described as the realm of Urien or Bagdemagus. Although it has otherwordly features, it may preserve a memory of the Celtic kingdom of Rheged. See SORHAUT.

ABOVE *Lancelot in prison at Gore, from* Lancelot du Lac *(French, early fourteenth century).*

~

GORLOIS

First husband of Igraine whose semblance Uther took when he first copulated with that lady. Gorlois was slain in battle against Uther. The building called Carhules near Castle Dore in Cornwall may have been called after a person named Gourles, perhaps the original of Gorlois.[11,46] *See* DIONETA.

GORMANT

According to *Culhwch*, Gormant was Arthur's brother on his mother's side. Gormant's father is called Rica, chief elder of Cornwall. The latter appears to occupy the position of Gorlois in the Welsh tradition.[17]

GORNEMANT DE GOORT

Prince of Graherz and a Knight of the Round Table. His three sons, Schenteflurs, Lascoyt and Gurzgi, all met violent ends. He trained Perceval, hoping he would marry his daughter Liaze, but it was not to be.[134]

GORVENAL

Born in Gaul, Gorvenal became the tutor and later the servant of Tristan. He married Brangien, Iseult's maidservant. When Tristan left Liones, Gorvenal became its king.[19] *See* PHARAMOND.

GOSWHIT

According to Layamon, the name of Arthur's helmet (goose white).[32]

GOTEGRIM

Brother of Guinevere. He carried her off when she refused to leave Arthur and go with Gasozein who claimed to be her husband.[155] Gotegrim backed Gasozein's claims and threatened to kill his sister.

GOWTHER

The hero of an Arthurian romance in whom good and evil, inherited from his parents, strove against one another for mastery. Good eventually proved the victor.

GRACIA

In the fourteenth-century *Birth of Arthur*, one of Arthur's nieces.

GRAERIA

In the fourteenth-century *Birth of Arthur*, one of Arthur's nieces.

GRAIL CASTLE

The castle, known as Carbonek, in which the Grail was housed.

GRAIL KINGS

German literature affords the following genealogy of the Grail Kings:

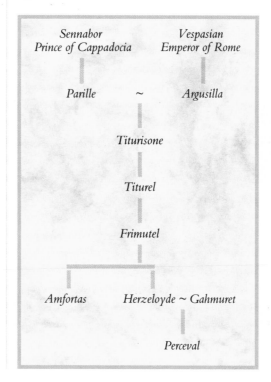

Sennabor
Prince of Cappadocia — Vespasian
Emperor of Rome

Parille ~ Argusilla

Titurisone

Titurel

Frimutel

Amfortas   Herzeloyde ~ Gahmuret

Perceval

ABOVE *The Holy Grail. The hero who achieves the Grail has been variously cited as Perceval, Galahad, Gawain and Bors.*

~

GRAIL

The Holy Grail was a vessel sought by the Knights of the Round Table. The word is derived from Old French *greal*, meaning a kind of dish. The earliest story of the Grail is that of Chrétien, in which Perceval is the hero. In this it is called 'a grail', a common noun, later becoming *the* Grail. Perceval's failure to achieve the Grail at first is due to his not asking the Grail questions (What is the grail? Whom does it serve?), thereby restoring the Maimed King to health and the land round about to fertility. The question that arises is, what sort of tradition lay behind the Grail story? In its final forms, the Grail was the cup used by Jesus at the Last Supper, the dish on the table at that event, or (in Wolfram) a stone. F. Anderson[39] has argued that the Grail was, in origin, the holy object of a nearly worldwide mystery cult which showed the Trinity symbolically. J.L. Weston[159] thought it part of a pagan fertility rite, involving a story

similar to that of Adonis. Certainly, the idea of a sickly king and a correspondingly sickly land seems to indicate some kind of fertility story but, while Miss Weston felt it must be of oriental provenance, it may be of local Celtic origin. It was thought to serve people with food and this calls to mind the notion of a cauldron of plenty, which is found in Celtic mythology, and reminds one of the Dysgl of Rhydderch, one of the Thirteen Treasures of Britain. The recorded expedition of Arthur to the Otherworld, apparently to obtain a cauldron, in *Preiddeu Annwfn* and, what is probably its variant, the story of Arthur's expedition to Ireland to obtain a cauldron in *Culhwch* may be early forms of the story of a Grail quest. However, it has been suggested that the story may originally have been built around a vengeance motif, as indicated by the Welsh *Peredur*. D.D.R. Owen[130] thinks that the original tale had to do with the naming of a hero

who had a cup proffered to him and was asked whom it should serve.

The idea of the Grail as a metaphor for the human body containing the Holy Spirit would seem to be a late development.

In recent times the Holy Blood/Holy Grail theory has become widely known because of its appearance in popular books. These argue that the Grail was a bloodline descending from Christ and they postulate that the Cathars or Albigensians, a heretical body of the Middle Ages, were much involved. However, as the Cathars regarded sexual reproduction as evil, they would hardly have cherished a line of descent. Elaborations of this theory have involved beings from outer space and pre-Columbian contact with America.

The Christian element in the story is widely thought to be a later overlay and is highlighted in works such as the *Queste*. P. Matarasso[113] suggests that the Grail experience in the *Queste* may well have involved some form of perception of God by Galahad.

The hero who achieves the Grail is Perceval in the Chrétien Continuations, in Wolfram and in *Perlesvaus*; Galahad in the *Queste* and its derivatives; Gawain in *Diu Crône*; and, in Malory, Galahad, Perceval and Bors achieve it together, Bors alone then returning to Arthur's court. J.L. Weston has argued that Gawain was the original Grail hero, later replaced by Perceval, while J. Matthews[119] takes the view that Gawain was replaced by Galahad.

According to the *Queste*, the Grail was carried to Heaven by a hand after Galahad's death.[6–9,17,22,24,31,34,48,56,63,91,94,107,121,159,162]

~

BELOW *Though the Grail is most usually shown within a Christian context, it also has links with pagan fertility rites.*

GRAIL PROCESSION

The procession observed by Perceval at the Grail Castle when the Grail was carried, according to Chrétien by a squire with a bleeding lance, two squires carrying ten-branched candle-sticks, a damsel with the Grail and a damsel with a plate. In the *Didot Perceval*, there was a squire with a lance, a damsel with two silver plates and cloths, and a squire with a vessel containing the blood of Jesus. The Welsh *Peredur* has two youths with a large spear from which blood flowed, followed by a maiden with a salver on which there was a head swimming with blood.[6,9,17]
See LANCE OF LONGINUS.

GRAIL SWORD

This sword, fashioned by Trebuchet, was shattered when it struck down Goon Desert, brother of the Fisher King. Making it whole was part of the Grail Quest.[64]

abens naows Septem. Elementum Aquae et Terr... de

...s naturam corrigens in vegno mineral...

...istonā. Benedichus dominius Deus nester

...inum. Cum eorundem in easdem opera...

...egatissious figūris depicit. Homo natus... ...manere...

...pore repletcur multi miserys Scb 14. Homo natis d...

...es annorum nostorum in ipsis septvaginka āni eru...

...lte Hominius actibus respondentes scilicet · Fortvous n...

...xiliān minōm tutela extens. Amißio comprehsum extr...

...in intrens limien superius logis aqueū afrītatur.

...Soū itti eudis... anus fr ornaut celos decem ad...

istonā · Benedichus dc...
iginum. Cum eorunde...
legatissious figūris de...
en pore repletcur mult...
les annorum nostoru...
epte Hominius actibus...
uxiliān minōm tutela...
nen intrens limien sup...
ro spū itti eudis. an...
us astruentbz pier ar H...

num nostorum in ipsis septvag...
minius actibus respondentes scilice...
minōm tutela extens. Amißio com...
ns limien superius logis aqueū...

effigieler habera
ptem. Elementum Aquae et Terrae.
rigens in vegno minerali. Utriusque
s dominus Deus nester qui dedit n
undem in easdem operahinibus et e
atissious figuris depicit. Homo natus de muliere b
pore repletur multi miserys Scb 14. Homo natis c
annorum nostorum in ipsis Septvaginta ani er
Hominius actibus respondentes scilicet. Fortuous
ilian minim tutela extens. Amissio comprehsum ex
n intrens limien superius logis aqueu afritatur.

geinosq; trioes
depurius effigueler
demain veber fidelis
asub peditz cherubm
tum Aquae et Terra
naturam corrigens in vegno minerali. Utriusqu
istonā. Benedichus dominus Deus nester qui dedit
gium. Cum eorundem in easdem operahinibus e
egatissious figuris depicit. Homo natus de muliere
n oore repletur multi miserys Scb 14. Homo natis

GRISANDOLE

A damsel named Avenable went to the court of Julius Caesar, disguised as a page, and calling herself Grisandole. She introduced Merlin to the court and eventually married Julius Caesar.[31]

GROCLAND

An island in the polar regions, colonized by Arthur, according to the *Itinerary* of Jacob Cnoyen. It may be identical with Greenland. The *Itinerary* claims that its inhabitants were twenty-three feet tall and that Arthur conquered the northern islands in about AD 530. There was a mountain range surrounding the Pole and channels went through this to form four indrawing seas. Four thousand of Arthur's men went into the indrawing seas, but none returned. In 1364, seven of these people, plus one of Flemish descent, were thought to have presented themselves at the court of King Magnus of Norway. In any case, the date is certainly wrong for, at this time, Norway was ruled by King Haakon VI. The 'King Magnus' mentioned was presumably his predecessor, Magnus VII (reigned 1319–55).

GROMER

A knight who, by magic, was made to resemble a Turk. He and Gawain went to the Isle of Man where, after some adventures, they slew the king and Gromer, restored to his original shape by decapitation, became king in his place. Gromer's story is told in the poem of *The Turk and Gawain* (*c.* 1500). Another bearer of this name was Gromer Somer Joure who once captured Arthur.

GRONOSIS

A son of Kay.

GROTTE D'ARTUS

A cave in Brittany where Arthur and his warriors are said to lie asleep, awaiting the time when they will be called to battle once again.

GUENDOLOENA

The wife of Merlin in *Vita Merlini*. She may be identical with Chwimleian, mentioned in *Afollonau*, one of the Welsh Myrddin (Merlin) poems.[121]

GUENGASOAIN

He was slain by Yder and Gawain to avenge Raguidel. Yder married his daughter. Guengasoain was guarded by a bear as he knew he could be overcome only by a pair of knights.[64]

GUENLOIE

A queen, wife of Yder.

GUIDERIUS

A king of Britain who, according to Geoffrey, was killed during the Claudian invasion and was succeeded by his brother, Arviragus.[11]

GUIGENOR

A grand-niece of Arthur. Her relationship to Arthur is shown below.

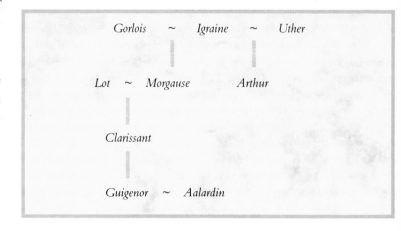

Gorlois	~	Igraine	~	Uther
Lot	~	Morgause		Arthur
Clarissant				
Guigenor	~	Aalardin		

PREVIOUS PAGE

THE GREEN KNIGHT,
Amanda Cameron.

~

GRAMOFLANZ

The husband of Itonje, one of the sisters of Gawain.[34]

GREAT FOOL

A nephew of Arthur and the hero of the Irish romance *Eachtra an Amadán Mor*. Because his brothers were killed for plotting against Arthur, he was raised in obscurity in the woods. When he grew up he became a mighty warrior, defeating Gawain, the Purple Knight, the Red Knight and the Speckled Knight.

GREAT SPIRITS SPRING

A spring to which Arthur, according to an American legend, went to drink the healing waters. It was at Windfall Run, USA.

GREENAN CASTLE

Situated about three miles from Ayr, this castle is built on the site of an Iron Age hill fort. N.L. Goodrich argues that this was the site of the original Camelot, though she also states that 'Camelot' was the name given to whatever stronghold Arthur was occupying at the time. She further identifies the site of Greenan Castle with Badon.[87]

GREEN KNIGHT

1. A character featured in the classic poem *Sir Gawain and the Green Knight* (fourteenth century) and its derivative *The Green Knight* (*c.* 1500). This knight came into Arthur's hall and asked any one of his knights to trade blows. Gawain accepted this challenge and he was allowed to strike first. He cut off the Green Knight's head. The latter calmly picked it up and told Gawain to meet him on New Year's Morning for his turn.

On his way to this meeting, Gawain lodged with a lord and each agreed to give the other what he had obtained during each day of Gawain's stay.

On the first day, when the lord was out hunting, Gawain received a kiss from his wife which was duly passed on. On the second day, he received a brace of kisses which were also passed on. On the third day he was given three kisses and some green lace which would magically protect him, but only the three kisses were passed on.

Having left the lord's residence, Gawain arrived at the Green Chapel where he was to meet the Green Knight. He knelt for the blow. The Green Knight aimed three blows at Gawain, but the first two did not make contact and the third but lightly cut his neck.

The Green Knight turned out to be the lord with whom he had been staying and he said he would not have cut Gawain at all had the latter told him about the lace. The Green Knight was called Bertilak and he lived at Castle Hutton. The tale bears a striking resemblance to an Irish narrative in which Cu Roi takes the part of the Green Knight and Cuchullain that of Gawain. The Green Knight may have been the Green Man, a wild man featured on inn signboards whose effigy was carried in civic processions.[26]

2. Sir Pertolepe, a knight who was defeated by Gareth.[19]

GREENLAND

This island, called Kalaallit Nunaat in Greenlandic, was conquered by Arthur, according to William Lambard in his *Archaionomia* (1568). Hakluyt, the travel writer of the sixteenth and seventeenth centuries, is of the opinion that Grocland was Greenland. Greenland may be meant by Granland, the territory ruled by Amangons in *Le chevalier as deus espées* (Old French).

ABOVE *The Green Knight Prepares to Fight Gareth,* William Russell Flint, *from Malory's* Le Morte d'Arthur. *The Green Knight, also known as Sir Pertolepe, before he was defeated by Gareth.*

~

GREGORY

A pope who once brought Merlin's orthodoxy into question. During his pontificate, a bishop called Conrad brought a charge of heresy against Merlin but the latter was acquitted.[85]

GREIDAWL

Father of Gwythr.[17]

GRELOGUEVAUS

The father of Perceval in the First Continuation of Chrétien's *Perceval*.[6]

GREY LADY

A ghost said to haunt Moel Arthur in Llanwrst, Clwyd. R. Holland in his book, *Supernatural Clwyd*, (Llanwrst 1989), suggests she was thought to be the protectress of Arthur's treasure which is said to be buried there.

GRIFFITH

A king of Wales who gained his throne by murder, but was ousted by Meriadoc, the true heir to the throne.[64]

GRIFLET

An Arthurian knight, the son of Do. His name is also rendered *Girflet*. He may be identical with Jaufré, the hero of a Provencal romance. In one version he, not Bedivere, was given the task of flinging Excalibur into the waters after Arthur's last battle. When he saw Arthur's tomb he became a hermit but he died shortly afterwards. Griflet's origins are Celtic: he is derived from Gilfaethwy, son of Don, in the *Mabinogion* story of *Math, Son of Mathonwy*, where he is the brother of Gwydion. As Gwydion seems to have been a British smith-god, Gilfaethwy was presumably also a deity. Griflet's father, Don, seems to come from Don, the goddess who was Gilfaethwy's mother in British tradition.[19] *See* ESCANOR *and* LORETE.

GRIMAL

The illegitimate son of Evelake.

GRINGALET

(In Welsh: Kincaled) Gawain's horse. Accounts vary as to how it came into Gawain's possession. He was thought either to have won it in a duel with Escanor Le Grand, though it was Escanor's nephew's possession, given him by the fairy, Esclarimonde; or else to have taken it from the Saxon King Clarion.[31,105]

GRISANDOLE

A damsel named Avenable went to the court of Julius Caesar, disguised as a page, and calling herself Grisandole. She introduced Merlin to the court and eventually married Julius Caesar.[31]

GROCLAND

An island in the polar regions, colonized by Arthur, according to the *Itinerary* of Jacob Cnoyen. It may be identical with Greenland. The *Itinerary* claims that its inhabitants were twenty-three feet tall and that Arthur conquered the northern islands in about AD 530. There was a mountain range surrounding the Pole and channels went through this to form four indrawing seas. Four thousand of Arthur's men went into the indrawing seas, but none returned. In 1364, seven of these people, plus one of Flemish descent, were thought to have presented themselves at the court of King Magnus of Norway. In any case, the date is certainly wrong for, at this time, Norway was ruled by King Haakon VI. The 'King Magnus' mentioned was presumably his predecessor, Magnus VII (reigned 1319–55).

GROMER

A knight who, by magic, was made to resemble a Turk. He and Gawain went to the Isle of Man where, after some adventures, they slew the king and Gromer, restored to his original shape by decapitation, became king in his place. Gromer's story is told in the poem of *The Turk and Gawain* (*c.* 1500). Another bearer of this name was Gromer Somer Joure who once captured Arthur.

GRONOSIS

A son of Kay.

GROTTE D'ARTUS

A cave in Brittany where Arthur and his warriors are said to lie asleep, awaiting the time when they will be called to battle once again.

GUENDOLOENA

The wife of Merlin in *Vita Merlini*. She may be identical with Chwimleian, mentioned in *Afollonau*, one of the Welsh Myrddin (Merlin) poems.[121]

GUENGASOAIN

He was slain by Yder and Gawain to avenge Raguidel. Yder married his daughter. Guengasoain was guarded by a bear as he knew he could be overcome only by a pair of knights.[64]

GUENLOIE

A queen, wife of Yder.

GUIDERIUS

A king of Britain who, according to Geoffrey, was killed during the Claudian invasion and was succeeded by his brother, Arviragus.[11]

GUIGENOR

A grand-niece of Arthur. Her relationship to Arthur is shown below.

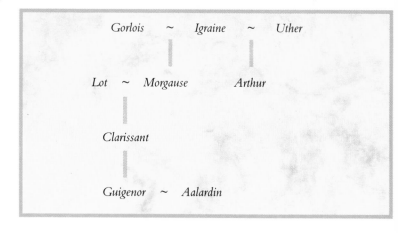

Gorlois ~ Igraine ~ Uther

Lot ~ Morgause   Arthur

Clarissant

Guigenor ~ Aalardin

GUIGNIER

The chaste wife of Caradoc Briefbras whose fidelity was shown by the mantle test. A boy brought a mantle to Arthur's court and asserted that it would fit only faithful wives. Various ladies tried it on but it fitted only Guignier. Guignier lost one of her breasts in dealing with a serpent magically wrapped around Caradoc's arm, but this was replaced by one made of gold with the aid of the knight Aalardin who had once been enamoured of her. *See* TEGAU EURFON

GUINALOT

The offspring of Eliavres and a bitch, with which he had been forced to copulate.

GUINEBAUT

The brother of Ban and the elder Bors. Something of a wizard, he made a magic chessboard and caused a dance to continue perpetually.

RIGHT *King Arthur, Prisoner of the False Guinevere, from* Lancelot du Lac *(French, early fourteenth century). The False Guinevere was able to deceive Arthur for a time into accepting her as his real wife.*

~

GUINEVERE, THE FALSE

Guinevere's identical half-sister, whom Leodegrance fathered on the same night as he fathered Guinevere. She claimed she was the true Guinevere and enticed Arthur into giving up her half-sister who took refuge in Sorelois. The False Guinevere and her champion Bertholai admitted in the end that they were deceivers and after two and a half years the real Guinevere was restored to Arthur.[31]

LEFT *Eliavres was forced to copulate with a bitch, by which he fathered Guinalot.*

GUINEVERE

(In Welsh: Gwenhwyvar) The wife of Arthur, daughter of King Leodegrance of Cameliard in Malory. Welsh tradition calls her father Gogrvan or Ocvran, while in *Diu Crône* he is called King Garlin of Galore. A late literary source, Thelwall's play *The Fairy of the Lake* (1801), suggests that she is the daughter of Vortigern. Wace makes her Mordred's sister. In Geoffrey, she is of Roman stock, and while Arthur was fighting the Roman war, Mordred abducted her and made himself king. In the later version of the Arthurian story she was the lover of Lancelot. Their intrigue discovered, Lancelot fled and Guinevere was duly sentenced to burning. Lancelot rescued her and war followed between him and Arthur. While Arthur was away, Mordred rebelled. Arthur returned to do battle with him and received his final wound. Guinevere took the veil.

However, there are different tales of her end. According to *Perlesvaus*, she died in Arthur's lifetime, while Boece averred she ended her days as a prisoner of the Picts. She and Arthur had a son called Loholt, though he was also said to be the son of Arthur and Lionors. The *Alliterative Morte Arthure* says that she and Mordred were the parents of two sons. B. Saklatvala has suggested she was really a Saxon named Winifred, and J. Markale[112] has opined that Kay and Gawain were originally amongst her lovers. Welsh tradition stated that Arthur was married, not to one, but to three Guineveres.

Some have argued that Guinevere is a mythical figure, representing the sovereignty of Britain, over which contenders fight; in this respect she is a parallel figure to Eriu, the goddess of the sovereignty of Ireland.

ABOVE

Guinevere and Lancelot.

~

C. Matthews[115] contends that this interpretation is supported by the legend of three Guineveres married to Arthur, saying these are not three separate persons but a single triune goddess. J. Matthews contends that Guinevere and Morgan are like two sides of a coin, the beneficent and maleficent aspects of sovereignty. Efforts to connect Guinevere with Findabair, daughter of the Irish goddess Maeve, have not proven successful.

Guinevere was very susceptible to being abducted and it has been suggested that her story is a parallel of the Irish story of Midir and Etain. In this, Etain was once an otherworldy bride of Midir but she retains no memory of this fact and is now married to an Irish king. Midir turns up to lure her back to the Otherworld. Similarly, it is said, Guinevere's abductor, be he Meleagaunce or Lancelot, Gasozein or Valerin, is merely taking her back to the Otherworld whence she came.

We are told in the *Mabinogion* that Guinevere had a sister named Gwenhwyvach; in French romance that she had an identical half-sister who, for a while, took her place; and in the German *Diu Crône* that she had a brother, Gotegrin.[155]

127

GUINGANBRESIL

The husband of Tancree, niece of Arthur.

GUINGLAIN

The son of Gawain and Ragnell. He appeared at Arthur's court ignorant of his name, so he was called Le Bel Inconnu ('The Fair Unknown'). A damsel turned up with a dwarf and asked for a knight to rescue her mistress, a princess, with 'the daring kiss'. Arthur sent Le Bel Inconnu. After a couple of adventures they came to the Golden Island where a fairy, Pucelle aux Blanche Mains, offered him her love, but they went on to the palace of the princess. There, Guinglain defeated a knight with a horned and fire-breathing horse, and darkness fell everywhere. A snake appeared and kissed him and he heard a voice tell him his name and that he was Gawain's son. He fell asleep and when he awoke a princess called Blonde Esmerée was there. She told him she had been the snake, whom he had released from enchantment by receiving her kiss. After a sojourn with Pucelle on the Golden Island, Guinglain married the princess.

GUINNION

Unidentified site of one of Arthur's battles.[21]

GUIOMAR

A nephew of Arthur and cousin of Guinevere, he fell in love with Morgan when she was lady-in-waiting to Guinevere. When Guinevere found out about this, she parted them.

GUIROMELANT

He was an enemy of Gawain and a lover of Gawain's sister, Clarissant, with whom, to Gawain's chagrin, Arthur arranged his marriage. Arthur then bestowed the city of Nottingham on him after his nuptials.

GUIRON THE COURTEOUS

A hero who appears in the anonymous *Palamedes*.[64] He was the essence of a gentleman, refusing the advances of the wife of his friend Danain and, when Danain had later carried off Bloie, Guiron's lover, sparing him when he caught up with them. We are told that Guiron was descended from Clovis, the Frankish king. His son by Bloie was called Calinan. He eventually retired to a cave where he died.[158]

ABOVE *The courteous Guiron takes leave of Arthur and Guinevere, from* Guiron le Courtois *(Flemish, late fifteenth century).*

RIGHT *Bay of Firth, Orkney.*

~

GUNDEBALD

The King of a mysterious realm called the Land From Which No One Returns. Meriadoc rescued the German emperor's daughter from him. ▣

GUNPHAR

King of the Orkney Islands, he voluntarily submitted to Arthur.[11] ▣

GUNTER

The King of Denmark, slain by Arthur for refusing to pay him tribute. ▣

GURGURANT

A cannibal king whose son was slain by a giant who was, in turn, slain by Gawain. The son's corpse was cooked and eaten by Gurgurant's followers. When Gurgurant became a Christian his name was changed to Archier. He became a hermit near the Grail Castle.[22] ▣

GURMUN

In Gottfried, the King of Ireland and father of Iseult. He was the son of an African king. The name probably comes from Gormund who, in Geoffrey, was an African king who conquered and established himself in Ireland.[13] ▣

GURZGI

One of the three sons of Gornemant de Goort.[134] ▣

GUYOMARD

The lover of Morgan Le Fay who, in Breton tradition, betrayed her. One story says she imprisoned Guyomard's lover's upper portion in a brazier and her lower portion in a block of ice. Another tale says she turned both Guyomard and his lover into rocks, now known as the Rocher des Faux Amants. ▣

GWALCHMAI *see* GAWAIN. ▣

GWALHAFED

In *Culhwch*, the son of Gwyar and brother of Gwalchmai, perhaps the original of Galahad.[17] ▣

GWARTHEGYDD

Son of Caw and counsellor of Arthur.[17] ▣

GWAWL

Daughter of Coel and, possibly, wife of Cunedda. ▣

GWEIR

The son of Gwestyl, variously described as a knight and an adviser of Arthur.[17] ▣

GWEIR GWRHYD ENNWIR

A maternal uncle of Arthur in *Culhwch*.[17] ▣

GWEIR PALADYR HIR

A maternal uncle of Arthur in *Culhwch*.[17] ▣

GWEN

1. In *Dream of Rhonabwy*[16,18] a mantle of invisibility belonging to Arthur.[17]
2. Arthur's maternal grandmother, the daughter of Cunedda, in Welsh tradition. ▣

GWENDDOLAU

According to the Welsh Myrddin (Merlin) poems, Merlin's lord at the battle of Arthuret. His retinue was described as one of the six faithful retinues of the island of Britain, for it continued to fight for six weeks after his death. In one of the *Triads* it states he had birds which had a yoke of gold and two corpses for dinner and supper. They were killed by Gall, son of Dysgyfdawd. In the *Vita Merlini* Merlin was on the side which opposed Gwenddolau at Arthuret. See THIRTEEN TREASURES. ▣

GWENHWYVACH

The sister of Guinevere in Welsh tradition. She struck Guinevere and this led to the battle of Camlann. In Thomas Love Peacock's *Misfortunes of Elphin* (1829), Gwenhwyvach is married to Mordred.[29]

GWENHWYVAR *see* GUINEVERE.

GWENWYNWYN

In *Culhwch*, Arthur's chief fighter.[17]

GWION

The son of Gwreang who was left by Ceridwen to stir her cauldron. Drops from it landed on his finger which he sucked and at once understood everything that had happened or was to happen. He fled to avoid Ceridwen, both pursuer and pursued changing into different shapes. Gwion eventually changed himself into a grain of wheat and she changed herself into a hen and swallowed him. She became pregnant with him and bore him as Taliesin. All this may represent an initiatory process, as C. Matthews suggests.[116] A certain similarity may be noted between Gwion and the Irish hero Finn (Fionn) mac Cool, who sucked his thumb when some of the essence of the Salmon of Knowledge was on it. The chewing of the thumb may recall a pagan practice of divination. R. Graves[88] considers that Gwion was a historical person who discovered poetic mysteries and began to compose poetry, using the name of the legendary Taliesin.[16,128]

ABOVE *The Blackbird of Cilgwri who, through the interpreter Gwrhyr, aided Arthur's search for Mabon.*

~

GWLADYS, SAINT

According to tradition she was the daughter of Brychan and was abducted by Gwynllym Filwk, King of Gwynllywg. Arthur saw Brychan giving chase, but aided Gwynllym, as they had reached his domains. Gwladys and Gwynllym eventually became the parents of Saint Cadoc.

GWRFODDU HEN

A maternal uncle of Arthur in *Culhwch*.[17]

GWRHYR

An interpreter at Arthur's court. When Culhwch and Arthur's men were searching for Mabon, they asked for Gwrhyr's help. Gwrhyr, who was able to speak the animals' tongues, asked the Blackbird of Cilgwri for directions. He referred them to the Stag of Rhedynfrc who passed them on to the Eagle of Gwernabwy who took them to the Salmon of Llyn Llw.[17]

GWRI *see* BORS.

GWRVAWR

An ancestor of Arthur in the maternal pedigree in *Bonedd yr arwr*.

GWYAR

A parent of Gawain. In the original Welsh tradition Gwyar may have been the father of Gwalchmai, but, when the Welsh came in contact with Continental tales that made Lot the father of Gawain, they may have decided Gwyar must have been his mother. Certainly, Gwyar is latterly so presented in Welsh sources. However, as 'Lot' is not really a personal name but a title or designation meaning 'Lothian-ruler', it is not impossible that he was actually called Gwyar. *See* DIONETA.

BELOW *One of the plentiful salmon from Gwyddno Garanhir's weir.*

~

GWYDDAWG

The killer of Kay who was, in turn, killed by Arthur in Welsh tradition.[17] ▣

GWYDDBWYLL

An early Celtic board game, which Arthur played against Owain.[17] It is the same as the Irish game *fidchell*, meaning 'wood sense'. The board was seen as the world in miniature and the match between Arthur and Owain may have been a ritual. ▣

GWYDDNO GARANHIR

The father of Elphin. He possessed a weir which yielded many salmon and a *mwys* or basket which could feed 100 persons at a time. In his recent book, *Taliesin* (1991), J. Matthews argues that Gwyddno may have been, in origin, a Celtic god. ▣

GWYDION

The magical creation of Taliesin was the work of Gwydion, according to one tradition. Gwydion (possibly a smith-god) appears as a shapeshifter in the *Mabinogion* and may be, in origin, a Celtic deity. ▣

GWYDRE

In *Culhwch*, a son of Arthur killed by the boar Twrch Trwyth.[17] ▣

GWYL

One of Arthur's three mistresses, according to *Triad* 57. She was also the daughter of Gendawd.[29] ▣

LEFT *The fierce boar Twrch Trwyth.*

~

GWY

Originally a Celtic god, the son of Nodens; in later belief, a warrior. He and his followers fought the followers of Gwythr, son of Greidawl, for the maiden Creiddyled. To stop the general bloodshed, Arthur made an agreement for the pair of them to fight each other at May Kalends (or May Day) until Doomsday. The winner then would obtain the hand of Creiddyled. Arthur made Gwyn ruler of the demons of Annwn to stop them destroying humanity.

Another story makes Gwyn suffer defeat by Saint Collen on Glastonbury Tor. He seems originally to have been the ruler of an Otherworld realm, of which Glastonbury Tor may have been a portal.[17,42] ▣

GWYNEDD

A medieval kingdom in North Wales, called in Latin Vendotia. The earlier kings are legendary, but about the Arthurian time are thought to have been Einion (until AD 443), Cadwallon I (AD 443–517) and the famous Maelgwyn (AD 517–47). Cadwallon is mentioned by Geoffrey as Arthur's contemporary. ▣

GWYNNLYM

King of Gwynllyg, he abducted Saint Gwladys whose father, Brychan, gave chase. Arthur, however, helped Gwynnlym to escape. Gwynnlym was the father of Saint Cadoc in Welsh tradition. ▣

GYNETH

In a modern work, Sir Walter Scott's *Bridal of Triermain* (1813), daughter of Arthur by the half-fairy Gwendolen. Because of her cruelty, Merlin had her fall into an enchanted sleep from which she was awakened by Sir Roland de Vaux. ▣

HAGS OF GLOUCESTER

Nine witches who lived with their mother and father. One of them trained Peredur (Perceval) in the use of arms. They had slain Peredur's cousin whose head had been seen by Peredur on a platter. Peredur and Arthur's men destroyed them.[17]

HARLEQUIN *see* HELLEKIN.

HART FELL

A mountain in Scotland which N. Tolstoy[150] argues was the dwelling place of Merlin.

HAVELIN *see* HOEL.

HEBRON

An alternative name for Bron. It may have been invented by Robert de Boron, to make Bron sound more Hebrew, as Hebron was a place name in Palestine.

HECTOR

In Greek legend, a Trojan hero, son of Priam, defender of his city against the besieging Greeks in the Trojan War. According to the text of the *Roman de Troie* (an Old French romance), Morgan Le Fay loved him but, spurned by him, turned against him.

TOP LEFT *Hector and Perceval unwittingly exhaust each other in combat, from* Lancelot du Lac *(French, early fourteenth century). Hector was the Trojan hero killed by Achilles.*

~

LEFT *Armed knights setting out to rescue Hector from the Chastel des Maries, from* Lancelot du Lac *(French, early fourteenth century).*

~

HELAIN THE WHITE

Son of Bors and the daughter of King Brandegoris. He eventually became Emperor of Constantinople.

HELAIUS

Nephew of Joseph of Arimathea and ancestor of Arthur on the maternal side, according to the pedigree of John of Glastonbury.[14]

HELIADES

One of the allies of Mordred to whom Mordred awarded the realm of Scotland.

HELIE

A damsel in service to Blonde Esmerée, she brought Guinglain to rescue her mistress. At first she despised Guinglain but, as time went on, her contempt turned to respect for his prowess.

HELIS

A cousin of Arthur, son of Arthur's uncle, Ardan.

HELLEKIN

In *Li Jus Adan* (thirteenth century) a fairy king who became Morgan Le Fay's lover. He was an established figure in Germanic lore, first mentioned by Ordericus Vitalis in his *Ecclesiastical History* (eleventh – twelfth century) in which he is described as a giant with a club leading the Wild Hunt. In later times in Italy Hellekin became the Harlequin (Arlecchino) of the Commedia dell'Arte. Harlequin actually appears in the Arthurian pantomime *Merlin* (1734) by Lewis Theobald.

HELMWIND

A sort of cyclone which occurs in the Lake District. In Cumbrian tradition it is associated with Arthur.[93]

HEMISON

The lover of Morgan Le Fay, this knight was killed by Tristan. Italian romance gave him a daughter by Morgan, Pulzella Gaia.[85]

BELOW *HELLEKIN, who became the Harlequin of the Commedia dell'Arte.*

~

HENGIST

Traditionally, the leader of the Saxon invaders of Britain who took service as a mercenary with Vortigern. He brought with him his brother, Horsa. Vortigern married Ronwen, Hengist's daughter and Hengist became King of Kent. Driven out of Britain by Vortimer, when the latter died he returned and again took service under his son-in-law. After Vortigern's death he was defeated by Ambrosius and slain by Ambrosius's ally, Count Eldol. This much is Geoffrey's account. The *Anglo-Saxon Chronicle* (a medieval list of Saxons in Britain), places his death in AD 488, but does not say how he died. Some of his earlier history may be gleaned from the Anglo-Saxon poems *Beowulf* and *The Fight at Finn's Burg*. These mention a Hengist who may be identical with the invader. He was a follower of Hnaef, King of the Danes. When they were visiting Hnaef's brother-in-law, Finn Focwalding, King of the Frisians, a fight

occurred and Hnaef was killed. Hengist became the leader of Hnaef's followers and entered the service of Finn, but later killed him.

Hengist is credited with sons named Hartwaker (who was thought to have succeeded him as ruler of German Saxony and to have reigned from AD 448–80),[40] Octa, Aesc and Ebissa, and daughters called Ronwen and Sardoine. He has generally, if not universally, been regarded as a historical character.[125] ▣

HENRY THE COURTLY

This character was the leader of the force sent to succour Jerusalem in the *Prophécies de Merlin.* ▣

HENWEN

In Welsh tradition, a pig whose offspring were going to cause trouble for Britain. When gravid, she was pursued by Arthur and she gave birth to various progeny. She eventually dived into the sea at Penryn Awstin.[29]
See CATH PALUG. ▣

HERI

In the Icelandic *Tristrams Saga*, he told King Mark about Tristan's affair with Iseult.[99] ▣

HERMESENT

Sister of Arthur, daughter of Igraine and Hoel.
See BELISENT *and* BLASINE. ▣

HERMIT KING

Either a maternal or paternal uncle of Perceval – sources are not in agreement – whom Perceval visited. His name was Elyas Anais. The title was also applied to King Pelles. ▣

HERMONDINE

A daughter of the King of Scotland, she married Meliador, one of Arthur's followers, after he had slain another suitor called Camal. ▣

LEFT *Hengist, said to have led the Saxon invasion of Britain.*

~

ABOVE *Henwen, reputed to be the mother of the cat monster Cath Palug.*

~

HEROWDES

An emperor of Rome who went blind and consulted Merlin who told him to slay the Seven Sages who were the imperial counsellors. When he did so, he was cured.[85]

HERZELOYDE

In Wolfram, the mother of Perceval. She first married Castris from whom she inherited Wales and Northgalis. She subsequently married Gahmuret, Perceval's father.[34]

HESPERIDES

In Irish romance Mador's father is the king of the Hesperides. In Greek mythology the Hesperides were the daughters of Atlas and their gardens were situated on Mount Atlas or on islands.[8]

HIND OF THE FAIRIES

In Erasmo de Valvasone's *La Caccia*, an animal which led Arthur into a cave, then out on the far side of the mountain, to Morgan's palace. He was shown the heavens and the earth to give him guidance for the future.[85]

HOEL

1. King of Brittany who was brought to Britain by Arthur to help him against the Saxons. He became ill during the campaign and was left at Alclud (Dumbarton) where he was besieged by the Scots and Picts. Arthur came to relieve him. He is presumably identical with the King Hoel of Brittany who was Tristan's father-in-law. Geoffrey calls him Arthur's nephew but L. Thorpe (Arthurian scholar) argues that this is a mistake and we must read 'cousin' for 'nephew', his mother really being the sister of Ambrosius rather than Arthur. Geoffrey does not name his mother but calls his father Boudicius. The traditional dates of the Breton kings say Hoel reigned from *c.* AD 510–45. The *Birth of Arthur*, a Welsh work of the fourteenth century, makes him a son of Arthur's sister Gwyar by Ymer Llydaw. The *Prose Tristan* gives him a son named Runalen. He is more well known as the father of Iseult of the White Hands and her brother Kahedrin.[11,13,19]
See GIANT OF MONT ST MICHEL.

2. In *Arthour and Merlin*, Igraine's first husband is called Hoel rather than Gorlois and their daughters are named as Blasine, Belisent and Hermisent. The *Vulgate Merlin* Continuation also mentions this Hoel, giving him the title Duke of Tintagel.[124]
See TWENTY-FOUR KNIGHTS.

HOLGER *see* OGIER.

HOLY GRAIL *see* GRAIL.

HONOREE

A sword unsheathed by Biausdous, the son of Gawain. This act enabled him to wed Biautei.

HONORIUS

Roman Emperor of the West in the fifth century. *See* CONSTANTINE.

HORN OF BRAN GALED

One of the Thirteen Treasures of the Island of Britain. Merlin had to acquire this one if he were to be given the others. It had originally belonged to a centaur slain by Hercules and its particular property was that it could contain any drink one wished.[29]

OVERLEAF
THE HOLY GRAIL,
Amanda Cameron.

~

Hic canet erranté Lunam, Solisq; labore
Arcturŭq; pluuiasq; hyad. gēinosq; triōes

Cherubin íste
las que fer al

m̄ humana depurtus effigue let anı̄ a rearūm ſi beber
tus moycpne demain vber ſide habens nows ſeptem. Elen

ABOVE *The River Humber.*
It has been suggested that this
river was the location of
Arthur's final battle.

~

HORSA

Brother of Hengist who accompanied him to Britain. He was slain by a cousin of Vortigern. His memorial was thought to have been a flint heap near Horsted (Kent).[11,161]

HUEIL

A son of Caw and brother of Gildas. He was an opponent of Arthur who eventually had him executed. Their feud began when Arthur stabbed Gwydre, Hueil's nephew. In one tale, he and Arthur fought and Arthur was wounded in the knee. Arthur told Hueil he would not slay him, provided Hueil never mentioned the wound, but he later did and Arthur had him killed.[46]

HUMBER

Scottish writers claimed Arthur's last battle was on this river.

HUNBAUT

A companion of Gawain when Arthur sent the latter on a mission to the King of the Isles. In the course of their adventures together, Hunbaut tended to show more caution than Gawain.[119]

HUNCAMUNCA

In Henry Fielding's *Tom Thumb* (1730), the name of Arthur's daughter.

HUNGARY

Arthurian romance assigned this country several kings. In *Claris et Laris* it was ruled by King Saris who captured Cologne but was killed by Laris. Elsewhere the king is called Jeremiah; Gawain married his daughter. Sagremor is styled the son of the King of Hungary. King Ditas of Hungary was listed among the followers of the Roman Emperor Thereus, when the latter attacked Arthur. In fact, Hungary did not really exist as a country until about the end of the ninth century – much later than the Arthurian period when the territory it contained was divided amongst Gepids, Heruli, etc.

HUNTING KNIGHT

A son of the King of Gascony, who came to Arthur's court to learn valour.

HUON

The hero of the romance *Huon de Bordeaux* (thirteenth century), set in Carolingian times. In this tale Oberon, king of the fairies, assigned his realm to Huon. Arthur, who had been living in Fairyland since his reign, had thought the kingdom would be his and was most disturbed, but Oberon, by threatening Arthur, ensured there would be peace between him and Huon.

HYGWYDD

A servant of Arthur who carried the cauldron of Diwrnach on his back when Arthur captured it.[17]

IBERT

A character in Wolfram, possibly identical with Iweret, who had a wife called Iblis. He castrated Klingsor.[30]

IBLIS

According to Ulrich, the wife of Lancelot. Ulrich may have coined the name from Sibile (a Sibyl).[34]

ICELAND

This island was part of Arthur's empire. Layamon says its king was Aeleus. He was married to the King of Russia's daughter and they had a son named Escol. Aeleus voluntarily submitted to Arthur and gave him Escol to be his man. Geoffrey gives Iceland a king called Malvasius.[11,32]

IDDAWG

Before Arthur's final tragic battle with Mordred at Camlann, the king sent Iddawg to Mordred with a message. However, Iddawg uttered it in such a way that it angered its recipient and he was therefore known as the Embroiler of Britain.[17]

IDRES

A king of Cornwall, one of the eleven rulers who rebelled against Arthur at the outset of his reign.[19]

IGRAINE

(In Welsh: Eigyr)

1. The mother of Arthur. She was the daughter of Amlawdd and she married Gorlois, by whom she had a number of daughters. (This husband is sometimes called Hoel.) Uther made her pregnant with Arthur while he was under a spell which made him resemble her husband. Later, when Gorlois was dead, Uther married her.[11,19] *See* GOLEUDDYDD *and* RIEINGULID.

2. In the *Vulgate Merlin*, the sister of Arthur with whom he committed incest.

ILAX *see* EREC

ILINOT

A son of Arthur mentioned by Wolfram. He ran away when he was a child. He was raised by Queen Florie of Kanadic and fell in love with her, but she expelled him from her country and he died.[34]

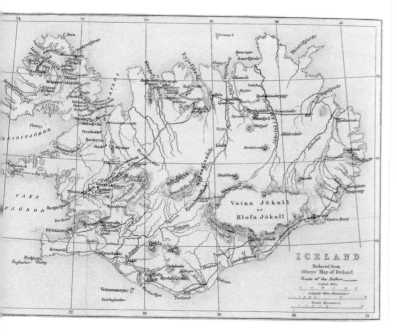

LEFT *Iceland is a country abounding with myths and legends.*

~

ILLAN

Illan was a traditional king of Leinster (Ireland) who was thought to have conducted raids in Britain. J. Morris[125] argues that he would have been one of the historical Arthur's enemies. The traditional regnal dates of Illan are AD 495-511, but the history of Leinster at this period is obscure and Illan may have reigned at an earlier period or not at all.[110]

ILLE ESTRANGE

A kingdom (otherwise called Estrangot) ruled by Vagor who kept Lionel a prisoner. Lionel was to fight the king's son, Marabron, but as Lionel was injured, Lancelot acted successfully as his substitute.

ILLTYD, SAINT

He founded the monastery at Llanilltud Fawr in Wales (now Llantwit Major). He was said to have been related to Arthur and to have served as a warrior under him.[80] *See* RIEINGULID

INDEG

One of the mistresses of Arthur, according to *Triad* [57]. She was the daughter of Garwy the Tall.[29]

INDRAWING SEAS

see GROCLAND

INOGEN

A daughter of Merlin with whom Arthur fell in love in Richard Hole's *Arthur* (1789).

IRELAND

Arthur is represented as having this country as part of his domains. Geoffrey describes how Arthur defeated the king of the country whom he names Gilmaurius. Elsewhere the king is represented as Anguish (the father of Iseult), Elidus, Marhalt or Gurmun. *Durmart* features an Irish queen named Fenise and informs us that the gonfalonier (royal standard-bearer) of Ireland was Procides, castellan of Limerick. Arthur overcame the Scots (Scotti), who were Irish invaders in Britain. In early Medieval Latin Scotus signifies an Irishman and, in the fifth century, many Scots from Ireland were settling in the country which today bears their name. They had also settled elsewhere in Britain. As to the actual rulers of Ireland in the Arthurian period, at that time the Irish kings of Tara had no effective, and perhaps even no theoretical, supremacy. They were Niall of the Nine Hostages (generally regarded as historical), Nath I (perhaps legendary), Laoghaire, Ailill Molt and Muircheartach I, with whom the eighteenth-century antiquary Keating, in some respects the Irish equivalent of Geoffrey, says Arthur had a treaty. The names Marhalt/Marhaus in the Tristan saga may preserve some memory of him. One of the kings of the southern Irish kingdom of Munster at this period was called Oengus – probably a different form of the name Anguish, borne by the King of Ireland in Malory.

IRION

A king, the father of Martha and father-in-law of Tristan's son Ysaie.[75]

IRONSIDE

The name of the Red Knight of the Red Lands, defeated by Gareth. He became a Knight of the Round Table and was the father of Sir Raynbrown.[19]

ISCA LEGIONIS
see CITY OF THE LEGION ▦

ISEO
In Spanish romance, the daughter of Tristan who married King Juan of Castile.[79] *See* TRISTAN THE YOUNGER ▦

ISEULT
1. The daughter of King Anguish of Ireland who was married to King Mark of Cornwall, but also, as the result of drinking a love potion, hopelessly enamoured of Tristan. When she heard of Tristan's death, she died of a broken heart. Her name is not Irish, but derived from Ancient British *Adsiltia* (she who is gazed on). Attempts to associate her with Chapelizod, Dublin, are due to a false derivation of that place name.

2. Tristan's wife, whom he married when he had parted with Iseult of Ireland, was called Iseult of the White Hands. She is variously called the daughter of Hoel of Brittany and Jovelin, Duke of Arundel. Tristan had nothing to do with her, as he still loved Iseult of Ireland, a fact she naturally resented. When Tristan was fatally wounded, he sent for Iseult of Ireland, hoping she could heal him. The ship sent for her was to have white sails if she were aboard on its return, but black sails if she had declined to come. Iseult of the White Hands, seeing the ship had white sails, lied about them to Tristan who died before his beloved's arrival, as a result of hearing the falsehood. There seem to be classical influences here – the stories of Paris and Oenone and of Theseus and Aegeus. The Icelandic version of the story says the second Iseult was Spanish and claims she was given to Tristan when he defeated the King of Spain.

3. The name of Tristan's god-daughter.

4. The Queen of Ireland, mother of Iseult, wife of Mark.[3,13,19,29,78,81] ▦

LEFT *Iseult,* William Gale (1823-1909).

~

ISOLDE

LEFT *Iseult, or Isolde,* Aubrey Beardsley (1872-98). Tristan loved Iseult of Ireland but married Iseult of the White Hands, with tragic consequences.

~

ISLE OF LIFE
A place, possibly identical with the Isle of Wight, where the ancient British kings Gaddifer and Perceforest enjoyed a prolonged existence.[75]

ITHER
Arthur's cousin, the son of Uther's sister, he had been raised by his uncle and became the King of Kukumarlant. He claimed Arthur's throne and stole a golden cup from him. He was killed by Perceval.[34]

ITONJE
A sister of Gawain who married King Gramoflanz.[34]

IVOINE
The original name, in French romance, of Moine (Constans).

ABOVE *The mysterious ancient Isle of Life may have been our Isle of Wight.*

~

IVOIRE
The sister of Ban who married King Constantine of Britain. They had three children: Ivoine (Constans), Pandragon (Ambrosius) and Uther.

IVOR
A huntsman who raised Meriadoc.

IWERET
The father of Iblis, wife of Lancelot, in Ulrich. He was the lord of Beforet. He raided the territory of Mabuz, Lancelot's foster-brother, and Lancelot subsequently killed him. He may be of Celtic origin, from Ywerit, the father of Bran, or is possibly identical with Ibert.[30]

JACK THE GIANT-KILLER

A hero of nursery tales, who was thought to have flourished in Arthur's time.

He commenced his career by killing a giant whom he trapped in a pit. He was then captured by the giant Blunderboar, but he killed him and his brothers. He also tricked a Welsh giant into killing himself. He became a servant of King Arthur's son and, in the course of his service, obtained a cap of knowledge, a wonderful sword, shoes of swiftness and a cap of invisibility. He continued to kill giants and eventually married a duke's daughter. He was given a noble dwelling by Arthur.

There is no evidence that Jack was a genuine hero of early tales, but he may be a composite of several such, invented around 1700.[127]

JAUFRÉ

This character, possibly identical with Griflet, is the hero of a romance bearing his name which tells how Taulat came to Arthur's court, killed a knight in front of the queen and said he would return each year to do the same. Jaufré was sent after him and, following various adventures, defeated him.

Jaufré married Brunissen, whom Taulat had made to suffer.[64]

JESCHUTÉ

In the story of Perceval we learn that his mother had told him to demand a kiss or a jewel from any lady he met. Chrétien tells us that, coming on a girl in a tent, Perceval demanded both. Wolfram gives us further information about the girl: her name was Jeschuté and she was the daughter of King Lac and therefore a sister of Erec. Her husband was Orilus, Duke of Lalander.[34]

JOAN GO-TO-'T

The mother of Merlin in the Elizabethan play *The Birth of Merlin* (published 1662, but written earlier), in whose composition Shakespeare may have had a hand. If so, it is possible that he was helped by W. Rowley (died 1626), although Rowley may well have written the entire play.

JOHFRIT DE LIEZ

The trainer of Lancelot as a warrior during his sojourn in Maidenland.[30]

JONAANS

An ancestor of Lancelot, noted for his virtue, he left Britain and went to Gaul where he married the daughter of King Maronex, from whom he obtained his kingdom.[24,31]

JONAS *see* MARK.

JORAM

In Wirnt von Grafenberg's *Wigalois* (a medieval manuscript), a king who left Guinevere a magic girdle, saying she could regard it as a present or else, if she preferred, he would come and fight for it. She asked him to do the latter. Joram came and defeated several champions, but to one of them, Gawain, he presented it. Gawain married Joram's niece, Florie.[33]

JOSEPH OF ARIMATHEA, SAINT

To the biblical data about him romance adds the following. He was a soldier of Pilate who gave him the cup from the Last Supper. After the Resurrection, he was thrown into a dungeon where Jesus appeared to him and gave him the cup which had fallen out of his possession. After the fall of Jerusalem to Vespasian's army, he was set free and, with his sister

Enygeus and her husband, Hebron or Bron, went into exile with a group of fellow travellers. They began to suffer from a lack of food owing to sin, so they held a banquet. Those amongst the company who were not sinners were filled with the sweetness of the cup of Jesus, the Grail. Bron and Enygeus had twelve sons, eleven of whom married. The twelfth, Alan, did not, so he was put in charge of his siblings, and they went out and preached Christianity. Bron was told to become a fisherman and was called the Rich Fisher. In Robert's version, Joseph entrusted the Grail to Bron, but did not accompany him to Britain. Elsewhere, we are told that Joseph crossed to Britain on a miraculous shirt. We are also informed that he and his followers converted the city of Sarras, ruled by King Evelake who, having become a Christian, was able to defeat his enemy, King Tholomer. (According to the various sources, the city of Sarras is located either in the East (Asia), or else in Britain. It may have been thought of as the place from which the Saracens derived their name. It is not known outside romance.) John of Glastonbury claims that Joseph brought two cruets containing the blood and sweat of Jesus to Britain, but he does not mention the Grail.

The romance *Sone de Nausay* says that Joseph drove the Saracens out of Norway, married the pagan king's daughter and became king himself. God made him powerless and the land became blighted. Fishing was his only pleasure and men came to call him the Fisher King. At last he was cured by a knight. He provided for the foundation of the Grail Castle-cum-Monastery with thirteen monks, typifying Christ and his twelve apostles.

The interpolations of William of

ABOVE *Joseph of Arimathea praying before a vision of Christ with five angels, from* Arthurian Legends, Lancelot Cycle *(Bologna, c.1270).*

~

BELOW *Joseph (appearing as a bishop) before Queen Sarracinto, from* Arthurian Legends, Lancelot Cycle *(Bologna, c.1270).*

~

Malmesbury's *History of Glastonbury* say Joseph was sent to Britain by Saint Philip who was preaching in Gaul. With regard to Gaul, there is a tradition which says that, with Mary Magdalene, Lazarus, Martha and others, Joseph was placed in an oarless boat which was divinely guided to Marseilles. J.W. Taylor says there is an Aquitanian legend that says Joseph was one of a party which landed at Limoges in the first century and that there is a Spanish tale relating how Joseph, with Mary Magdalene, Lazarus and others, went to Aquitaine. Taylor also cites a Breton tradition that Drennalus, first bishop of Treguier, was a disciple of Joseph. Taylor adduces these traditions as part of an attempt to show that Joseph came first to Gaul, then to Britain. It is worth nothing, however, that the tradition of Mary Magdalene and Lazarus coming to Marseilles is not now regarded seriously by most hagiologists.[80]

Joseph was said, not only to have come to Britain, but to have settled at Glastonbury where he was given land by King Arviragus. A local tradition, perhaps not older than the nineteenth century, says he buried the cup of the Last Supper above the spring in Glastonbury and hence the water has a red tinge. A tradition amongst certain metalworkers was that, sometime before the Crucifixion, Joseph actually brought Jesus and Mary to Cornwall. Benjamin[51] suggests that Joseph may be identical with Joachim, the father of the Virgin Mary in the *Protevangelium of James*, an apocryphal work; but the two names are quite distinct in origin.[77] In the *Estoire* Joseph is given a son, Josephe. In *Sone de Nausay* he had a son named Adam, while Coptic tradition claims he had a daughter, Saint Josa.[19, 31,42,89,95,103]

JOSEPHE

The son of Joseph of Arimathea, first mentioned in the *Estoire*. When Joseph and his followers crossed the sea to Britain the pure ones did so on Josephe's outspread shirt. He consecrated Alan his successor as Grail Keeper and was buried in Scotland. The *Queste*, however, has him living long enough to give Communion to Galahad.[31]

JOSHUA

1. The son of Brons and nephew of Joseph of Arimathea. He married the daughter of King Kalafes of the Terre Foraine, of which he later became king. He succeeded his brother Alan as guardian of the Grail.[31]

2. The son of Helaius, he is recorded as an ancestor of Arthur according to the pedigree of John of Glastonbury.[14]

JOVELIN

In Gottfried, the Duke of Arundel and father of Iseult of the White Hands.[13]

JOYOUS GARD

Lancelot's castle in the north of England, which he captured. After he had rescued her, he took Guinevere there. It was originally called Dolorous Gard and later reverted to that name.[19]

JUAN

In Spanish romance, King of Castile. He married Iseo, the daughter of Tristan. His sister, Maria, married the younger Tristan.[79]

JUDWAL *see* TREMEUR.

JULAIN

In *Perlesvaus*, the husband of Yglais and mother of Perceval.[22]

JULIUS CAESAR

Roman statesman, born 100 BC, made ruler of Rome 49 BC and assassinated 44 BC. In the *Vulgate Version* he is given the title of emperor (which he never actually held) and is made the contemporary of Arthur. Merlin visited his court in the form of a stag. Caesar had had a dream and Merlin told him that the Wild Man of the Woods could divulge its meaning. The latter was captured by Merlin and Grisandole and told Caesar that the dream was about his wife's adultery. The romance of *Huon de Bordeaux* makes Caesar the father by Morgan Le Fay of Oberon.[31]

ABOVE *Julius Caesar. The Vulgate Version (thirteenth century), both elevates Caesar to emperor and makes him a contemporary of Arthur.*

~

ABOVE *Gawain and companions before Dolorous Gard (Joyous Gard).*

ABOVE *Lancelot (on a white horse) attacking the Knights of Dolorous.*

LEFT *Lancelot and companions leaving Joyous Gard. All from* Lancelot du Lac *(French, early fourteenth century).*

~

KADIEN

An ancestor of Arthur in the maternal pedigree found in the Welsh *Bonedd yr arwr.*

KADWR

A paternal ancestor of Arthur in the Mostyn MS 117.

KAHEDRIN

The son of Hoel of Brittany. Tristan was his bosom friend and married his sister, Iseult of the White Hands. Kahedrin, however, fell in love with Iseult of Ireland and wrote letters and poems to her. She replied innocently, but Tristan misunderstood and Kahedrin had to jump from a window to avoid his wrath, landing on a chess game which Mark was playing below. Kahedrin eventually died of love for Iseult.[4,13]

KALAALLIT NUNAAT

see GREENLAND.

KALAFES

King of Terre Foraine who was cured of leprosy by Alan, son of Bron. He became a Christian and took the baptismal name of Alfasein. His daughter married Joshua, another son of Bron. Kalafes was speared through the thighs for watching the Grail service and died shortly afterwards.[31]

KALEGRAS

In the Icelandic *Tristrams Saga*, the name of Tristan's father and also Tristan's son by Iseult of the White Hands, his wife. It is said that the younger Kalegras eventually became King of England.[99]

KANAHINS

Lancelot's squire.[158]

KAPALU *see* CATH PALUG.

KARADAN

The husband of one of Arthur's sisters (name not known). Their son, Arthur's nephew, was called Aguisant.[31]

KARADAWC *see* KARADOC

KARADOC

An ancestor of Arthur found in two pedigrees in the Welsh *Bonedd yr arwr.* He is presumably the same as the Kradoc and Karadawc found in other manuscripts.

KARDEIZ

In Wolfram, one of the twin sons born to Perceval.

KAY

(In Welsh: Cai) Arthur's foster-brother, son of Ector. His name is often said to be a form of the Roman Caius, but it may be of Irish origin as suggested by R. Bromwich.[19]

In earlier sources Kay was one of Arthur's doughtier champions but, in late romance, he is given a somewhat churlish character. Indeed, in *Perlesvaus*, he murdered Arthur's son Loholt and joined Brian des Illes in a rebellion against Arthur. He claimed that it was he, not Arthur, who pulled the sword from the stone, but Ector compelled him to tell the truth.

The obscure Welsh poem *Pa gur* may imply that he killed the Cath Palug. He married Andrivete, daughter of King Cador of Northumberland.

Kay is credited with sons called Garanwyn and Gronosis and a daughter called Kelemon. His horse was named Gwinam Goddwf Hir. Geoffrey says he was made Duke of Anjou.

In the *Chroniques d'Anjou et du Maine* by J. de Bourdigne, we are told he was a Saxon who served Uther and hated other Saxons because, unlike them, he was a Christian.

There are different accounts of his death: throughout Welsh literature it is claimed that he was killed by Gwyddawg who was, in turn, killed by Arthur; but he is also said to have been killed by the Romans or in the war against Mordred.[19,22,83] *See* CASTLE KEY *and* GIANT OF MONT ST MICHEL. ▣

KEHYDIUS

Form of Kahedrin used by Malory. ▣

KELEMON

A daughter of Kay in Welsh tradition. ▣

KELLIWIC

A Cornish stronghold of Arthur, it was possibly identical with Castle Killibury. Alternatively, it may have been Callington, Celliwith or Kelly Rounds.[46] ▣

KENT

In Vortigern's time, the kingdom of Gwyrangon, but given by Vortigern to the Saxons. In the Arthurian period Kent would seem to have been under Anglo-Saxon rule and at this time, according to the *Anglo-Saxon Chronicle*, may have been ruled by King Aesc, who may have been the son of Hengist who reigned AD 488–512. William of Malmesbury says Aesc did not enlarge his father's kingdom, but had to defend it. This implies he had a formidable foe, such as Arthur, with whom to contend. Bede says the barbarians who settled in Kent were Jutes.

ABOVE *The county of Kent was originally an entire saxon kingdom.*

~

KILLAURUS

The place in Ireland from where, according to Geoffrey, Merlin brought the Giants' Dance, the stones of Stonehenge. Giraldus Cambrensis, in his *Topography of Ireland*, identified it with Kildare. In modern times T.C. Lethbridge in his *Legend of the Sons of God* (1972) has argued ably that Tipperary is intended. N. Tolstoy identifies it with Uisnech, the sacred centre of Ireland. ▣

KILYDD

The father of Culhwch. He was the father of Goleuddydd, Arthur's aunt. ▣

KING ARTHUR'S BED

A natural feature on Bodmin Moor (Cornwall), once supposed to have been Arthur's place of repose. ▣

KING ARTHUR'S FOOTPRINT

A footprint-like indentation at Tintagel, presumably once thought to be the print of Arthur's foot. ▣

KING ARTHUR'S HALL

Megalithic remains in Cornwall, associated in folklore with Arthur. ▣

KING ARTHUR'S HUNTING LODGE

Arthur was supposed to have used this hill fort as his headquarters when hunting on Goss Moor (Cornwall). ▣

KING WITH A HUNDRED KNIGHTS

One of the eleven rulers who rebelled against Arthur, this king is variously called Berrant le Apres, Aguysans and Maleginis. *Due Tristani* seems to imply that he came from Piacenza and that his wife was called Riccarda.[19,85] ▣

KLINGSOR

In Wolfram, the Duke of Terre de Labur; this appears to have been in Italy as its capital was Capua. After being castrated by King Ibert of Sicily, he became a wizard.

Klingsor's character is not so black as it is represented by Wagner in his opera *Parzifal*. He is portrayed as courteous, a man whose word was his bond; one tradition makes him a bishop. He kept Arthur's mother and other queens captive, but they were rescued by Gawain.[31]
See ARNIVE. ▣

KNIGHT OF THE FAIR COUNTRY

A brother of Arthur, he married the daughter of Earl Cornubas of Wales and was the father of the Great Fool. ▣

KNIGHT OF THE DRAGON
see SEGURANT. ▣

KNIGHT OF THE LANTERN

Slayer of the Black Knight who was the son of the King of the Carlachs. Also, the title of the son of Libearn. ▣

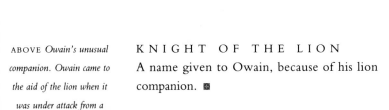

KNIGHT OF THE LION

A name given to Owain, because of his lion companion. ▣

KNIGHT OF THE OLD TABLE *see* SEGURANT. ▣

KNIGHT OF THE SLEEVE

The hero of the Dutch romance *Ridder metter Mouwen*, he won the hand of Clarette at a tournament at Arthur's court.[109] ▣

KNIGHT OF THE TWO SWORDS

A title given to Balin. ▣

ABOVE Owain's unusual companion. Owain came to the aid of the lion when it was under attack from a serpent. This has similarities with the legend of St. Jerome who is said to have removed a thorn from a lion's paw, the animal then became his companion.

~

KNIGHTS OF THE FRANC PALAIS

An order of knights founded by Perceforest, they were eventually wiped out by the Romans. ▣

KRADOC *see* KARADOC. ▣

KUSTENHIN

Kustenhin is an early Welsh form of the name Constantine, used to designate Constantine, grandfather of Arthur. Kustenin and Kustennin are variant forms. ▣

KUSTEN(N)IN *see* KUSTENHIN. ▣

KYNAN

An ancestor of Arthur in the maternal pedigree found in the Welsh *Bonedd yr arwr*. ▣

KYNOR

Variant form of Kynuawr. ▣

KYNOTUS

Arthur made Kynotus Rector of Cambridge.[123] ▣

KYNUAWR

Arthur's great-grandfather on the paternal side, according to Mostyn MS 117. ▣

KYNVARCH

In Welsh legend the father of Urien of Rheged by Nefyn, daughter of Brychan. ▣

KYNWAL

An ancestor of Arthur in the maternal pedigree found in the Welsh *Bonedd yr arwr*. ▣

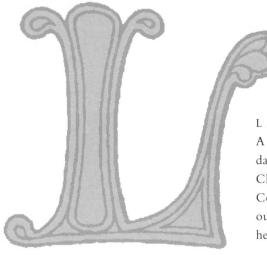

LABEL

A king of Persia whose daughter became a Christian and married Celidoine. He is variously made to die at a hermitage or in battle.

LABIANE

The niece of King Mark, she was violated by him and, as a result, gave birth to Meraugis. Mark murdered the unfortunate Labiane.[64]

LAC

King of Estregales and ruler of the Black Isles. He was a Knight of the Round Table. His family tree is as follows:

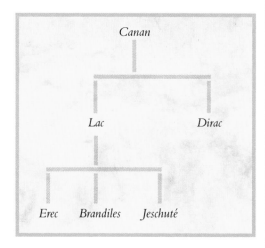

```
                    Canan
                      |
        +-------------+-------------+
        |                           |
       Lac                        Dirac
        |
   +----+--------+
   |    |        |
 Erec  Brandiles  Jeschuté
```

LADIS

Ruler of Lombardy in Arthurian romance.

LADON

Elderly King of Gascony, married to Lidoine, sister of Laris.[64]

LADY OF THE FAIR HAIR

A fairy whom Arthur delivered from the Fish-Knight. He later became her lover.[15]

LAHELIN

The brother of Orilus who robbed Herzeloyde of Wales and Northgalis after Gahmuret's death. His name is a German form of the Welsh Llewelyn.[34]

LAILOKEN

A wild man in Celtic tradition whose career bears some resemblance to that of Merlin. He was for a time at the court of Rhydderch Hael, revealed to King Meldred that his wife was adulterous and made a prophecy concerning his own death. It is possible Lailoken was merely a nickname for Merlin, as Lailoken resembles the Welsh word for a twin and Merlin was thought to have a twin sister.[109,150]

LAKE DISTRICT

S.G. Wildman[163] has suggested that this picturesque region of Cumbria was the birthplace of Arthur or at least the place where he was brought up.

RIGHT *Coniston Water, Cumbria. The enchanting scenic beauty of the Lake District has been associated with Arthur's early life.*
~

LADY OF THE LAKE

LEFT *The Lady* *of the Lake, Amanda* *Cameron.*

FAR LEFT TOP *The Lady* *of the Lake and Lancelot* *at dinner.*

FAR LEFT MIDDLE *The* *Lady of the Lake finds* *Lancelot mad and starving.* *All from* Lancelot du Lac *(French, early fourteenth* *century).*

~

LEFT *The Lady of the* *Lake carrying the child* *Lancelot to safety.*

~

This mysterious female gave Arthur his sword Excalibur. She stole Lancelot when a child and cured him when he went mad. She may be a Celtic lake divinity in origin, perhaps of the same kind as the Gwagged Annwn – lake fairies in modern Welsh folk-lore. In Ulrich, the fairy who raised Lancelot is the mother of Mabuz. As Mabuz is probably identical with the Celtic god Mabon, it would seem that the fairy must be Morgan Le Fay who was, earlier, Mabon's mother, Matrona. A lady of the lake, perhaps a different one, was killed by Balin.[19,30]

LAMBOR
The King of Terre Foraine or Logres, he was killed by Brulan (Varlan) and both his and Brulan's lands were blighted, forming the Waste Land of the Grail stories. He may be identical with Lambord, Arthur's maternal great-grandfather in the pedigree of John of Glastonbury.[14,31]

LAMORAK
Pellinore's son, Perceval's brother and a Knight of the Round Table. He slept with Morgause and was killed by her son, Gawain.

LAMBORD
An ancestor of Arthur in the pedigree of John of Glastonbury.[14]

LANCE OF LONGINUS
The weapon used to wound Jesus on the Cross. It was carried in the Grail Procession and was also sought by Arthur's warrior daughter, Melora.

LANCELOT

1. The grandfather of Sir Lancelot of the Lake. He married the daughter of the King of Ireland. King Ban and King Bors were his sons.

2. Arthur's champion and right-hand man. He was the son of King Ban by his wife Elaine. After his father's death, he was left near a lake by his mother and was taken by the Lady of the Lake, who raised him. He became Arthur's trusted companion and a Knight of the Round Table. He fell in love with Guinevere and commenced to have an affair with her; he was also the object of the affections of Elaine of Astolat who died of love for him. Another Elaine was the daughter of King Pelles and, when Lancelot

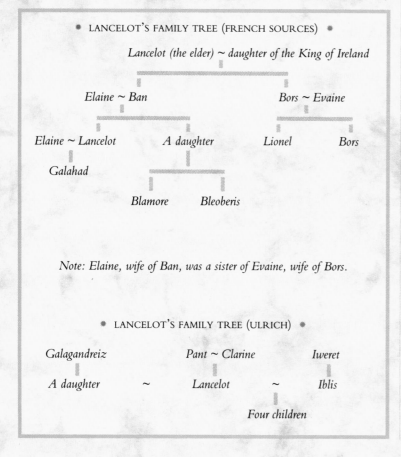

* LANCELOT'S FAMILY TREE (FRENCH SOURCES) *

Lancelot (the elder) ~ daughter of the King of Ireland

Elaine ~ Ban   *Bors ~ Evaine*

Elaine ~ Lancelot   *A daughter*   *Lionel*   *Bors*

Galahad

Blamore   *Bleoberis*

Note: Elaine, wife of Ban, was a sister of Evaine, wife of Bors.

* LANCELOT'S FAMILY TREE (ULRICH) *

Galagandreiz   *Pant ~ Clarine*   *Iweret*

A daughter   ~   *Lancelot*   ~   *Iblis*

Four children

visited Carbonek, he saved her from a tub of boiling water. Brisen, her nurse, arranged for her to sleep with him, while he thought she was Guinevere. As a result, Galahad was conceived. When this happened a second time, Guinevere discovered the pair in *flagrante* and sent Lancelot away from Camelot. He went mad, but was cured by the Grail. When Guinevere was abducted by Meliagaunce, son of King Bagdemagus, Lancelot pursued him in a cart, a humble mode of conveyance in which the knight was reluctant to travel. He had to cross a sword bridge to reach the castle and find Meliagaunce. The two fought, but Bagdemagus pleaded with Guinevere that his son's life would be spared, so their combat was stopped, to be taken up again in a year's time. Later, Meliagaunce accused Guinevere of adultery with Kay. Lancelot fought the accuser as her champion and, once again, Bagdemagus had to plead for his son's life. Eventually, Lancelot slew Meliagaunce in combat at Arthur's court.

When Lancelot and Guinevere were at last discovered together, Lancelot fled, but returned to rescue Guinevere from the stake, killing Agravain, Gaheris and Gareth in the process. War between him and Arthur followed but was broken off when Arthur had to return to deal with Mordred's rebellion.

This version of Lancelot's adventures, found in French sources and Malory, differs markedly from that of Ulrich who says he was the son of King Pant of Gennewis and his wife, Clarine. Pant was killed in a rebellion and Lancelot was stolen by a fairy and raised in Maidenland. The fairy would not tell him his name until he had fought Iweret of Beforet. Johfrit de Liez trained him in the use of weaponry and he married the daughter of Galagandreiz. The fairy's son, Mabuz, a wizard, was having his territory raided by Iweret. Lancelot killed Iweret and married

LEFT *Lancelot's mother, Queen Elaine, taking refuge in an abbey, welcomes her daughter.*

BELOW LEFT *The young Lancelot learning to shoot.*

ABOVE RIGHT *Elaine, Lancelot and the young Galahad, on their way to the abbey where Galahad is to be raised.*

RIGHT *Lancelot threatening to kill Elaine, daughter of King Pelles, who has deceived him.*
All from Arthurian Legends, Lancelot Cycle *(French, fourteenth century).*

Iweret's daughter Iblis, with whom he had four children. He eventually won back his father's kingdom.

Did Lancelot originate in Celtic imagination or was he a Continental invention? It is popularly supposed that he has no Celtic counterpart. His name is generally thought to be a double diminutive of the German word *Land*; but R.S. Loomis[109] has argued that Lancelot is the same character as the one called Llwch Lleminawc in *Preiddeu Annwfn*, in which he accompanies Arthur to the Otherworld. This expedition may be the same as the one to Ireland in *Culhwch* in which Llenlleawc, an Irishman, aids Arthur to steal the cauldron belonging to Diwrnach. The identification of Lancelot with Llwch Lleminawc/Llenlleawc is opposed by R. Bromwich[29] who argues that neither of these forms was used to translate Lancelot from other languages into Welsh; for this purpose the names Lanslod and Lawnslot were employed. However, this may not be so severe an objection as it might appear. It is possible that the Continentals could have translated Lleminawc/Llenlleawc into the similar-sounding Lancelot but, when Welsh writers came on this form, they may have failed to realize it represented an original Welsh name and retranslated it as Lanslod/Lawnslot. Certainly the presence of Mabuz, who is probably the Celtic god Mabon, indicates a Celtic origin for Ulrich's story. It is thought that the basic saga of Lancelot may have dealt with the fairy captivity episode which is common to French and German sources. *See* COLGREVANCE, ILLE ESTRANGE *and* TWENTY-FOUR KNIGHTS. ✦

LEFT *Sir Lancelot Gives his Shield into Elaine's Keeping, Arthur A. Dixon. Here the mounted Lancelot presents the archetypal image of the chivalrous knight.*

~

LEFT *Guinevere banishing Lancelot after discovering his relationship with Elaine.*

~

LEFT *Lancelot mad with love for Guinevere, with Galehaut and companion.*

~

LEFT *Lancelot wandering and mad, arrives at a pavilion. He strikes the shield and a dwarf appears to take his sword.*

~

LEFT *Physicians declare Lancelot cured by the Grail. All from* Lancelot du Lac *(French, early fourteenth century).*

~

LANCEOR

A son of the King of Ireland whom Arthur sent to inflict retribution on Balin for slaying the Lady of the Lake. Balin killed him and his distraught lover Colombe committed suicide. King Mark of Cornwall came by, saw their bodies and entombed them.[19]

LANCIEN

The place of Mark's residence, now Lantyan (Cornwall).

LAND FROM WHICH NO ONE RETURNS *see* GUNDEBALD.

LANSDOWN HILL

Near Bath, this is possibly the site of the battle of Mount Badon. It was called Mons Badonicus in early times. In the Middle Ages what was said to be Arthur's skeleton was found there.

BELOW *Beckford's Tower at Lansdown Hill, near Bath.*

LANSLOD *see* LANCELOT.

LANTRIS *see* ALCARDO

LANVAL

One of Arthur's knights. He was approached by a mystery lady who became his lover, but made him promise to keep the matter a secret. Guinevere tried to seduce him and, when rebuffed, accused him of making overtures to her. He was put on trial and told to produce his lover to prove he was enamoured of someone other than the queen. He could not, but the mystery lady arrived at the last moment to save him and they left for Avalon.

His story is found in Marie de France's *Lanval* (twelfth century) and in the English works *Sir Landeval* (fourteenth century), *Sir Lambewell* (sixteenth century) and *Sir Lamwell* (sixteenth century).[20] *See* BLANCHARD.

LAPIS EXILLIS

The name given to the Grail by Wolfram[34] who regards it as a stone. The term means 'worthless stone' and is probably an alchemical variant of the philosopher's stone.

LAPLAND

According to Hakluyt's *Travels* (sixteenth century), the eastern border of Arthur's empire.

LAR

The dead husband of Queen Amene. His ghost guided Wigalois on his way to aid Amene against the evil Roaz.[33]

LARIE

Daughter of Lar and Amene, she married Wigalois.[33]

LARIS

The son of Henry, Emperor of Germany, he is one of the heroes of *Claris et Laris* and was in love with Marine, daughter of Urien. The rival suitor, King Tallas of Denmark, besieged Urien. Arthur arrived and raised the siege, but Laris was captured by the Danes and had to be rescued by Claris and others. Tallas was defeated by Arthur, and Laris became King of Denmark.[64] *See* LIDOINE.

LASCOYT

One of the three sons of Gornemant de Goort. Like his brothers, he met a violent end.[34]

LAUDINE

The lady of the fountain, widow of Esclados, who married Owain.[5]

LAUFRODEDD

The knife of Laufrodedd was one of the Thirteen Treasures of the Island of Britain.[29]

LAUREL

The wife of Agravain. She was the niece of Lionors and Lynette.[19]

LAVAINE

The son of Bernard and brother of Elaine of Astolat. He became a follower of Lancelot.[19]

LAWNSLOT *see* LANCELOT.

LAZILIEZ

An ancestor of Perceval.[34]

LEODEGRANCE

King of Cameliard and father of Guinevere. It was he who gave the Round Table to Arthur.[19]

LEFT *Sir Lancelot and Elaine*, Arthur A. Dixon. *Elaine's brother, Lavaine, was a follower of Lancelot.*

~

LEUDONUS *see* LOT.

LEVANDER

A servant of the King of Africa, he was sent by the King to help Arthur's daughter Melora on her quest.[8]

LIANOUR

A duke, ruler of the Castle of Maidens.

LIBAN

A daughter of King Ban and mother of illegitimate twins by Pandragus.

LIBEARN

The stepmother of Alexander, Prince of India, she turned him by magic into the Crop-Eared Dog.

LICAT ANIR

A mound at Archenfield which marked the burial place of Arthur's son, Amr. The length of the mound was said to vary each time it was measured.[21]

LICONAUS *see* ENID.

LIDOINE

In *Claris et Laris*, the sister of Laris and daughter of Henry, Emperor of Germany. Her first husband was King Ladon of Gascony, a man of advancing years, after whose demise she was captured by Savari, King of Spain. Arthur rescued her and she married Laris's companion, Claris.[64]

LIGESSAC

A fugitive from Arthur who took sanctuary with Saint Cadoc for ten years.

LILE

The lady of Avalon who brought to Arthur's court a sword that only Balin could drawn from its scabbard. When he had done so, she asked him to return it. When he refused, she foretold it would bring about his destruction and kill his dearest friend.[19]

LINNUIS

The scene of four of Arthur's battles in the catalogue of Nennius. It may be identical with Lindsey.

LION

Lions occur in various Arthurian tales. Although the animal (*Panthera leo*) is unknown in Britain, Boece, a historian who lived in Scotland in the sixteenth century, claims that lions once existed in Scotland. Breunor slew one, as did Gawain. Owain had a lion as a com-panion and the story of Androcles may have been an influence here. The lions mentioned as having been slain by Kay on Anglesey in *Pa gur* may have been creatures of a supernatural nature.

LION THE MERCILESS

The original owner of Arthur's pet parrot, from whom Arthur won it.[15]

LIONEL

The son of the elder Bors and the brother of the younger Bors, he was a fierce character to whom Arthur gave the throne of Gaul. After Arthur's death, he was slain by Melehan, son of Mordred.[19] *See* COLGREVANCE *and* ILLE ESTRANGE.

BELOW *Lancelot and the rescued Lionel (in blue), arriving at an abbey, from* Lancelot du Lac *(French, early fourteenth century).*

~

LIONES

The kingdom ruled by Meliodas, Tristan's father, thought by some to be identical with Lyonesse. In the *Vulgate Version*, Lot is said to be its king; if this is the case then Liones is also Lothian. Its early history is supplied by the *Prose Tristan*: one of its kings, Pelias, was succeeded by his son, Lucius. Lucius was succeeded by Apollo who unwittingly married his mother but later wed Gloriande, by whom he became the father of Candaces who, in time, became king of both Liones and Cornwall.[11,31,158]

BELOW *Caradoc Briefbra's horse, Lluagor.*

~

LIONORS

The daughter of Sevain, she was the mother of Arthur's son, Loholt. Malory calls her the mother of Arthur's illegitimate son Borre, possibly identical with Loholt.[19,31]
See LAUREL.

LISTINOISE

A kingdom that became the Waste Land when its monarch, Pellehan, was given the Dolorous Stroke.

LIT MERVEILE

A wondrous bed. Gawain went to rescue certain captives from a palace and, on entering, he saw the bed scudding around on its own. Gawain jumped onto it and it shot from wall to wall, dashing itself against them. When it ceased its gallivanting, 500 pebbles were unleashed at Gawain from slingstaves. Crossbow bolts were then aimed at him but happily his armour was sufficient to protect him.

OVERLEAF *LOHENGRIN, Amanda Cameron.*

~

LLACHEU

A son of Arthur mentioned in Welsh tradition. He was identified with Loholt, but they were probably different characters originally.

LLAMREI

Arthur's mare.

LLEFELYS

King of France. *See* DINAS EMRYS.

LLENLLEAWC

The name of a companion of Arthur in *Culhwch*. An Irishman, he helped Arthur to seize the cauldron which belonged to Diwrnach. He is to be identified with Llwch Lleminawc in *Preiddu Annwfn*. There is a possibility he was the prototype of Lancelot.[17,23]

LLEU *see* LOT.

LLONGAD GRWRM FARGOD EIDYN

The killer of Addaon, son of Taliesin.[17]

LLONGBORTH

Arthur's men took part in a battle here. The Red Book of Hergest says Gereint was killed in this fracas, but the preferred text of the Black Book of Carmarthen does not mention this.

LLUAGOR

Caradoc Briefbras's horse.

LLWCH LLEMINAWC
see LANCELOT *and* LLENLLEAWC.

LLYCHLYN

Welsh name for Scandinavia but, like the analogous Irish Lochlann, it may originally have signified an Otherworld realm. Blaes, a character in the *Triads* who is apparently identical with Blaise, the master of Merlin, is called the son of the Earl of Llychlyn.

Hic canet errante Luna
Arcturuq; pluuiasq; hyad. g
Cherubin iste in humana dep
las que fer artus moyepne den
anima redinin si beber Rotasub
habens raows septem. Elementum A
Ars naturam corrigens in regno minor
Historia. Benedichus dominius Deus noster
ignum. Cum eorundem in easdem operat
legatissibus figuris depicit. Homo natus de
in pore repletur multi miserys Sob 14. Homo nu
nes annorum nostorum in ipsis septuaginka ani ei
septe Hominus actibus respondentes scilicet. Fortvors minor
auxilian minim tutela extens. Amissio comprehsum extra
nen interens lumien cuperius logis agneu allustatur. Theologis

ante Lunam, Solisq; labores
...sq; hyad. gēinosq; triões
...humana depurtus effigueler
...us moycpne demain veber fidelis
...si beber Rotasub peditz cherubm
...s Septem. Elementum Aquae et Terrae
...m corrigens in vegno minerali. Utriusq
...benedichis dominus Deus nester qui dedit
... Cum eorundem in easdem operahinibus e
...tissious siguris depicit. Homo natus de muliere
...pore repletcur multi miserys Scb 14. Homo natis
...vus logis qqueu affritatur ih ipsis Septuaginta āni e
...anus ftr ornauit celos decem c...pondentes scilicet. Fortvors
...apraentbz pier arlum empnul i quo est twn...ens. Amiβio comprehsum e

LLYGADNUDD EMYS
Maternal uncle of Arthur.[17]

LLYN BARFOG
A lake in Gwynedd where Arthur is said to have fought an afanc.

LLYR MARINI
An ancestor of Arthur, both paternal and maternal, who occurs in Welsh pedigrees. In origin he may have been a divinity of the sea (Welsh: *llyr*) who was regarded as the ancestor of a number of royal houses. He would seem to be the original of Shakespeare's King Lear.[10] *See* CARADOC, CARADOC BRIEFBRAS *and* MANAWYDAN.

LLYWARCH HEN
A celebrated Welsh poet who may have flourished about the year AD 600. He was said to have been a cousin of Urien of Rheged. Traditions variously place him among the North Britons or in Powys. He may once have figured in independent tales but later been drawn into the Arthurian circle. He was listed as one of the Twenty-Four Knights of Arthur.

LOGISTILLA
A sister of Morgan in Ariosto's *Orlando Furioso*.[2]

LOGRES
The name of England in Arthurian romance. It comes from Lloegr, the Welsh name for England, perhaps derived from Anglo-Saxon *legor*, an element found in the place name of Leicester. The derivation of this *legor* is puzzling.

LEFT *Lohengrin, whose boat was drawn by an angel in the guise of a swan.*

~

LOHENGRIN
The son of Perceval in Wolfram and one of the Grail community. Lohengrin went to Brabant in a boat drawn by an angel, disguised as a swan, to aid Elsa, the duke's daughter, against Frederic de Telramund, who claimed she had promised to marry him. Lohengrin defeated Telramund in combat and married Elsa but cautioned her not to ask his name. They had two children but Elsa eventually posed the forbidden question, whereupon Lohengrin left her. Lohengrin subsequently married Princess Belaye of Lizaborye, but he was murdered by armed men sent by her parents who thought he had enchanted her. Belaye died of grief. The country's name was changed to Lothringen (Lorraine) in his honour. Lohengrin's adventures are told by Wolfram and in a subsequent anonymous poem (*Rigomer*).

LOHOLT
A son of Arthur, he was a Knight of the Round Table. He is variously called the son of Guinevere or of Lionors. He was murdered by Kay in *Perlesvaus*, the author of which may have invented this episode.[22]

LOMBARDY
In Arthurian romance, the territory of King Ladis. This region had not yet been conquered by the Lombards, however, in the Arthurian period.

LORE
The Lady of Garadigan who brought a sword-belt to Arthur's court and asked everyone to try to unfasten it. Meriadeuc was the only one able to do this.[64]

LORETE
The sister of Griflet.

ABOVE *Celtic knotwork from the Pictish school.*

~

~

LORIE

Gawain's mistress in *Rigomer*. ◼

LORIGAL

The offspring of Eliavres and a mare, with which he had been forced to copulate. ◼

LOT

The King of Lothian, Orkney and Norway, father of Gawain and his brothers, husband of Arthur's sister Anna (according to Geoffrey) or Morgause (according to Malory). In Geoffrey he is represented as a supporter of Arthur, already King of Lothian, whom Arthur placed on the throne of Norway. The idea that he was King of Orkney seems a later development. Elsewhere, however, it is stated that he took part in the rebellion against Arthur at the start of his reign. He was killed by Pellinore and a resultant discord existed between Lot's sons and those of Pellinore.

The name Lot (in its earlier form Leudonus) simply means 'Lothian-ruler' and need not be taken as a personal name (see also GWYAR). It seems certain that there was a king in the Lothian area in the fifth century whose head-quarters were at Traprain Law, near Edinburgh.

Lot's sons in Arthurian lore included Gawain, Gaheris, Agravain, Gareth and Mordred, and his daughters were Soredamor and Clarissant. The *Enfances Gauvain* says that the young Lot was a page at Arthur's court and that he had an intrigue with Morgause, as a result of which Gawain was conceived. The *Life of St Kentigern* says that he was the father of Thaney, Kentigern's mother – assuming that the same Lot is being referred to. Boece claims Lot was the king of the Picts. As to his ancestry, John of Fordun in his *Chronica Gentis Scotorum* claims he was descended from Fulgentius, one of Geoffrey's early kings of Britain. However, John of Glastonbury gives the line of descent from Petrus, one of Joseph of Arimathea's companions. ◼

✳ LOT'S FAMILY TREE ✳

Petrus

Erlan

Melianus

Arguth

Edor

Lot

✳ DESCENDANTS OF LOT ✳

Lot

Gawain *Eries* *Agravain* *Gaheris* *Gareth* *Soredamor* *Clarissant*

Cligés *Guigenor*

Guinglain *Florence* *Lovel*

✳ DESCENDANTS OF LOT (WELSH TRADITION) ✳

Lot ~ Anna

Cywyllog ~ Mordred *Perferren ~ Bugi* *Denw ~ Owain* *Tenwi*

two sons *Beuno*

LOTTA

In the *Tavola ritonda*, Queen of Ireland and mother of Iseult. ◼

LOVEL

A son of Gawain who was one of the party that surprised Lancelot and Guinevere together. He was slain by the escaping Lancelot. ◼

LUCAN

Arthur's butler and one of his knights. He was the Duke of Gloucester and brother of Bedivere. After Arthur's final battle, he tried to help Bedivere to lift the king but, as he was so badly wounded, he fell dead. A variant of this is that Arthur embraced him but he was so badly wounded that the embrace killed him.[19]

LUCIUS

1. The Roman emperor who fought against, and was defeated by, Arthur. Geoffrey is rather vague as to his actual status and calls him *procurator*; he implies he was inferior to the Emperor Leo in Constantinople. Wace and Malory both style him emperor.[11,19]

2. An early King of Liones, son of Pelias. *See* ALIFATIMA.

LUFAMOUR

The lover of Perceval in the English verse romance, *Sir Perceval of Galles.*

LUGUAIN

The loyal servant of Yder who eventually became a knight.

LUNETE

Nimue's cousin. She learned magic from Nimue and put up a fountain in the Forest of Broceliande, to be defended by her lover.

LYBIUS DESCONUS

An illegitimate son of Gawain, his mother kept his ancestry a secret. He went to Arthur's court and was made a knight. He was sent to rescue the Lady of Sinadone, which he did, accompanying the damsel Ellen. This character is identical with Guinglain, Lybius being his nickname. Lybius Desconus means 'the Fair Unknown One'.

LYNETTE

Her sister, Lyonesse, was besieged by the Red Knight of the Red Lands. She obtained Gareth from Arthur's court to rescue her but at first her manner towards Gareth was derisory, and improved only as the adventure progressed.[19] *See* LAUREL.

LYONESSE

1. A lady besieged by the Red Knight of the Red Lands. Gareth rescued her and in due course she married him.[19]

2. A lost land said to have existed beyond Cornwall. Some thought it identical with Liones, the kingdom of Tristan's father, but this may originally have been Lothian (Leoneis), later confused with a region of Brittany (Leonais). As to the lost land itself, a legend told that, when Arthur had fallen in his last battle, Mordred pursued the remnant of his army into Lyonesse. The ghost of Merlin appeared, the land sank and Mordred's forces were destroyed. Arthur's men, however, reached what are now the Isles of Scilly and survived. Did such a land exist? Reference is made to it in Camden's *Britannia* (1586) and Carew's *Survey of Cornwall* (1602). Earlier, the medieval Arab geographer Idrisi uses the word *Dns* for a place that is perhaps the Scillies. *Dns* may be a scribal mistake for *Lns* (Lyonesse). In Roman times the Scillies seem to have been a single island partially overrun by the sea. This may be the origin of the legend. Readers of Tennyson may remember that he sets Arthur's final battle in Lyonesse.

LYPPAUT

Lord of Bearosche and father of Obie and Obilot.[34]

BELOW *Dame Lyonesse Comes Forth, Arthur Rackham (1867-1939). She married her defender and protector, Gareth.*

~

MABON

In the poem *Pa gur* two of Arthur's followers are so called: one the son of Modron, described as the servant of Uther Pendragon, and the other the son of Mellt. This may be a duplication, the same character having Modron for a mother and Mellt for a father. *Culhwch* says he was abducted when he was three nights old. It was necessary for Culhwch to find him, as part of his quest. Arthur attacked his prison, while Kay and Bedivere rescued him. Similarly named characters are Mabonagrain in Chrétien's *Erec et Enide* and Mabuz in Ulrich's *Lanzelet*. In origin, these characters are perhaps all the same. Mabon, the son of Modron, is undoubtedly the Celtic god Maponos (perhaps the equivalent of the Irish Mac ind oc), Modron originally being the Celtic goddess, Matrona, and Mellt perhaps a hypothetical god called Meldos. C. Matthews[116] regards the story of Mabon as a mystery cycle. G. Ashe[146] argues that Merlin may have acted as a prophet of the god Maponos, while J. Matthews[119] feels that the history of Gawain replays the story of the god. Mabon is also referred to as a sorcerer. *See* BLONDE ESMERÉE *and* MARSIQUE.

MABONAGRAIN

An opponent of Erec, Mabonagrain was a prisoner of sorts in a castle with an airy wall and he was the lover of a lady who dwelt there. When Erec overcame him, Mabonagrain told him to blow a horn and this freed him from his imprisonment. It seems likely that Mabon is the original of this character, especially as the motif of liberation from imprisonment occurs in the story.[5]

MABUZ

In Ulrich, the son of the Lady of the Lake. His territory was being raided by Iweret, and Lancelot came to succour him. He is very likely identified with Mabon; this would, in turn, identify the Lady of the Lake with Modron/Morgan.[30]

MACSEN WLEDIG

see MAXIMUS.

MADAGLAN

A king in *Perlesvaus*, who, after the death of Guinevere, demanded that Arthur yield him the Round Table as he was Guinevere's relation; otherwise, he required Arthur to marry his sister. He was twice defeated by Lancelot.[22]

MADAN

King of Bulgaria in Arthurian romance.

MADOC

In the poem *Ymddiddan Arthur a'r Eryr*, Arthur's nephew, Eliwlod, appears in the shape of an eagle. Eliwlod's father is called Madoc, implying that Madoc was Arthur's brother-in-law. A possible reference to Madoc, son of Uther, appears in the *Book of Taliesin*. A Madoc or Maduc appears as an opponent of Arthur in French romance. *See* TALIESIN.

MADOR

A Knight of the Round Table and Grail quester, surnamed *de la Porte* (of the Door). In *Eachtra Mhelóra* he is called the son of the King of the Hesperides.

MAELGWYN *see* MELKIN.

MAEN ARTHUR

The name of a stone which can no longer be identified which had a hollow in it where Arthur's horse had stepped. It was in the vicinity of Mold (Clwyd). Another stone called Maen Arthur is in Maen Arthur Wood near Llanafan (Dyfed).

MAGLORE

A companion of Morgan, according to *Li jus Adan* (a thirteenth-century French romance).

ABOVE

LANCELOT FIGHTS
MADOR IN DEFENCE OF
GUINEVERE'S HONOUR,
N.C. Wyeth.
Mador (in blue) losing a
battle to Lancelot.

ABOVE *Lancelot seated*
on the floor beside the
Lady of Malehaut, from
Lancelot du Lac (French,
fourteenth century).

~

MAID OF THE NARROW WOOD

She fell in love with Gawain but, when the latter did not reciprocate her sentiments, she tried to kill him.

MAIDENLAND

The country where Lancelot was raised by his foster-mother, a water fairy. It parallels the Irish Celtic Otherworld land called Tir na mBan (Land of Women).[30]
See JOHFRIT DE LIEZ.

MAIMED KING

One of the two characters into whom the Fisher King was divided in the *Vulgate Version*. He is called Parlan, Pelleam, Pellehan or Pelles. His injury was variously ascribed to a wound by Balin or to a punishment for drawing the Sword of Strange Hangings.

MALDUC

A wizard who said he would free Guinevere from the clutches of Valerin if given Erec and Gawain as prisoners. He freed Guinevere and duly received the prisoners but they were rescued by Lancelot.[155]

MALEGINIS
see KING WITH A HUNDRED KNIGHTS.

MALEHAUT

A city of Arthurian Britain. The Lord of Malehaut was called Danain the Red. His wife, Bloie, the Lady of Malehaut, was the lover of Belinant and the mother of Dodinel. Elsewhere Bloie is called Eglante, *see* DODINEL. The city was supposedly in the realm of the King with a Hundred Knights.

MAN, ISLE OF

In Arthurian times, this island was ruled by various Celtic kings about whom we know very little. According to Arthurian romance, Gromer, an enchanted knight, became King of Man with the help of Gawain. It was at Castle Rushden on the island that Merlin was said to have defeated giants and buried them in the caves beneath the castle. There has been a recent attempt to identify the Isle of Man with Avalon.[87]

MANAEL

Son of Castellors and ancestor of Arthur, according to the pedigree of John of Glastonbury.

MANAWYDAN

The son of Llyr. He is mentioned in *Culhwch* as a follower of Arthur, but is in origin a Celtic sea-god corresponding to the Irish Manannán mac Lir. The *Mabinogion* calls him the brother of Bran.[17]

MANGOUN

The King of Moraine, he sent Caradoc a horn which would expose any infidelity on the part of his wife.[31]

MARABRON

The son of King Vagor of the Ille Estrange, he was defeated in battle by Lancelot.

MANTLE OF INVISIBILITY

Arthur's mantle became one of the Thirteen Treasures of the Island of Britain.[29]

MANUEL

The hero of a German romance, *Manuel und Amande*, of which no complete copy survives. Manuel, who was of Greek origin, married Amande at Cardueil. Arthur was there at the time.

~

MAPONOS

An early Celtic god, son of Matrona, the original of Mabon in Arthurian lore.

MARAGOZ

Steward of King Elyadus of Sicily who slew his master, causing the queen to flee. She gave birth to Floriant who became the foster-son of Morgan.

MARC

Marc was the son of Ysaie the Sad and grandson of Tristan. He married Orimonde, daughter of the Amir of Persia.[75]

MARDOC

A character who appears on the Arthurian bas-relief in Modena Cathedral where he is represented on the battlements with Winlogee (possibly Guinevere). He may be identical with Mordred.[85]

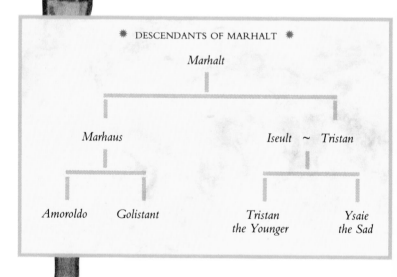

❋ DESCENDANTS OF MARHALT ❋

Marhalt

Marhaus — Iseult ~ Tristan

Amoroldo — Golistant — Tristan the Younger — Ysaie the Sad

MARHALT

King of Ireland and father of Marhaus (according to Malory). The chronology in Malory is a little odd: when Marhaus fought Tristan he was the brother-in-law of the Irish King Anguish, yet only later does his father, Marhalt, ascend the throne. The family tree below shows Marhalt's descendants drawn from a variety of sources. One wonders if names such as Marhalt and Marhaus might preserve some genuine memory of the fifth-century King of Tara, Muircheartach I.

MARHAUS

The brother of Iseult, slain by Tristan in combat. Malory tells us that, prior to this, he had been a follower of Arthur and had killed the giant, Taulurd. Gottfried supplies us with the information that he was a duke and Eisner[78] feels that his combat with Tristan was based on that of Theseus and the Minotaur. He had sons named Amoroldo and Golistant.[19,13]

See MARHALT.

MARIA

In Spanish romance, the sister of King Juan of Castile. She married Tristan the Younger after he rescued her from an African potentate.[79]

MARINAIA *see* ALDAN.

MARINE

The daughter of Urien, loved by Laris.

MARIUS

According to Geoffrey, he was an early King of Britain, the son of Arviragus. *See* SODRIC.

MARJODOC

The steward of Mark, at first friendly towards Tristan, but, when he discovered Tristan's intrigue with Iseult, he turned against him.[13]

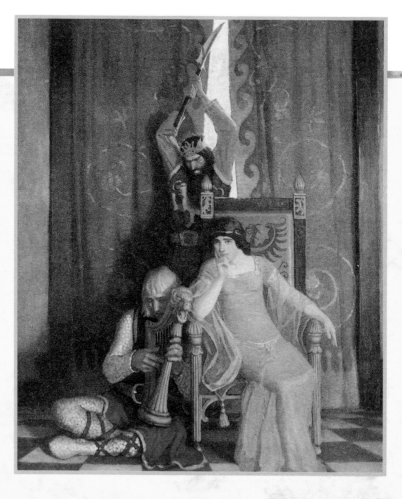

LEFT *TRISTAN
SLAIN BY KING MARK,
N.C. Wyeth.*

~

MARK

King of Cornwall, uncle of Tristan and husband of Iseult. He is generally presented as something of a tyrant, Malory calling him 'bad King Mark'. In Welsh his name (March) means a horse and Beroul informs us he had horse's ears – a characteristic he shares with other legendary personages. *The Dream of Rhonabwy* tells us that he was Arthur's cousin while, in the *Triads* we learn that Tristan was his swineherd. In the story of Tristan, Mark did not find out for some time of his nephew's affair with his wife. One version says that, on the deaths of the lovers, Mark had them interred in a single grave. However, in Malory, Mark is the slayer.

Various tales tell what befell him after Tristan's death. According to an Italian romance (*La vendetta che fe messer Lanzelloto de la morte de miser Tristan*), Lancelot invaded Cornwall and killed Mark. Elsewhere it is said that the younger Tristan overcame him; or that he was placed in a cage and from there had to view the graves of Tristan and Iseult; or that, when Lancelot died, he invaded Logres and subsequently destroyed most of Camelot and the Round Table, but himself fell at the hand of Pamlart, a descendant of Ban; or that Bellangere, son of Alisander the Orphan killed him.

BELOW *HOW KING MARKE FOUND SIR TRISTAN, Aubrey Beardsley
(1872-98), from* Le Morte d'Arthur.

The question arises as to whether Mark was identical with a historical Cornish ruler called Cunomorus, who reigned also on the far side of the Channel in Brittany. The ancient inscription on a stone at Castle Dor (Cornwall) may read (though this is uncertain) *Drustans hic iacit cunomori filius* (Here lies Tristan, son of Cunomorus). If the reading is accurate, it may mean that, in the original version, Tristan was more closely related to Mark than subsequent story tellers were prepared to allow. The writer Wrmonoc says Cunomorus was also called Mark and he may have thought him identical with March, son of Meirchiaun, King of Glamorgan. A story tells that this Cunomorus had been warned that one of his sons would kill him, so he murdered his wives when they became pregnant. One wife, Trephina, daughter of Warok, chief of the Venetii, actually gave birth before Cunomorus had her decapitated. However, he performed this task after the birth and her son (Judval or Tremeur) was left to die. Gildas restored Trephina to life. They went back to the castle (Trephina carrying her head) and the battlements fell on Cunomorus, killing him. At a more prosaic historical level, we are told that Cunomorus supported Chramm, son of the Frankish King Clothair, in a rebellion in which both he and Chramm fell (AD 560).[125] However, M. Dillon and N.K. Chadwick state that Cunomorus fell while fighting people who had rebelled against him.[74]

King Mark lives on in Breton tradition. He is thought to ride a winged horse (*mormarc'h*) when the sea off Penmarc'h (Mark's Head, a headland in Brittany) is stormy. 🏵

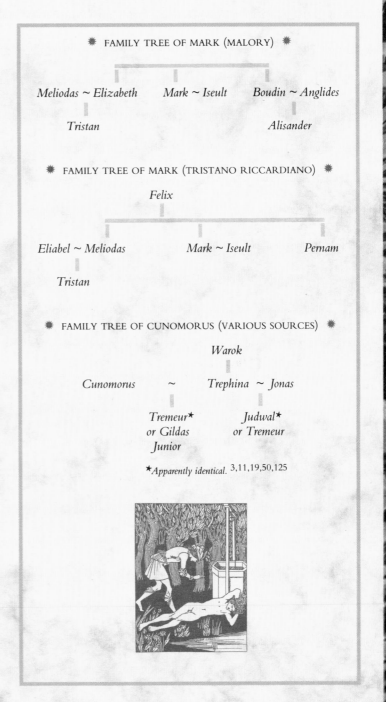

✳ FAMILY TREE OF MARK (MALORY) ✳

Meliodas ~ Elizabeth   Mark ~ Iseult   Boudin ~ Anglides

Tristan   Alisander

✳ FAMILY TREE OF MARK (TRISTANO RICCARDIANO) ✳

Felix

Eliabel ~ Meliodas   Mark ~ Iseult   Pernam

Tristan

✳ FAMILY TREE OF CUNOMORUS (VARIOUS SOURCES) ✳

Warok

Cunomorus   ~   Trephina ~ Jonas

Tremeur*   Judwal*
or Gildas   or Tremeur
Junior

★*Apparently identical.* [3,11,19,50,125]

MARK
King of Glamorgan. *See* LABIANE *and* MERCHIAUN. ▣

MARLYN
The son of Ogier and Morgan Le Fay; hence, Arthur's nephew. ▣

MARMYADOSE
A sword won by Arthur from Rience. It had once belonged to Hercules and had been wrought by the Roman smith-god, Vulcan. *See* RIENCE. ▣

MARONEX
A King of Gaul. *See* JONAANS. ▣

MARRION
One of Morgan's sisters, according to *Bataille Loquifer.* ▣

MARROK
One of the Knights of the Round Table whose wife changed him into a werewolf for seven years. ▣

MARSIQUE
A fairy who obtained the magic scabbard of Excalibur for Gawain who had fought the sorcerer Mabon over her. ▣

MARTHA
The daughter of King Irion and the wife of Tristan's son Ysaie.[75] ▣

MATRONA
An early goddess of the Celts, worshipped in Britain and Gaul where her name survives in the River Marne, near the source of which she had a sanctuary.[74] It is thought that she is the original of Morgan. ▣

MAXIMUS
A Roman emperor, known in Welsh tradition as Macsen Wledig. He was said by Geoffrey – who calls him Maximianus – to have made Conan Meriadoc the ruler of Brittany. [11,17,45] ▣

MAZADAN
According to Wolfram, Arthur's great-grandfather and also an ancestor of Perceval. He was a fairy, husband of Terdelaschoye.[34] ▣

MAZOE
A sister of Morgan.[12] ▣

MEDRAWT *see* MORDRED. ▣

MELCHINUS *see* MELKIN. ▣

MELEAGAUNCE
(In Welsh: Melwas) A knight, son of King Bagdemagus, who abducted Guinevere, taking her to his territory. Only his father prevented him from raping her. Lancelot rescued her. There are different versions of what befell Meleagaunce. In one, he subsequently imprisoned Lancelot but the latter escaped and slew him. In another version, he and Lancelot fought a single combat over Guinevere, Lancelot winning and killing his opponent. A Welsh version of the abduction story tells how Melwas, ruler of Somerset, carried Guinevere off to Glastonbury. Arthur laid siege to it but the abbot and Gildas prevailed upon Melwas to return his captive.[19,42] ▣

MELEHAN
A son of Mordred. When Mordred was dead, he and his brother seized the kingdom, but they were defeated by Lancelot. He was killed by Bors.[31] ▣

BELOW *Marrok transformed into a werewolf.*

~

RIGHT *Galahad takes leave of the wounded Melianus,* from Arthurian Legends, *Lancelot Cycle (French, thirteenth century).*

BELOW *King Meliodas attempts to remount in the midst of battle, from* Guiron le Courtois *(Flemish, late fifteenth century). Meliodas was Tristan's father.*

~

MELIADICE

A descendant of Arthur and heroine of the romance *Cleriadus*, published in Paris in 1495. She was the daughter of the English King Philippon and married Cleriadus who became Philippon's successor.[75]

MELIADOR

Son of the Duke of Cornwall, he was a personage at Arthur's court. He married Hermondine, daughter of the King of Scotland, after killing another suitor, Camal.

MELIANT DE LIS

A knight whose father had been killed by Lancelot and who, consequently, viewed Lancelot with much venom. Lancelot ultimately served him as he had his father.

MELIANUS

An ancestor of Lot.[14]

MELIODAS

1. King of Liones and father of Tristan. In his youth he had carried off the Queen of Scotland, which led to war between him and Arthur. In Malory, he is the brother-in-law, in Italian romance the brother, of Mark of Cornwall. *Tristano Riccardiano* calls the father Felix.

Meliodas first married Elizabeth, Tristan's mother, and, after her death, wed a daughter of Hoel of Brittany. Another of Hoel's daughters was to marry Tristan. This would therefore make Iseult of Brittany both sister-in-law and daughter-in-law to Meliodas. Meliodas was eventually killed by knights of the count of Norhout.[19,85] *See* PERNAM.

2. A natural son of King Meliodas of Liones and the Queen of Scotland. His mother set him adrift and he was raised by the Lady of the Lake.

MELJANZ

King of Liz, he went to war against Duke Lippant when the latter's daughter rejected him.[34]

MELKIN

John of Glastonbury mentions a vaticinator (one who foresees the future) called Melkin, who lived before Merlin and uttered a prophecy about Glastonbury, couched in obscure Latin, which is difficult to interpret. It may refer to Glastonbury as a place of pagan burial and to a future discovery of the tomb of Joseph of Arimathea. It has been suggested that Melkin is to be identified with Maelgwyn, a sixth-century ruler of Gwynedd. Henry VIII's royal antiquary, John Leland (c. 1503–52) claimed to have seen Melkin's book at Glastonbury Abbey.[14]

MELLT

The father of one of the two Mabons listed as being followers of Arthur.

MELODIAM

A son of King Pellinore.

MELORA

In an Irish romance, a daughter of Arthur who fell in love with Orlando, son of the King of Thessaly. Mador, who was jealous, bribed Merlin to get rid of him and Merlin complied, persuading his servant, the Destructive One, to imprison the hapless prince. Only the Lance of Longinus, the carbuncle of the daughter of the King of Narsinga, and the oil of the pig of Tuis could dispose of the enchantments that surrounded him. Melora, dressed as a knight, defeated the King of Africa on behalf of the King of Babylon who gave her the Lance and sent Levander, his servant, to accompany her.

They were imprisoned by the King of Asia but escaped with the aid of a guard, Uranus, and obtained the porcine oil from their captor. They lured the King of Narsinga and his daughter, Verona, on to a ship, but all became friends and the carbuncle was secured. Melora freed Orlando and they went to Thessaly, while Levander married Verona.[8]

MELOT

According to Gottfried, Melot was an Aquitanian dwarf who spied for Mark on Tristan and Iseult. He is called Aquitain by Eilhart.[13]

BELOW Sir Gareth's Dwarf, Melot, N.C. Wyeth.

~

MENW

An enchanter in Arthur's service. In *Culhwch*, Arthur assigned him to help the hero, Culhwch, in case he and his party needed to be made invisible.[17] ▣

MERAUGIS

King Mark of Cornwall violated his niece, Labiane, and as a result she gave birth to Meraugis. Mark then murdered Labiane and abandoned Meraugis in the woods, but he was raised by a forester and grew to be a Knight of the Round Table. After Arthur's last battle, he became a hermit with Bors and others.[64] ▣

LEFT *The Kings Arthur, Ban and Bors parting, from* Lestoire de Merlin *(Bologna, early fourteenth century). Bors, like Meraugis, then became a hermit.*

~

MERCHIAUN

The father of King Mark of Glamorgan. This Mark may have been the original of, or confused with, Mark of Cornwall. ▣

MERIADEUC

A knight who obtained a second sword because he was the only one able to unfasten a sword-belt which Lore, Lady of Garadigan, brought to Arthur's court. He was therefore known as the Knight of the Two Swords (a title also given to Balin). He eventually married Lore.[64] ▣

MERIADOC

He was the son of King Caradoc of Wales. The latter was succeeded by Griffith who had secured the throne by murder. Griffith sent Meriadoc and his sister Orwen to the woods to be killed, but the executioners did not carry out their task. Meriadoc was subsequently raised by Ivor the Huntsman and his wife Morwen. Urien, here called the King of Scots, abducted Orwen and married her. Meriadoc went to Arthur's court and, with that king's help, he ousted Griffith and gained his rightful throne which he handed over to Urien. Meriadoc went abroad and rescued the daughter of the Emperor of Germany from Gundebald, king of the Land From Which No One Returns, and married her.[164] ▣

MERLIN

(In Welsh: Myrddin, Latinized as Merlinus because the more natural Merdinus would have connected it with Latin *merdus*, 'dung'.) Arthur's magician and counsellor, in many ways the architect of his reign. In the classic form of the tale, Merlin was begotten by an incubus. Robert says the devils of Hell had determined to set on earth an evil being to counterbalance the good introduced by Jesus Christ. Happily, the child was promptly baptized so he was not evil! Vortigern, King of Britain some time after the Roman withdrawal, was haplessly trying to build a tower for, whenever it was erected, it would collapse. The king's counsellors told him he would need to sacrifice a fatherless child to remedy this. Such children were hardly thick on the ground but Merlin, now a youth, was popularly supposed to be sireless so he was secured for this purpose. However, he pointed out that the real reason for the collapse was the existence of a pool beneath the foundations. Digging revealed the truth of this and a brace of dragons emerged, one red and one white; these caused Merlin to utter a series of prophecies.

When Aurelius Ambrosius defeated Vortigern he wished to put up a monument. Merlin advised him to make an expedition to Ireland to procure certain stones and these were erected on Salisbury Plain as Stonehenge. After the death of Aurelius, when Uther came to the throne, Merlin arranged for him to seduce Igraine by magically making him take the shape of Igraine's husband, Gorlois. He took the child, Arthur, born of this union, and arranged the sword-in-the-stone contest, whereby Arthur became king. The rules of this contest stipulated that whosoever could pull a certain sword out of a stone would be acknowledged king. Many tried but none succeeded. Arthur was attending a joust as Kay's squire and found he had forgotten Kay's sword. He came upon the sword in the stone and drew it out to give to Kay. Ector, Arthur's foster-father, saw this and realized what it signified. Arthur drew out the sword once more, in public, and this led to his enthronement.

After this, according to Malory, Merlin became infatuated by Nimue (elsewhere called Viviane), whom he taught magical secrets which she used to imprison him. Geoffrey, however, has him active after Camlann, bringing the wounded Arthur to Avalon. He then went mad after the battle of Arthuret and became a wild man, living in the woods. According to Giraldus Cambrensis, this was because of some horrible sight he beheld in the sky during the fighting. He had been on the side of Rhydderch Hael, King of Cumbria, who was married to Merlin's sister, Ganieda, and three of Merlin's brothers had died in the battle. After a time, Ganieda persuaded Merlin to give up his life in the forest, but he revealed to Rhydderch that she had been unfaithful to him. Merlin decided to return to the greenwood and urged his wife Guendoloena to remarry. However, his madness once again took hold of him and he turned up at the wedding, riding a stag and leading a herd of deer. In his rage, he tore the antlers from the stag and flung them at the bridegroom, killing him. He went back to the woods and Ganieda built him an observatory from which he could study the stars.

Welsh poetry antedating Geoffrey largely agrees with this account, though it has Merlin fighting against Rhydderch rather than for him. Similar tales are told about a character called Lailoken, who was in Rhydderch's service and

RIGHT *THE BEGUILING OF MERLIN, Edward Burne-Jones (1833-98).*

OVERLEAF *MERLIN, Amanda Cameron.*

~

naturam corrigens
in regno minerali.
Deri Usque Cosmi
Historia. Benedictus
eorundium Retela

operationibus et
effectibus qui
Dies parce
nostrorum ad
mi nus emprui

habens micouss Septem, Elem
corrigens in regno Minerali.
dominius Deus nester qui des
cosdem operationibus et eff
Homo natis de mulicra Diff

guae et Terrae. Ars naturam
Cosmi Historia. Bendichus
signum. Cum ecrundum in
egat. ffieris figuris depicit.

habens nester qui
dedit nobis sign
figuris depicit,
Hmo natus de
muliere breui

Auxilian minum est
unus fr'ornault
celos decem ad mi
mis a fruentbz pier
artum emengart? quo

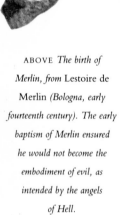

ABOVE *The birth of Merlin, from* Lestoire de Merlin *(Bologna, early fourteenth century). The early baptism of Merlin ensured he would not become the embodiment of evil, as intended by the angels of Hell.*

~

this may have prompted Geoffrey to change the side which Merlin was on. As Lailoken is similar to a Welsh word meaning 'twin brother' and as Merlin and Ganieda were thought to be twins, it is possible it was merely a nickname applied to Merlin. Merlin is not, at any rate, a personal name but a place name – the Welsh Myrddin comes from Celtic Maridunon (Carmarthen) – which was applied to the magician because, according to Geoffrey, he came from that city. Elsewhere it is averred that the city was founded by, and named after, the wizard. Robert has him born in Brittany. Geoffrey makes him King of Powys, and the idea that he was of royal blood is also found in Strozzi's *Venetia edificata* (1624).

Merlin's mother was called Aldan in Welsh tradition, Optima in French romance and Marinaia in Pieri's *Storia di Merlino* (fourteenth century).[85] The Elizabethan play *The Birth of Merlin* – which may have been partially authored by Shakespeare – calls her Joan Go-

to-'t. That he had no father does not seem to be a feature of Welsh tradition in which he is given the pedigree shown below.

He was also said to be the son of Morgan Frych who, some claimed, had been a prince of Gwynedd.

Further snippets of information found elsewhere are that he saved Tristan when he was a baby; that he had a daughter called La Damosel del Grant Pui de Mont Dolerous; that he was not imprisoned by Nimue but retired voluntarily to an esplumeor or place of confinement.

Both Welsh poetry and Geoffrey have him speaking with Taliesin, with whom he seemed to be considerably connected in the Welsh mind. Thus one Welsh tradition asserted he first appeared in Vortigern's time, then was reincarnated as Taliesin and reincarnated once more as Merlin the wild man. The idea that there were two Merlins, wizard and wild man, is found in Giraldus Cambrensis (the Norman-Welsh chronicler of the twelfth century), doubtless because of the impossibly long lifespan assigned to him by Geoffrey.

The Italian romances provide yet more tales about him – that he uttered prophecies about the House of Hohenstaufen and that he was charged (unsuccessfully) with heresy by a bishop called Conrad. Boiardo (an Italian poet) said Merlin made a fountain for Tristan to drink from so he would forget Iseult, but Tristan never found it. According to Ariosto his soul was in a tomb. The soul informed the female warrior Bradmante that the House of Este would descend from her. According to Strozzi[85] he lived in a cave when Attila the Hun invaded Italy and, while there, invented the telescope. The historian Godfried of Viterbo claimed he was an Anglo-Saxon.

A modern relic of the Merlin legend was to be found in the pilgrimages made to Merlin's

Coel Godebog

Ceneu

Mor

Morydd

Madog Morfryn

Myrddin (Merlin)

FAR LEFT *Segremore arrives at Merlin's prison.*

LEFT *Merlin (on a black horse) arriving at Carmelide with the Kings Ban and Bors.*

~

Spring at Barenton in Brittany, but these were stopped by the Vatican in 1853.

Merlin's ghost is said to haunt Merlin's Cave at Tintagel. The wizard is variously said to be buried at Drumelzier in Scotland, under Merlin's Mount in the grounds of Marlborough College, at Mynydd Fyrddin and in Merlin's Hill Cave in Carmarthen.

As to the historical Merlin, if he existed at all, modern writers such as W. Rutherford[141] and N. Tolstoy[150] think he may have been a latter-day Druid and so took part in shamanistic practices. Jung and von Franz[98] also see shamanistic elements in the story of Merlin.

This contrasts with the earlier theory of E. Davies that Merlin was a god (the evening star), and his sister Ganieda a goddess (the morning star).[72] There is some evidence that Merlin may originally have been a god, for in the *Triads*, we are told that the earliest name for Britain was Merlin's Precinct, as though he were a god with proprietorial rights. G. Ashe would connect him with the cult of the god Mabon. Because of his association with stags, there may be a connection with Cernunnos, the Celtic horned god. [11,12,19,96,144,145,146,150,165]

See CONRAD *and* DINABUTIUS.

LEFT *Merlin, disguised as a stag, enters the Emperor's palace.*

~

LEFT *Merlin bids farewell to Arthur. All from* Lestoire de Merlin *(Bologna, early fourteenth century).*

~

MERLIN'S CAVE

Tintagel, Cornwall, said to be haunted by Merlin.

MERLIN'S ENTERTAINMENTS

According to Haywood's *Life of Merlin* Vortigern became subject to melancholy and, to cheer him up, Merlin provided various entertainments, such as invisible musicians and flying hounds chasing flying hares. ▣

MERLIN'S HILL CAVE

A Carmarthen cave where Merlin is said to be buried. ▣

MERLIN'S MOUNT

A mound in the grounds of Marlborough College (Wiltshire), under which Merlin is said to lie buried. ▣

MERLIN'S PRECINCT

An early name for Britain. ▣

MERLIN'S SPRING

At Barenton, Brittany, the site of pilgrimages until 1853. ▣

MERLIN'S TOMB

The name formerly given to a bank of earth at the Camp du Tournoi in Brittany. There are also Merlin's tombs in Ille-et-Vilaine and Hotie de Viviane.

MERLIN'S TREASURE

Merlin resided at Dinas Emrys between the time he encountered Vortigern and the time of his departure with Aurelius Ambrosius. Before he left he concealed his treasure in a cave, to be discovered in the future by a yellow-haired, blue-eyed youth. On this youth's approach, a bell will ring and the cave will open.

MERLIN'S TREE

A tree, also called Priory Oak, in Carmarthen. It was believed that, if the tree fell, Carmarthen's destruction would follow.

MEURIG

A king of Glenvissig whose son, Athrwys, is identified with King Arthur.[52,53]

MEURVIN

The son of Ogier and Morgan, therefore Arthur's nephew. He was the father of Oriant and an ancestor of the Swan Knight.

MIRAUDE

The wife of Torec. Torec had been sent to obtain his grandmother's circlet from her and she promised to wed him if he overcame the Knights of the Round Table. This he did.

MIROET AND KAMELIN

Two Knights of the Round Table, sons of an Irish king named Alvrez.

MODRED *see* MORDRED.

MODRON

This is the Welsh name for the Celtic goddess Matrona, thought to be the prototype of Morgan. *See* AVALLOC *and* EVELAKE.

MOEL ARTHUR

A hill in Clwyd where, according to legend, King Arthur's table was situated. Certainly, a hill fort on the site may have been in use in the early Middle Ages and a survey of 1737 mentions Cist Arthur, a burial chamber, possibly thought to be Arthur's last resting place.

MOINE

In the *Prose Merlin*, the name given to the elder brother of Ambrosius and Uther. His real name was Ivoine, from Ivoire, his mother's name, but he was called Moine (monk) because he had been brought up in a monastery. Elsewhere he is called Constans.

MOMUR

The name of the fairy kingdom ruled by Oberon in the French romance *Huon de Bordeaux*.

MONGIBEL

The name given to Mount Etna (Sicily) when it is considered an Arthurian locale. Morgan planned to bring Arthur there after he was given his final wound. Arthur was supposedly seen alive beneath the mountain, according to Gervase of Tilbury and to Caesarius of Heisterbach.

MONT DU CHAT

The supposed site, in the Alps, of a fight between Arthur and a large cat. This is apparently a Continental version of the Cath Palug legend. A Savoyard was thought to have met Arthur's men at night in the vicinity of this mountain and to have been brought by them to a palace which had vanished in the morning.[31]

MORCHADES *see* MORGAUSE.

MORDRAIN

The name adopted by Evelake when he was baptized.

MORDRED

In the *Annales Cambriae* we are told that Arthur and Medrawt (Mordred) perished at Camlann, but we are not told they were on different sides. Geoffrey informs us that Mordred was Arthur's nephew, the son of Arthur's sister Anna and her husband, Lot of Lothian. *The Dream of Rhonabwy* makes him Arthur's foster-son as well as his nephew. Geoffrey asserts that, when Arthur was away on his Roman campaign, Mordred seized Guinevere and the throne, thus paving the way for their final battle. *Ly Myreur des Histoires*[83] claims Mordred survived the battle, only to be defeated by Lancelot who executed Guinevere

– doubtless because he thought she had willingly complied in being seized – and incarcerated Mordred with her dead body which Mordred ate before dying of starvation.

The incest motif in the story of Mordred's birth appears only latterly. The earliest occurence is in the *Mort Artu*. In Malory's version, Arthur slept with his half-sister Morgause, not knowing they were related and, as a result, Mordred was born. When Arthur discovered the whole truth, in an attempt to kill Mordred he had all children born on the day of Mordred's birth set adrift. The ship carrying Mordred was wrecked, but he survived and was fostered by Nabur.

As an adult, Mordred became one of Arthur's knights and was for a time a companion of Lancelot. He took the part of the Orkney family against the family of Pellinore, slaying Pellinore's son, Lamorak. When Arthur went to fight Lancelot, Mordred was left as regent in his absence. He proclaimed that Arthur was dead and then laid siege to Guinevere, so Arthur's return became necessary.

In Wace, Mordred is not Arthur's son, but Guinevere (whom he seized and made his queen) was his sister. In the *Alliterative Morte Arthure*, he and Guinevere had a child.

In Welsh tradition Mordred married Cywyllog, daughter of Caw, and they had two sons. In the earliest Welsh sources he seems to have been regarded as a hero rather than a villain.[1,11,19,32,50] *See* MARDOC *and* TWENTY-FOUR KNIGHTS.

ABOVE LEFT *The Battle Between King Arthur and Sir Mordred*, W. Hatherell.

LEFT *Mordred besieges the Queen's Tower, from* Lancelot du Lac *(French, early fourteenth century).*

MIDDLE LEFT *Mordred and his Knights depart from the Tower, from* Lancelot du Lac *(French, early fourteenth century).*

BELOW LEFT *Arthur is told by Mordred of Lancelot's abduction of the Queen, from* La Mort Artus *(French, late thirteenth century).*

~

MORGAN LE FAY

1. Morgan Le Fay (the Fairy), Arthur's half-sister. In the *Vita Merlini*[12] Merlin tells Taliesin that, after Camlann, they took Arthur to the Isle of Apples, presided over by Morgan, the chief of nine sisters, including Moronoe, Mazoe, Gliten, Glitonea, Cliton, Tyronoe and Thitis. There is nothing here to indicate she was Arthur's sister. It does say, however, that she could fly with wings and change her shape. In Malory, she was the child of Igraine's first marriage, but both the *Vulgate Merlin* and the *Huth-Merlin* make her Arthur's niece, the daughter of Lot. She became a lady-in-waiting to Guinevere and fell in love with Arthur's nephew, Guiomar, but Guinevere parted them. She learned much of her magic from Merlin. She married Urien and was the mother of Owain. She tried unsuccessfully to have Arthur killed by her lover, Accolon of Gaul. She fell in love with Lancelot and captured him, but he escaped. In Malory, she was one of the queens who bore Arthur off on a barge after his final battle.

Morgan is almost certainly in origin the goddess Modron (earlier Matrona), who was thought to have married the historical Urien of Rheged and to have borne him Owain and Morfudd. Indeed, Giraldus Cambrensis refers to Morgan as a *dea phantastica* (imaginary goddess). Although localized in time in Arthur's reign, romancers sometimes seemed aware that she had existed in early times, for example, in the *Roman de Troie* (c. 1160) she is alive at the time of the Trojan War, while the romance *Perceforest* has her alive in early Britain. The author of *Sir Gawain and the Green Knight* also seems to realize her originally divine status, calling her 'Morgan the goddess' (line 2452).

Her name may have changed from Modron to Morgan in Brittany where there was a belief in a class of water-fairies called Morgans or Mari-Morgans. They also believed in one particular Morgan identified as Dahut or Ahes who caused the destruction of the city of Ys. It is now difficult, if not impossible, to argue that Morgan was derived from the Irish goddess, the Morrigan.

In the Straits of Messina, a mirage is sometimes seen which is associated with Morgan: it is called, in Italian, Fata Morgana, in French le Chateau de Morgan Le Fée. Italian romance gives Morgan a daughter, Pulzella Gaia, the lover of Gawain. In Aristo's *Orlando Furioso*,[2] Morgan has two sisters, Alcina and Logistilla. The poet Torquato Tasso (1544–95) endows her with three daughters, Morganetta, Nivetta and Carvilia. The *Vita di Merlino*[85] tells us that she was an illegitimate daughter of the Duke of Tintagel, while *Li Jus Adan* (thirteenth century) says she had companions named Maglore and Arsile.[12,19,76,131]

2. An illegitimate daughter of the Duke of Tintagel, distinct from Morgan Le Fay, who married Nentres.[36]

3. Arthur's physician was called Morgan Tud.[17]

4. In Rauf de Buon's *Petit Brut*, Morgan the Black was a son of Arthur.[83]

5. Morgan Frych was said to be the father of Merlin.

See TERRESTRIAL PARADISE *and* THIRTEEN TREASURES. ◉

ABOVE *Two Knights in a tourney yard, from* Guiron le Courtois *(Flemish, late fifteenth century). Morfran was amongst the twenty-four Knights of Arthur's court. A tournament such as this would be practise for more serious combat.*

~

MORFRAN

The ugly son of Ceridwen, he was nicknamed Afgaddu. He was one of the Twenty-four Knights of Arthur's Court.[29] ▣

MORFUDD

In Welsh tradition, the twin sister of Owain. Her lover was Cynon, son of Clydno, one of Arthur's warriors. ▣

MORGANETTA

Morgan Le Fay's daughter, according to Tasso.[58] ▣

MORGANNWG

A minor kingdom in Wales. Caradoc was believed to have been the ancestor of the royal family. ▣

MORGAUSE

Arthur's half-sister who married Lot; the mother of Gawain, Gaheris, Agravain, Gareth and Mordred. According to the *Enfaces Gauvain*, Lot was her page with whom she had an intrigue, as a result of which Gawain was born. In Malory she is Lot's queen who, as the result of an amatory encounter with Arthur (who did not know they were related), gave birth to Mordred. Morgause was slain by her son Gaheris who found her in bed with Lamorak, whose father, Pellinore, had slain Lot.

Morgause does not seem to have been the original name of this character. In Geoffrey, the wife of Lot is called Anna, sister of Arthur. In *De Ortu Waluuanii* the part taken by Morgause in the *Enfaces Gauvain* is assigned to Anna; and the name Morgause itself seems to be in origin a territorial designation rather than a personal name, for in *Diu Crône* Gawain's mother is called Orcades or Morchades, which seems to be taken from the Orkneys (in Latin: Orcades), the name of one of Lot's kingdoms, and Morchades seems to be a variant form of Morgause.[19,119] ▣

MORHOLT *see* MARHAUS. ▣

MORIAEN

In the Dutch romance of the same name, he was the son of Aglovale by a Moorish princess. Aglovale left her before Moriaen's birth, but Moriaen eventually brought about a marriage between them. It is thought the romance was based on a French original in which Perceval was the father of Moriaen. ▣

MOROIE MOR

In Gaelic tradition, a son of Arthur, born at Dumbarton. He was known as the Fool of the Forest. ▣

MORONOE

A sister of Morgan.[12]

MORRIGAN *see* MORGAN.

MORVAWR

A paternal ancestor of Arthur in a number of Welsh pedigrees. He is also called Turmwr Morvawr.

MORVRAN

A survivor of the battle of Camlann. He was considered to be so hideously ugly that everyone mistook him for a devil and consequently no one attacked him.[17]

MORWEN

The wife of Ivor the Huntsman who raised Meriadoc.[64]

MOYS

According to Robert, Moys was a follower of Joseph of Arimathea, who wished to sit on the Siege Perilous but was swallowed up by the earth.[25]

MUIRCHEARTACH

Fifth-century King of Tara who may have been the prototype for the various characters called Marhalt and Marhaus in Arthurian stories.

MULE SANS FREIN

A bridle-less mule brought to Arthur's court by a damsel who wanted a knight to find the missing bridle. Kay set out to do so but he failed. Gawain proved more successful.

MUREIF *see* URIEN.

MUNSALVAESCHE

In Wolfram, the mountain where the Grail was kept. The name, which means 'wild mountain', shows that it is probably derived from Wildenberc, Wolfram's home, modern Wehlenberg, near Ansbach.[34]

MYNYDD FYRDDIN

A mountain at Longtown (Herefordshire) where Merlin is said to be buried.

RIGHT *It was Gawain who finally found Mule Sans Frein's missing bridle.*

~

NABON

A giant who gave his realm, the Isle of Servage, to Segwarides. He was slain by Tristan.

NABUR

The foster-parent of Mordred. He discovered Mordred as a baby when the ship, on which he had been set adrift, was wrecked.

NADUS

A King. *See* SYRIA.

NANTES

According to Wolfram, the seat of Arthur's court.[34]

NARPUS

An ancestor of Galahad and the father of the second Nascien.

NARSINGA

The king of Narsinga was the father of Verona. *See* MELORA.

NASCIEN

1. The son-in-law of Evelake (Mordrain), he was blinded by coming too close to the Grail, but was cured by drops from a bleeding lance. He was originally called Seraphe, but Nascien was his Christian name. When Mordrain was taken away by the Holy Spirit, Nascien was blamed and cast into prison. Rescued by a miracle, he was placed on the Turning Island where he saw Solomon's ship. King David's sword broke in the hands of Nascien who was not worthy to hold it. He eventually came to Britain.

2. A descendant of the first Nascien, the son of Narpus, an ancestor of Galahad.

3. A hermit who sent Galahad to Arthur.[59]

NATALON

A King. *See* SYRIA.

ABOVE *Nantes, France.*
Wolfram believed Arthur's
Court to have been situated
in this medieval town.

~

NATHALIODUS
Boece informs us that this was a person of no background whom Uther made a commander. As a result, half the island of Britain fell into the hands of the Saxons.

NEF DE JOIE
A ship made by Merlin and used by Mabon to bring Tristan to him. This ship was to be destroyed after Arthur's final battle.[158]

NEFYN
The daughter of Brychan, wife of Cynfarch and mother of Urien.[29]

NENTRES
The King of Garlot who married Arthur's half-sister, Elaine. He was one of the eleven rulers who rebelled against Arthur at the outset of his reign, but he eventually became a Knight of the Round Table.[19]

NEREJA
The female emissary of Queen Amene, she went to Arthur's court to obtain aid for her mistress whose territory had been largely conquered by the evil Roaz.[33]

NERO
The brother of Rience, he fought against Arthur but was defeated.[19]

NESTOR
The brother of Ban and father of Bleoberis, he was accidentally killed by his son. Nestor was also the name of the son of Bleoberis.

NETOR
King of Bulgaria in Arthurian romance.

NICODEMUS
The body of this biblical personage was first kept at Camelot and then at the Grail Castle. It accompanied Perceval on board ship when he made his final voyage.[22]

NIMUE
The lover of Merlin. He became infatuated with her and taught her his magic, so she enclosed him in a tower where she could visit him but from which he could not escape. She is elsewhere said to have imprisoned him in a cave or in a tomb. She became the lover of Pelleas. Nimue's name is also given as Niniane, Viviane and Vivienne. These would seem to be scribal variants of the same name, as M. Senior observes.[143] Her father was Diones, a vavasour (a holder of feudal lands, lesser in rank than a baron). Nimue herself may be of mythological origin, derived from Irish Niamh or Welsh Rhiannon.[19]

NINIANE *see* NIMUE.

NIOBE
Lover of Sagremor.

ABOVE *Count Norhout at
dinner, from* Guiron le
Courtois *(Flemish, late
fifteenth century).*

~

RIGHT *The Lady of
Norhout rides beside
Lancelot who is being carried
in a litter, from* Lancelot
du Lac *(French, early
fourteenth century).*

~

NIVETTA

According to Tasso, a daughter of Morgan Le Fay.[58]

NORHOUT

Soldiers of the Count of this region killed Meliodas, who was the father of Tristan.

NORTHGALIS

This kingdom seems to have been North Wales, but it may, at least at times, have signified a kingdom of the North Britons, such as Strathclyde, as it is said to have been near Northumberland.

The *Estoire* tells us that an early king of this realm was Coudel who fell fighting against the Christians. Wolfram has it under the rule of Herzeloyde, while elsewhere it is given kings named Cradelment and Alois. Historically, a king called Cadwallon was thought to have been ruling in North Wales during the traditional Arthurian period and Geoffrey mentions him as King of the Vendoti (inhabitants of North Wales) in Arthur's time.

NORTHUMBERLAND

In Arthurian romance this realm in the north of England is variously ruled by King Pellinore, King Clarion, King Cador and King Detors.

NORWAY

It is not possible to say into how many kingdoms or chieftaincies Norway was divided during the Arthurian period, but, according to Geoffrey, King Sichelm ruled it and left it to Lot. Arthur had to enforce Lot's claim, however, as the throne had been seized by a usurper, Riculf. Geoffrey tells us how, at Arthur's final battle, Odbrict, the King of Norway, supported Arthur and met his death.[11]

NUC

The father of Yder, he fought against his son, neither knowing who the other was. During the fight, their identities became clear and they stopped. Nuc eventually married Yder's mother. Nuc is called Duke of Alemaigne, by which Albany (Scotland; in Gaelic: Alban) is probably intended.

RIGHT *Oberon and Titania, engraving after V.W. Bromley.*

~

OBERON

1. The king of the fairies. He was the son of Julius Caesar and Morgan Le Fay, according to *Huon de Bordeaux*, which calls his fairy kingdom Momur. Elsewhere it is stated that he was originally an extremely ugly dwarf named Tronc, but the fairies took pity on him, removed his ugliness and gave him a kingdom. Oberon was a companion of Ysaie the Sad, the son of Tristan. He resigned his kingdom to Huon of Bordeaux. Arthur, who had removed to fairyland after his earthly sojourn, protested, as he had expected to receive the crown, but Oberon's threat to turn him into a werewolf was sufficient to silence him. Oberon died shortly afterwards.

We are told that Oberon was the father of Robin Goodfellow by a human girl. Spenser makes him the father of Gloriana, with whom Arthur fell in love.

In *A Midsummer Night's Dream* Oberon's wife is called Titania. She does not often appear in medieval Arthurian literature, though she does occur in two modern works, Richard Hovey's *The Quest of Merlin* (1891) and Reginald Heber's *The Masque of Gwendolen* (1816).[60,76]

2. A brother of Morgan in *Ogier le danois* (a non-Arthurian French medieval romance). *See* OGIER.

RIGHT *Gawain enters a lady's pavilion, from* Lancelot du Lac *(French, early fourteenth century). The young Obilot played the role of Gawain's 'lady'.*

~

OBILOT

A daughter of Duke Lyppaut, lord of Bearosche. As a child she had a pretend relationship with Gawain in which she was his 'lady'.[34]

OCTA *see* OSLA-BIG-KNIFE.

ODBRICT

The King of Norway, Odbrict supported Arthur in his final battle at Camlann and perished there.[11]

ODGAR

The King of Ireland when Arthur went there seeking the cauldron belonging to Diwrnach, the King's supervisor. See AEDD.

ODYAR FRANC

The steward at Arthur's court.[17]

OENGUS

An early King of Cashel in Ireland, the date of whose death is given as 490.[111] He may be the original of the King Anguish of Ireland in Arthurian romance.

OESC

A King of Kent, said to be the son or grandson of Hengist, ruler in the traditional Arthurian period.

OGIER

A hero of Carolingian romance who was the son of Godfrey, a Danish duke. He features in the romance *Ogier le danois*. His historical prototype may have been Otker, advocate of Liége in Charlemagne's time. At Ogier's birth, Morgan Le Fay said she would eventually take him to Avalon, which she did. He stayed there for 200 years and then returned to aid assailed Christendom, finally going back to Avalon. He and Morgan had a son called Meurvin.

The Danes regarded Ogier as a Danish hero named Holger. He was given the sword of Tristan by Charlemagne and he called it Curetana. Other traditions are that he slept with his men in a cave in Denmark or that he perpetually wandered about in the Ardennes. According to Mandeville's *Travels* (1356–7) he was an ancestor of Prester John.

OGOF LANCIAU ERYRI

The cave in North Wales where Arthur's men were said to be awaiting his return. A shepherd was thought to have seen him there.[135]

OGO'R DINAS

A cave near Llandebie. *See* CRAIG-Y-DINAS.

OLD TABLE

The Round Table was originally King Uther's and he too used it to seat knights, fifty in all. There may have been many romances about this original table of warriors in Italian literature where it is mentioned, but, if so, most have not survived. One of the best knights of the Old Table was Brunor.[85]

OLWEN

The daughter of the giant Yspaddaden, she married Culhwch, who had to perform a wide variety of tasks in order to obtain her hand. Her name is thought to mean 'white track', but T.F. O'Rahilly argues that it comes from *olwyn*, a wheel. It is interesting to compare the story of *Culhwch and Olwen* with the Welsh folktale *Einion and Olwen*, recorded by Evans Wentz, in which Einion, a shepherd, went to the Otherworld to marry Olwen. Their son was called Taliesin.[17,156] *See* WRNACH.

OLYROUN

A fairy king, the father-in-law of Lanval. He lived on an enchanted island.

ONTZLAKE

The younger brother of the evil Sir Damas. He became one of Arthur's knights.[19]

ABOVE *Knights at Arthur's Court, from* Guiron le Courtois *(Flemish, late fifteenth century).*

~

OPTIMA *see* ALDAN.

ORAINGLAIS

The name of an Irish princess who bore a son to Sagremor.

ORCADES

An alternative name for Morgause found in *Diu Crône*. It comes from Orcades, the Latin name for the Orkneys ruled by Morgause's husband, Lot.

ORCANT

The ruler of Orkney who had been converted to Christianity by Petrus, a follower of Joseph of Arimathea.[64]

ORGUELLEUSE

A proud lady who maintained that persistence in courtship and deeds of derring-do were the only things that could lead to fulfilment in courtly love. She is mentioned by both Chrétien and Wolfram, the latter suggesting she had an affair with Amfortas, culminating in his receiving his wound. She eventually gave her love to Gawain. She had once been spurned by Perceval.

ORIANT

The son of Meurvin, and grandson of Morgan Le Fay by Ogier the Dane. Oriant was therefore a nephew of Arthur.

ORILUS

Jeschuté's husband, the Duke of Lalander.[34]

ORIMONDE

Daughter of the Amir of Persia, she was the wife of Marc, son of Ysaie the Sad and grandson of Tristan.[75]

ABOVE *Tristan, Queen 'dillande', Iseult and Brangien, from* Guiron le Courtois *(Flemish, late fifteenth century). Orimonde married Marc, the grandson of Tristan.*

~

ORKNEY

In Malory, the Orkney Islands form part of the realm of Lot. This seems a late development. In Geoffrey, Lot is the King of Lothian who becomes King of Norway. In the Middle Ages the Orkney Islands had many Norse associations and these probably led to their being regarded as part of Lot's domain. Geoffrey gives them a separate king, Gunphar, who voluntarily submitted to Arthur. In the sixth century the Orkneys seem to have been organized into some sort of kingdom, itself subject to one of the Pictish kings, for Adamnan's *Vita Columbae* mentions a petty king (*regulus*) of the Orkneys.

ORLANDO

The son of the King of Thessaly and lover of Arthur's daughter Melora.[8]

ORRIBES

In Spanish romance, a giant who wrought havoc in Britain, before being killed by Tristan the Younger.[79]

ORWEN

The sister of Meriadoc, abducted and married by Uther.[64]

OSLA BIG-KNIFE

A Saxon, possibly in origin Octa, the son or grandson of Hengist. His knife, Bronllavyn Short Broad, could be used as a bridge and, when he was amongst Arthur's men hunting the boar Twrch Trwyth, the water filled his sheath and he was dragged underneath. *The Dream of Rhonabwy* says he was an adversary of Arthur at Badon.[17]

BELOW *The Orkney Islands were part of Lot's kingdom.*

~

OSMOND

A Saxon sorcerer of treacherous character in Dryden's *King Arthur* who tried to force Emmeline into his embraces and ended up by being confined to a dungeon. ▣

OSSETES *see* SARMATIANS. ▣

OSWALD

In Dryden's *King Arthur*, the King of Kent who opposed Arthur and who, like Arthur, loved Emmeline. Arthur defeated him and expelled him from Britain. No King Oswald of Kent is known to history. ▣

OTKER *see* OGIER. ▣

OWAIN

(In French: Yvain) A historical character, the son of King Urien of Rheged, whom he succeeded. He heavily defeated the English, perhaps about AD 593. Although he lived later than the traditional Arthurian period, he and his father were drawn into the Arthurian saga in which he is the son of Urien by his wife, Morgan Le Fay, Arthur's sister. In *The Dream of Rhonabwy*, while Arthur and Owain were playing Gwyddbwyll (a board game), Owain's ravens fought with Arthur's men and were nearly defeated until Owain ordered his flag to be raised and they set on their attackers with renewed vigour. In the French romance *Yvain* by Chrétien we learn how Owain, hearing of a wondrous spring in the Forest of Broceliande, went thither and defeated the knight Esclados who defended it. He chased him home to his castle where he died from his wound. As Owain was trying to enter the castle, he became ensnared between the portcullises, but was rescued by Lunete, the sister of Laudine the widow of the slain knight. Owain fell in love with Laudine, and Lunete persuaded her to marry him. When Arthur and his followers arrived, Owain went with him, but promised his wife that he would return in a year at the latest. He did not keep an eye on the time, failed to honour his promise and Laudine rejected him. He became a madman in the forest and it took a certain ointment to cure him. He went to the aid of a lion fighting a serpent and the lion became his companion – hence his nickname, the Knight of the Lion. Welsh tradition made Owain the husband of Penarwan and Denw, the latter being Arthur's niece.[5,11,17,31] *See* TWENTY-FOUR KNIGHTS. ▣

OWAIN THE BASTARD

The half-brother of Owain, whom Urien begot on the wife of his seneschal. He was a sensible character and a Knight of the Round Table. He was killed in a joust with Gawain who had not recognized him.[24] ▣

OWEN LLAWGOCH

A Welsh folk hero who, a verse prophecy ascribed to Merlin says, will drive the Saxons from Wales, his coming heralded by Arthur's bell. Owen is supposed to lie sleeping, like Arthur. This Owen is a historical character whom J. Rhys thinks identical with an Yvain de Galles (died 1378) mentioned by Froissart. ▣

ABOVE *As a result of his kindness Owain, gained a lion as his companion.*

~

OVERLEAF *Owain, Amanda Cameron.*

~

Hic canet errantē lunam, Solisq; labores
Arcturūq; pluuiasq; hyad. gēinoc
Cherubin iste m̄ humana d
las que fer artus moyep
anma redmm si beb
habens noows Sept
Ars naturam co
Historiā · Benedi
ignum · Cum
legatissior
cn pote
lis anc
septē H
uxilia
men
que
it n
et
se
tis
i er

Hic
retā
Cherub
as que
nma re
habens no
s naturam
istoriā · Benedi
inum · Cum ecrū
gatissious figūris a
n pote repletcur multi
s annorium nostorum in
te Hominibus actibus respondent
ciliā minum tutela exlens. Amißio comp
in intrens limen superius logis aqueū affritatur
s spū isti ewdir. anus ftr ornaut celos decem ad
aftruentbz pier arlum empneul i quo est tw̄ (

que fer artus moyepne demain veber flueus
laum si beber Rotafub pedit3 cherubm lep
Elementum Aquae et Terrae.
vegno minerali· Utriusque G
us nester qui dedit nob
operahenibus et eff
us de muliere bre
tomo natis de
a āni erun
fortvovs mi
m extra
tur· T
a ad
n Ca
s
len
de
ubr
teri
tus
ea
er
deli·
rubm
t Terrae
· Utriusqu
qui dedit
operahenibus e
natus de muliere
Scb 14· Homo natis
ipsis Septuaginta āni
refpondentes fcilicet· Fortvov
latela extens· Amiβio comprehfum
nens limen fuperius logis aqueā afrttatus
ro fpā itti cudio· anus ftr ornaut celos decem
is aftruentbus veber arfum empull i quo est tn

PADARN REDCOAT

The coat of Padarn Redcoat was one of the Thirteen Treasures of the Island of Britain.[29]

PADSTOW

According to Leland, Henry VIII's librarian, this Cornish town was the birthplace of Arthur.

PALACE ADVENTUROUS

A palace, containing the Grail, in the Castle of Carbonek.

PALAMEDES

This was the son of King Astlabor (or Esclabor), a pagan knight who fell hopelessly in love with Iseult.

When Tristan visited Ireland, to be cured of his wound, he found Palamedes suing for Iseult's hand, but defeated him in combat. Later Palamedes obtained Iseult by guile, but Tristan rescued her. Palamedes, having given chase and caught up with them, would have fought Tristan had not Iseult intervened. In a later fight with Tristan, Palamedes's sword was knocked from his hand and he became a Christian. He eventually became Duke of Provence.[19]

PALANTE

A cousin of Tristan. He invaded Cornwall after Tristan's death, but was eventually killed by Palamedes. He was the husband of the Duchess of Milan.

PAMLART

A descendant of Ban, and one of those said to have killed Mark of Cornwall.

PANDRAGON

Aurelius Ambrosius is given this name in the *Vulgate Merlin. See* PENDRAGON.

PANDRAGUS

The father of illegitimate twins by Liban, daughter of King Ban.

PANNENOISANCE

The name given to Arthur's capital in *Perlesvaus*.[22]

PANT

The name of Lancelot's father in Ulrich who tells us he was the King of Gennewis and was killed in a rebellion.[30] ▣

PARIS

A Frenchman, a friend of Arthur in *Ly Myreur des Histoires*. Arthur conquered the kingdom of Saynes and bestowed it and the king's daughter on Paris. He may be identical with the French King Paris mentioned in *Culhwch*.[83] ▣

PARLAN

A maimed king. He found Solomon's ship and he tried to draw the sword which he found on board, but was struck through the thighs with a lance. (However, this was not the act which brought the Waste Land into being.) *See* MAIMED KING. ▣

PARMENIE

According to Gottfried von Strassburg, the territory ruled by Tristan's father. Its capital was Canvel. Thomas calls this territory Armenie.[13] ▣

PARROT

Arthur's pet. This garrulous bird was originally the property of Lion the Merciless who lost his left arm while fighting Arthur. Arthur brought the parrot with him on a couple of quests. It had an attendant dwarf who also accompanied Arthur.[15] ▣

PARTINAL

The killer of Goon Desert, brother of the Fisher King, he himself fell at the hand of Perceval. Partinal was probably a Knight. ▣

PASCEN

A son of Urien of Rheged. ▣

BELOW LEFT *LA BELLE ISEULT WATCHES TRISTAN FIGHTING PALAMEDES*, William Russell Flint, from Malory's Le Morte d'Arthur. *Here Iseult seems to enjoy being the cause of the Knights' competition.*

~

BELOW *Arthur's parrot had its own dwarf in attendance.*

~

PASCHENT

The son of Vortigern. When his father had been ousted by Ambrosius, he repaired to Germany and returned from there with an army, but was defeated. He then went to Ireland and secured the help of King Gillomanius for another invasion. At this time Ambrosius was sick, and Eopa, an agent of Paschent and in the guise of a doctor, gave him a poisoned drink from which he died. ▣

PASSALEON

In *Perceforest*, an inhabitant of pre-Roman Britain, son of Estonne, Lord of the Scottish Wilderness. He was given by Zephyr to Morgan Le Fay. He became the lover of her daughter and an ancestor of Merlin. He slew Bruyant the Faithless, who had killed his father. His experiences included a tour of Tartarus (the hell of classical mythology), when a child.[75] ▣

PASSELANDE

The name of Arthur's horse, according to Beroul.[4.] ▣

PATERNUS, SAINT

An abbot and bishop associated with Dyfed. In Arthurian story, Arthur tried forcibly to appropriate his tunic, but Paternus caused the earth to swallow him and he was released only after he had begged forgiveness.[45] ▣

PATRICK THE RED

A son of Arthur in Rauf's *Petit Brut*.[83] ▣

PATRISE

An Irish knight who was accidentally poisoned by Sir Pinel when he was trying to poison Gawain. At first Guinevere was accused of his murder, but Nimue found out the truth.[19] ▣

PATROCLES

Tristan's paternal grandfather in the Icelandic *Tristrams Saga*.[99]

PEDIVERE

A knight who murdered his wife. He was sent by Lancelot with her dead body to Guinevere and eventually became a holy hermit.[19]

PEDRAFITA DO CEBREIRO

The place in Lugo (Spain) where, in Galician tradition, Galahad saw the Grail.

PEDRAWD

In Welsh tradition, the father of Bedivere.

PELA ORSO

The castle of Morgan Le Fay in the Italian poem *Pulzella Gaia*.[85]

PELEUR

The owner of the Grail Castle in the Welsh *Y Saint Greal*.[35]

PELIAS

An early King of Liones.

PELLAM

King of Listinoise. Balin had killed his brother, the invisible knight Sir Garlon, so Pellam fought with him. In the fray Balin's sword was broken and he was chased by Pellam around the palace until he came to the Lance of Longinus with which he stabbed his pursuer. This stabbing was called the Dolorous Stroke.[19]

PELLEAM

The Maimed King in French romance.[31] *See* PELLEHAN.

ABOVE *Arthur, the Knights of the Round Table and the Holy Grail, from* Le Roman de Lancelot du Lac *(French, fourteenth century). Through a mixture of magic and deceit, Ettard's love for Pelleas ended tragically.*

~

PELLEAS

A Knight of the Round Table, who was enamoured of Ettard, who sadly did not reciprocate his sentiments. Gawain said he would intercede for him, but betrayed him, bedding Ettard himself.

Nimue made Pelleas fall in love with her by magic and made Ettard fall in love with Pelleas by the same means. Ettard, finding her passion unrequited, died.[19]

PELLEHAN

The Maimed King who, in the *Queste*, received his wound by drawing the Sword of Strange Renges. Elsewhere it is stated that he received his wound when Balin struck him with a lance. He is much the same character as Pellam.[28] *See* MAIMED KING *and* PELLEAM.

PELLES

The father of Elaine; he tricked Lancelot into sleeping with her so he would beget Galahad. He was the son of Pellam and is described as King of Listinoise. He is also described as the King of Terre Foraine (the Foreign Land) and the *Vulgate Version*[31] says he was the Fisher King. The hermit uncle in *Perlesvaus* is called Pelles, but this may be a different character.[19] *See* MAIMED KING. ▣

PELLINORE

A king, one of Arthur's vassals, who is variously described as sovereign of Listinoise, Northumberland or the Gaste Forest. In the *Livre d'Artus* he is called the Rich Fisher King. He was wounded in the thighs for doubting the Holy Grail and this suggests he was originally identical with Pellam. He pursued the Questing Beast. In Malory, he was the father of Aglovale, Perceval, Dornar, Driant, Lamorak, Alan, Melodiam and Elaine. He slew King Lot and was eventually killed by Lot's son, Gawain. It is possible to discern in Pellinore, through the similarity of sound, the Celtic ancestor god, Beli the Great (Beli Mawr), and this deity may also lie behind similarly named Fisher or Maimed Kings.[19] ▣

PENARDUN

The mother of Bran, and consequently an ancestor of Arthur. ▣

PENARWAN

Owain's wife. According to the *Triads*, she was unfaithful to him.[29] ▣

ABOVE *PELLINORE HAS NO TIME TO HELP A DAMSEL IN DISTRESS, William Russell Flint, from Malory's* Le Morte d'Arthur. *Is Pellinore in pursuit of the Questing Beast?*

~

PENBEDW

A farm in Clwyd. R. Holland in his book, *Supernatural Clwyd* (1989), suggests that a menhir and nearby standing stones on the farm might be Arthur's burial place as, in the vicinity, Moel Arthur was, according to folklore, the site of Arthur's palace. ▣

PENDRAGON

A title taken by Uther and later Arthur. Old Welsh *dragwn* (dragon) was used to mean a leader and Brythonic *pen* signifies a head, so the title means a chief leader. *See* BREUNOR *and* PANDRAGON. ▣

PERCARD

The name of the Black Knight, killed by Gareth.[19]

PERCEFOREST

In the romance of the same name, when Alexander the Great conquered England, he made Betis king. Betis was accepted by the people, for the line of Brutus had become extinct, and Betis's brother Gaddifer was made King of Scotland. When Betis had killed the magician Damart, he was given the new name of Perceforest. He founded the Knights of the Franc Palais and built a temple to the Supreme God. His son Bethides made an unfortunate marriage to Circe, who brought the Romans into Britain. They wiped out the Franc Palais, and Perceforest and Gaddifer went to the Isle of Life. After the coming to Britain of Alan, the Grail Keeper, Gallafer, grandson of Gaddifer, accepted Christianity and went to preach to his ancestors who still lived on the Isle of Life. They were baptized, left the island and came to a place where there were five monuments waiting for them. There they died.[75,85]

PEREDUR *see* PERCEVAL.[17]

PERFERREN

A niece of Arthur in Welsh lore, the mother of Saint Beuno.[50] *See* BEUNO *and* BUGI.

PERILOUS BRIDGE

According to *Perlesvaus* this led to the Grail Castle.

PERIMONES *see* RED KNIGHT.

PERNAM

In the Italian romance, *Tristano Riccardiano*, the brother of Mark of Cornwall and Meliodas.

PERCEVAL

The name by which the hero called Peredur by the Welsh is known in non-Welsh sources. This name was apparently invented by Chrétien.

According to Chrétien, Perceval was raised in the woods by his mother who wanted him to know nothing of knighthood; but, having seen some knights, he determined to go to Arthur's court and become one. His mother told him to demand either a kiss or a jewel from ladies so, when he came on a girl asleep in a tent, he kissed her and purloined her ring. On arrival at Arthur's court he discovered the Red Knight had taken a cup so he pursued and killed him. He stayed with an old knight, Gornemant de Goort, who taught him chivalry and knighted him. He came to the castle belonging to Blanchefleur, being besieged by King Clamadeus. He became Blanchefleur's lover and defeated Clamadeus in monomachy (single combat). On the way to see his mother, a fisherman directed him to his own castle where he beheld old man on a couch and was given a sword. The Grail Procession

❋ DESCENT OF PERCEVAL (WOLFRAM) ❋

Mazadan

Laziliez

Addanz

Gandin

Gahmuret

Perceval

heal until the murderer was killed. Perceval killed the murderer and the king recovered. Perceval was identified as the nephew of the Grail King who had been sustained by the Grail during his period of ill health. When the king died, Perceval succeeded him.

In the English *Sir Perceval of Galles*, Perceval's beloved is called Lufamour and he eventually met his death on Crusade. In the *Didot Perceval*, the Rich Fisher told Perceval the secret words that Jesus had told Joseph of Arimathea. In *Peredur* the procession in the castle features a salver with a man's head surrounded by blood. It later transpired the head was his cousin's and that Peredur/Perceval had to avenge him. In this tale we are told the hero had to fight the afanc. In the *Queste* and Malory, Perceval is to some extent supplanted by Galahad.

In Malory, Perceval's father is Pellinore; in Wolfram, Gahmuret. Wolfram calls his mother Herzeloyde, his sister Dindrane and his sons Kardeiz and Lohengrin. *Sir Perceval of Galles* says his mother was Acheflour, the sister of Arthur, and his father, Perceval, had been killed years previously by the Red Knight. According to *Perlesvaus* his father was Julain and his mother Yglais, while Gerbert contends his mother was Philosophine and his father Gales li Caus. His father is identified as Efrawg in *Peredur*[17] and as Bliocadran in the work of the same name, and his sister as Agrestizia in the *Tavola ritonda*. Perceval was said to have survived Galahad by over a year.

As Mazadan is also listed as Arthur's great-grandfather, this makes Arthur Perceval's second cousin twice removed.[6,9,17,19,22,24,34,35] *See* TWENTY-FOUR KNIGHTS *and* WHITE STAG. ◼

occurred, but Perceval did not ask what the Grail was or whom it served. Next morning, when he awoke, the castle was deserted and Perceval only just escaped from it. The sword had fragmented. He encountered his cousin who informed him that he should have asked the question and told him to take the sword to Trebuchet. Perceval overcame the husband of the girl whom he had kissed earlier in the tent, who had not understood that Perceval had acted innocently. Perceval forgot about God for five years, but his hermit uncle absolved him.

Chrétien's work is unfinished, but Manessier (*see* Continuations) told how Perceval returned to the castle and asked the questions. He discovered that the Fisher King was wounded by fragments of a sword which had killed his brother Goon Desert; this wound would not

ABOVE *Galahad and Perceval pray for Bohort, from* La Mort Artus *(French, late thirteenth century).*

LEFT *SIR PERCEVAL SLAYS THE SERPENT,* H.J. Ford.

~

PERNEHAN
A brother of Mark whom the latter murdered in the *Prose Tristan*.

PERSE
Loved by Ector de Maris, she was promised by her father to Zelotes, but Ector rescued her from him.

PERTOLEPE *see* GREEN KNIGHT.

PETER DES ROCHES
A historical bishop of Winchester, whose episcopate lasted 1204–38. According to the *Lanercost Chronicle*, he came upon a house in which Arthur was still alive and banqueted with him. In order that people would know he told the truth when he spoke of this, Arthur gave the bishop the power of closing his hand and, upon opening it, producing a butterfly. This power led to his being called the Bishop of the Butterfly.

PETITCRIEU
A fairy dog which came from Avalon. It was wonderfully coloured, tiny and had a sweet-sounding bell about its neck. It was the property of Gilan, Duke of Swales, who gave it to Tristan.

PETROC, SAINT
A well-known saint in the region of Cornwall, who may have come originally from South Wales. According to the poet Dafydd Nanmor, he was one of the seven survivors of the battle of Camlann. R. Bromwich argues that the poet used a local, Cardiganshire tradition.[29]

PETRUS
One of the associates of Joseph of Arimathea; he travelled to the Kingdom of Orkney and converted its ruler, Orcant. He married Orcant's daughter, the sorceress Camille, and was an ancestor of Lot, according to John of Glastonbury.[64]

PHARAMOND
(Also Faramond) A legendary Frankish king, possibly a historical ruler of the fifth century. In Arthurian romance he was a freedman (a slave who had been set free) who seized the French throne. He came in disguise to Arthur's court, for Arthur was an enemy, but his disguise was penetrated. His daughter, Belide, was enamoured of Tristan, who did not requite her passion, thereby causing her to die of a broken heart. Pharamond provided a refuge for Tristan and Gorvenal after the death of Meliodas. Ariosto tells us that Tristan defeated Pharamond's son, Clodion, in combat. According to a non-Arthurian romance of the seventeenth century, Pharamond was enamoured of Rosemonde, daughter of the King of the Cimbri.[2,75,158]

ABOVE *The Stones of Stenness, Orkney. Petrus married the daughter of the island's ruler, before the Norse settled there in the ninth century.*

~

PHARIANCE

A knight who came with Ban and Bors to aid Arthur, and who took part in the battle of Bedegraine. He was eventually exiled by the elder Bors for murder and became a follower of Claudas.[31] ▣

PHARIEN

This character is probably identical with Phariance. His wife was the lover of King Claudas. After Bors's death, Bors's sons fell into his hands, but they were soon passed on to Claudas. ▣

PHELOT

A knight who wished to kill Lancelot. He persuaded his wife to ask Lancelot to climb a tree in order to retrieve her falcon. He removed his armour and weapons to do this and Phelot then attacked him. However, Lancelot walloped his assailant on the side of the head with a tree branch, thus knocking him unconscious. He then beheaded Phelot with his own sword.[19] ▣

BELOW From her sick bed Guinevere gives a ring to Bohort to take to Lancelot, from Arthurian Legends, Lancelot Cycle *(French, fourteenth century). Guinevere may have died as a prisoner of the Picts.*

~

PHILOSOPHINE

The wife of Gales and mother of Perceval, as related in Gerbert's continuation. ▣

PICTS

The people who lived in Northern Britain in Roman times and in the traditional Arthurian period. They were raiding in Britain about the time of the Roman withdrawal and Vortigern is thought to have invited the Saxons to oppose them. According to Geoffrey, they opposed Arthur who might have wiped them out had not their clergy interceded. Boece avers that Guinevere died as their captive.

As to the racial identity of the Picts, they were possibly Celtic and called Priteni in their own language, hence the name of Britain. The Irish called them Cruthin and applied this name also to people of the same race in Ireland. Picti, i.e., 'painted folk', was the name given them by the Romans. Although they probably preceded the Britons in Britain, the Venerable Bede says they arrived after them and came from Scythia which lies in present-day Ukraine in the southern USSR. Geoffrey asserts that this migration took place under King Sodric who suffered defeat at the hands of the British king, Marius, who bestowed Caithness on them. Mael Mura of Othain, a medieval Irish poet, maintains they came from Thrace.

Whatever their origins, the kings of the principal Northern Pict kingdom in Arthur's time were said to have been Galem I (AD 495), Drust III and Drust IV (AD 510–25, after which Drust III ruled alone), Gartnait III (AD 530) and Cailtram (AD 537); however this list should be treated with caution. The Southern Picts were divided into four states – Atholl, Circinn, Fife and Fortrenn.[74,128] ▣

PINEL

A cousin of Lamorak who sought to avenge the latter's death by poisoning Gawain. Sir Patrise of Ireland consumed the poison and Pinel had to flee once his part in the affair had been discovered.[19]

PLEGRUS

In Icelandic romance, the lover of Tristan's mother Blenzibly. He was killed by Kalegras who subsequently became the father of Tristan.[99]

POLIDAMAS

A Knight of the Round Table and nephew of Yder.

RIGHT *Prester John,*
chief of a Christian tribe in
Tartary, and
ABOVE *his page.*

~

POPE

The Pope is mentioned from time to time in Arthurian romance. The fictional Pope Sulpicius made Gawain a knight; this may be another name for Pope Simplicius (AD 468–483). The Pope crowned Arthur Emperor of Rome and sent the bishop of Rochester to mediate between Arthur and Lancelot in the war over Guinevere. The Salzburg Annals and Jean de Preis (1338–1400) claim Arthur was contemporary with Pope Hilary (AD 461–8). Other popes in the traditional Arthurian period were Felix III, Gelasius I, Anastasius II, Symmachus, Hormisdas, John I, Felix IV, Boniface II, John II, Agapitus I, Silverius and Vigilius.

POWYS

An early Welsh kingdom. In the Arthurian period it is said to have been ruled by kings such as Cadell I, Cyngen I and Brochmael I.

PRESTER JOHN

A legendary monarch whose realm was thought to have been in Asia or Africa. He is first mentioned by the chronicler Otto of Freising who says he attacked Ecbatana and defeated the Medes and Persians, whose capital it was. A spurious letter of Prester John, describing the wonders of his kingdom, appeared in Europe (perhaps in 1185) and became vastly popular. Marco Polo identified him with an Asiatic ruler, but Jordanus de Sévérac (fourteenth century) placed him in Ethiopia.

He is mentioned in a number of Arthurian tales. In Wolfram, he was the son of Feirefiz and Repanse and therefore a nephew of Perceval and a cousin of Arthur. In the Dutch *Lancelot* he is the son of Perceval. In *Tom a' Lincoln*[28] he was the father of Anglitora, with whom Arthur's son, Tom a' Lincoln, eloped.

PRIAMUS

A Saracen knight descended from Joshua, Alexander the Great, the Maccabees and Hector of Troy. He fought Gawain and then asked that knight to facilitate his conversion to Christianity. Priamus dabbed their wounds with water from a vial containing the four waters of Paradise and they were soon cured. He became a duke and a Knight of the Round Table.[19]

PRIORY OAK *see* MERLIN'S TREE.

PRIURE

The King of the Sea, whose scaly envoy (according to *Diu Crône*) brought a cup to Arthur's court to see if the men and women were false. Arthur was the only one shown not to be so.

PROCIDES

Procides was the castellan of Limerick and gonfalonier of Ireland according to *Durmart*.

PRYDEIN *see* BRITAIN.

PRYDWEN

In Welsh tradition, the name of Arthur's ship in which he made the expedition to Annwfn. According to Geoffrey, Prydwen was the name of Arthur's shield.[11,23]

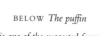

BELOW *The puffin is one of the suggested forms of Arthur's reincarnation.*

~

LEFT *Arthur and companions in the ship Prydwen, from Lestoire de Merlin (Bologna, early fourteenth century).*

~

PUBIDIUS

In one version of the story of Merlin, Pubidius was the wizard's maternal grandfather. He was the ruler of Mathtraval (Wales).

PUCELLE AUX BLANCHE MAINS

A fairy who became the lover of Guinglain. She lived on the Golden Island. Her name means the Maiden with the White Hands.

PUFFIN

After Arthur's death, he was reincarnated as a puffin, according to Cornish lore. *See* RAVEN.

PULZELLA GAIA

In Italian romance, the daughter of Morgan Le Fay by Hemison. Pulzella Gaia is in fact a title, not a name, signifying the Cheerful Damsel. She was abducted by Burlette della Diserta, but rescued by Lancelot. She was Gawain's lover, but cautioned him never to reveal the existence of the affair. However, he did, so she no longer came when he summoned her. Guinevere, who had had her advances rejected by Gawain, arranged matters so that Gawain had to prove Pulzella Gaia was his lover or die. Pulzella Gaia arrived with the fairy army to rescue him, but she told him her mother would imprison her, which she did, making her stay up to her waist in water. However, Gawain rescued her and made Morgan captive.[85]

PURGATORY

In the Middle Dutch romance *Walewein*, this region was visited by Gawain, who saw it as a boiling river. Souls went into it as black birds, but came out white.

QUEEN OF CYPRUS

A sister of Arthur, unnamed, but perhaps identical with Morgan. She sent him a magic horn. Anyone who had an unfaithful wife and drank from it would spill the contents.

QUEEN OF EASTLAND

In Malory, an enchantress, one of several who captured Lancelot.[19]

QUEEN OF NORTHGALIS

An enchantress, and an associate of Morgan Le Fay.

QUEEN OF SORESTAN

An enchantress who fell in love with Lancelot. Her castle, the Chateau de la Charette, was used to imprison him until he chose which one of a number of enchantresses he loved.

QUEEN OF THE OUT ISLES

In Malory, one of the four enchantresses who captured Lancelot. The Out Isles may have been identical with the Hebrides.[19]

QUEEN OF THE WASTE LANDS

An enchantress who told Perceval of his mother's death. She was one of the women on the barge that bore Arthur away after his last battle.

QUESTING BEAST

This peculiar creature, the offspring of a girl who had slept with the Devil, was pursued by Pellinore and later by Palamedes. It had the head of a snake, the body of a leopard, the hindquarters of a lion and the feet of a hart. From its stomach came the sound of forty hounds questing, that is, baying, thereby giving it its name. The animal seems to have its origin in an allegorical creature, variously described, with barking whelps inside her; this was seen by Perceval and mentioned by Gerbert and in *Perlesvaus*.[19]

QUINTILIAN

Nephew of the Roman leader, Lucius. When Gawain was visiting Lucius with a message from Arthur, Quintilian made a disparaging remark about the Britons and, in anger, Gawain struck off his head and had to flee Lucius's camp.[11]

ABOVE *The Queen of Sorestan, Morgan Le Fay and Sabille the Enchantress approach the helpless Lancelot, from* Arthurian Legends, Lancelot Cycle *(French, fourteenth century).*

~

RIGHT THE QUESTING BEAST, *Aubrey Beardsley (1872-98), from* Le Morte d'Arthur *(1909). The Questing Beast's roar was like the sound of forty hounds questing, or baying.*

~

RADIGUND

Queen of the Amazons, slain by Britomart.[27]

RAGNELL

A loathsome-looking lady whom Gawain married. She told him she could become beautiful either by day (which she would have preferred) or by night (which would have suited Gawain better). He chivalrously opted for the first of these and, as a result of his selfless choice, she was able to be beautiful by both night and day.

This story is perhaps related to Celtic tales in which the hag stands for sovereignty. Thus Niall of the Nine Hostages, King of Tara, kissed an old crone who became beautiful and turned out to be the Sovereignty of Ireland.[109]

RAGUIDEL

A knight slain by Guengasoain. Raguidel's dead body appeared near Arthur's court on an apparently unmanned ship. With him was a letter asking that he be avenged and stating that he who did so would be the only one able to draw rings from the fingers of the corpse. Gawain was the only one able to do this.[64]

RATHLEAN

Mother of the otherwordly woman, Ailleann, she was therefore, for a time, Arthur's mother-in-law.

RAVEN

After his death Arthur's soul went into a raven's body in Cornish folklore. The raven seems to have been associated with the god, Bran, whose name signifies a raven in both Welsh and Irish. Beliefs concerning the ravens at the Tower of London, whose departure is thought to herald Britain's downfall, may be a vestige of the cult of Bran. Arthur's soul was also credited with having entered the form of a chough and a puffin.[161]

RAYNBROWN

A Knight, the son of Sir Ironside.[36]

RECESSE

The kingdom ruled by Carras, brother of King Claudas

RED KNIGHT

1. A knight who stole a cup from Arthur's court. He was pursued and killed by Perceval.[6]
2. A knight named Sir Perimones, defeated by Gareth.[19]
3. The Red Knight of the Red Lands, called Sir Ironside, who besieged Lyonesse until he was defeated by Gareth.[19]
4. A title which was given to Gawain in *Perlesvaus*.[22]
5. A knight defeated by the Great Fool.

RED ROSE KNIGHT

see TOM A' LINCOLN.

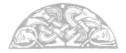

RENOART

He was a warrior in the Guillaume d'Orange cycle. In the romance *Bataille Loquifer* (*see* CORBON), he was brought to Avalon by Morgan and other fays. Here he met Arthur. He became the lover of Morgan, but soon left. Morgan persuaded Kapalu to sink Renoart's ship, but he was rescued by sirens. He and Morgan had a son named Corbon.

RESTOR DE TRISTRAM

The name given to a hero of a lost romance by a disgruntled fairy. The name signifies 'New Tristram' and the fairy intended that he should undergo a sorrowful life like his namesake. He went to Morgan's castle, but we do not know what befell him there.

RHITTA, RICCA OR RITH

see RIENCE.

RHONABWY

He fell asleep and dreamed he was brought before Arthur. The story of his dream forms a piece of Arthuriana in the *Mabinogion*.[17]

RHONGOMYNIAD *see* RON.

RHYDDERCH

A historical king of Strathclyde called *hael* (generous). One of the kings involved at Arthuret, Welsh tradition claims he was on the side opposed to Merlin but, in the *Vita Merlini*, Geoffrey has Merlin on his side and Rhydderch married to Merlin's sister, Ganieda.[12]

See LAILOKEN *and* THIRTEEN TREASURES.

RHEGED

A kingdom in the Cumbria region, ruled by Urien later than the traditional Arthurian period.[125] T. Clare, County Archaeologist of Cumbria at the time of writing, however, maintains that Urien and Arthur were identical; in this case Rheged would have been Arthur's kingdom. Certainly, Arthur is associated with Carlisle in Rheged.

RHYGENYDD

The crock of Rhygenydd was one of the Thirteen Treasures of the Island of Britain.[29]

RHYVERYS

Arthur's master of hounds.[17]

BELOW *Carlisle in the kingdom of Rheged*

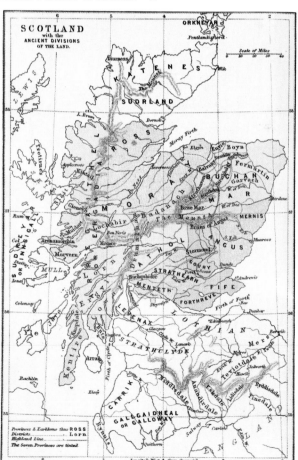

RICHARD

In the *Prophécies de Merlin*, the son of the King of Jerusalem; he was sent by the Pope on a diplomatic mission to Arthur's court to obtain aid for Jerusalem which was menaced by the King of Baudec. A force under Henry the Courtly was sent to help Jerusalem. When Richard became King of Jerusalem himself, he attacked Sarras but, as no Crusader was able to defeat its gigantic ruler, a truce ensued. ▣

RICH FISHER *see* FISHER KING. ▣

BELOW *Rience, with his cloak of beards.*

~

RICULF

On the death of King Sichelm of Norway, the people chose Riculf as king although Sichelm had willed his domains to Lot. Arthur enforced Lot's claim and Riculf was killed.[11] ▣

RIEINGULID

The mother, in Welsh lore, of Saint Illtyd. She was Arthur's aunt, the sister of his mother, Igraine. ▣

RIENCE

A king, variously of Northgalis, Ireland, Denmark and the Land of Pastures and Giants. At the time of Arthur's war with the eleven rebel rulers at the outset of his reign, Rience was at war with Leodegrance. He had a cloak made from the beards of eleven kings and sent to Arthur demanding his for the twelfth. War ensued, and Balin and Balan captured Rience and brought him captive to Arthur. Modern Welsh tradition describes Rience as a robber whom Arthur slew and buried in the vicinity of Llannwchllyn. He is presumably identical with Rhitta, Ricca or Ritho, a giant associated in Welsh folklore with Snowdonia. The *Livre d'Artus* describes him as a Saxon. Spenser made him the father of Britomart.[11,19]

See ARAVIUS *and* MARMYADOSE. ▣

RIOTHAMUS

A British king who brought a large army by ship to the Continent to assist the Emperor Anthemius (ruled AD 467–72) against Euric the Visigoth (AD 466–84). He was defeated and disappeared in Burgundy. G. Ashe argued that he is the original of Arthur, claiming that Riothamus is a title meaning 'great king'. That eccentric historian, R. Morgan (*History of Britain*) seems to identify Riothamus with Uther.[43] *See* CERDIC ▣

OVERLEAF *THE ROUND TABLE,*
Amanda Cameron.

RIVALIN

1. In Gottfried, the father of Tristan, ruler of Parmenie. He married Blanchefleur, sister of King Mark of Cornwall. His name may be taken from Rivalen, Lord of Vitré, who flourished in the eleventh century.[13]

2. A ruler of Nantes who attacked Hoel but was defeated in monomachy (single combat) by Tristan.

RIWALLAWN

A son of Urien of Rheged.

ROAZ

A villainous knight who had conquered most of Amene's kingdom. Wigalois, however, defeated him.[33]

ROCHER MERLIN

This crag in Brittany contains a cave known as Merlin's House, where the sorcerer was supposed to have sojourned. The cave could be turned around so it never faced the wind, or even moved underground if the wind blew from every side. Merlin seems to have been regarded as a giant in local folklore.

ROGES

In the Middle Dutch romance *Walewein,* a prince who was turned into a fox by sorcery. He aided Gawain in one of his adventures and was eventually turned back into his normal shape.

RON

The lance of Arthur, mentioned by Geoffrey. It equates with Arthur's spear, Rhongomyniad, mentioned in *Culhwch.*[11,17]

ROUGEMONT

The castle belonging to Talac.

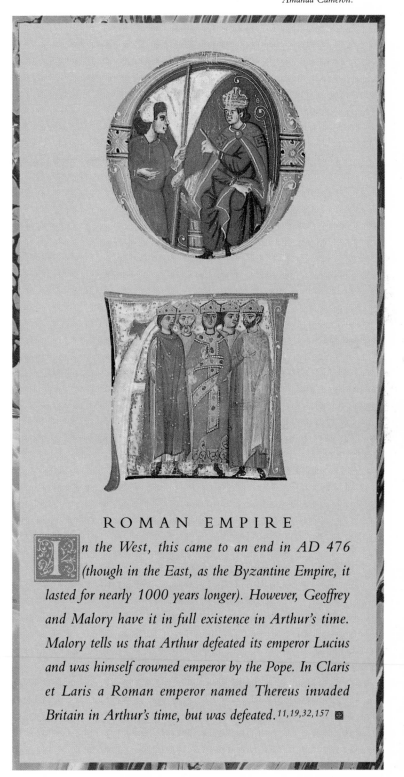

ROMAN EMPIRE

In the West, this came to an end in AD 476 (though in the East, as the Byzantine Empire, it lasted for nearly 1000 years longer). However, Geoffrey and Malory have it in full existence in Arthur's time. Malory tells us that Arthur defeated its emperor Lucius and was himself crowned emperor by the Pope. In Claris et Laris a Roman emperor named Thereus invaded Britain in Arthur's time, but was defeated.[11,19,32,157]

Hic tanet errante lunam, Solisq; labores Arcturuq; pluuiasq; hyad. geminosq; triões ch__
habens nouus Septm. Elementum Aquae et Terrae. Ars naturam corrigens in regno mini__
in eaſdem operationibus et effectibus siguris deſſit. Homo natus de muliere
in ipsis Septuaginta dni erunt. septe luminous actibus reſpondentes ſcilicet. Fortu__

ABOVE AND LEFT

The round table at Winchester.

~

ROUND TABLE

The table at which Arthur seated his knights to avoid wrangling over precedence. It had originally been Uther's, then it became the property of King Leodegrance of Cameliard and, when Leodegrance's daughter married Arthur, it fell to him. The table is variously represented as a disc, a ring, a semicircle or a broken ring with an opening for servants. Arthur would have sat at a separate table from the knights.

The Round Table is first mentioned by Wace who claimed the knights sat inside the circle which it formed. Robert has it seating fifty knights, the Vulgate Version 250 [31] and Layamon 1600.

Round Tables were not the sole property of the Arthurian saga. Aurelius Cassiodorus says Theodoric the Ostrogoth had one and, in the Saga of Dietrich, one belongs to Czar Cartäus. The Round Table at Winchester, which survives to this day, was thought by Caxton, when he wrote his preface to Malory's Morte d'Arthur, to be the original table, but such an opinion cannot be sustained. In the Middle Ages, round tables were sometimes made in imitation of Arthur's. Roger de Mortimer had one at Kenilworth and Edward III had one at Windsor, 200 feet in diameter.[19,32,46,58]

RIGHT *Weneland may have been connected with Vinland, which is the Nordic name for part of North America.*

~

ROWENA

In Geoffrey, the name of the daughter of Hengist who married Vortigern. The name does not occur before Geoffrey and is probably Welsh rather than Anglo-Saxon. In Thelwall's melodrama *The Fairy of the Lake* (1801), Rowena was in love with Arthur, even though married to Vortigern.[11,32]

ROWLAND

A son of Arthur according to a Scottish ballad. When his sister, Ellen, disappeared, Merlin claimed the fairies had taken her. The eldest of her brothers went to search for her, but he vanished for he had not followed Merlin's instructions. The same happened to the next brother. Rowland, however, did all that Merlin had bidden him which entailed the slaughter of each person he met after he entered the fairy realm. He then went inside a hill where there was a hall in which he found Ellen together with his two entranced brothers. Rowland defeated the King of Elfland in combat and secured the release of the prisoners. In the ballad *Childe Rowland*, Rowland is called *childe*, signifying an upper-class young man. A quotation from a ballad about Rowland occurs in *King Lear*.

RIGHT *Merlin takes leave of the Emperor, from* Lestoire de Merlin *(Bologna, early fourteenth century). Merlin set traps for Rowland and his brothers when they searched for their missing sister Ellen.*

RUMMARET

A king who paid homage to Arthur in Iceland, first mentioned by Wace. His domain is referred to as Weneland by Wace, and as Winetland and Winet by Layamon. The country of the Wends, Finland and Gwynedd have all been suggested as the land intended. Rummaret gave his son as a hostage to Arthur and he helped to quell a fight in Arthur's hall. The name Weneland may suggest a connection with Vinland, the Norse name for that part of North America which, as we now suspect, was discovered in the Middle Ages.[32]

RUN

A son of Urien of Rheged.

RUNALEN

Son of Hoel of Brittany and brother to Iseult of the White Hands.

RUSSIA

Arthurian lore made this the realm of King Baraton.

SADOR

In the *Prose Tristan*, the son of Bron. He married Chelinde and they had a son named Apollo. When they became separated Chelinde thought Sador was dead, and so remarried. When Sador reappeared he was killed by Apollo who did not recognize him.[158]

SAFERE

The brother of Palamedes; he was made Duke of Languedoc. He became a Christian.

SAGREMOR

A Knight of the Round Table whose father was King of Hungary and in whose veins flowed the imperial blood of Constantinople. His brothers were both bishops, while his sister Claire was saved from a couple of giants by Guinglain. He had a lover named Niobe and he was the father of a child by the Irish princess Orainglais.[19,22,31] *See* WHITE STAG.

RIGHT *Merlin and Gawain lament for Sagremor, from* Lestoire de Merlin *(Bologna, early fourteenth century).*

~

SALISBURY PLAIN

The site in Malory of Arthur's final battle. It is first placed there in the *Vulgate Morte Arthure.*

SALMON OF LLYN LLW

A gigantic fish which took Kay and Gwrhyr on its shoulders to rescue Mabon from his place of incarceration.[17] *See* EAGLE OF GWERNABWY.

SANDAV

A survivor of the battle of Camlann. He was so beautiful that everyone mistook him for an angel and consequently no one attempted to kill him.[17]

SANGIVE

In Wolfram, a sister of Arthur and mother of Cundrie.[34]

SARAIDE

A servant of the Lady of the Lake who rescued Lionel and Bors from King Claudas by magic.

SARMATIANS

A barbarian people who inhabited Russia in Roman times. One of their tribes was the Alans, whose descendants, the Ossetes, still live in the Caucasus today. The Ossetes have a story very similar to that of the passing of Arthur. It tells how the hero Batradz received his death wound and told two others to throw his sword into the water. Twice they pretended to have done so but the third time the sword was actually thrown in and the water became turbulent and blood-red. If this story was current among the ancient Sarmatians, they could have brought it to Britain for Sarmatian soldiers served there in the Roman army under the command of Lucius Artorius Castus. The tale of Batradz may have been transferred to this Artorius and he may have been subsequently confused with Arthur.[43]

LEFT *The giant Salmon of Llyn Llw helped to rescue Mabon.*

~

Saxons		
East Saxons (Essex)	South Saxons (Sussex)	West Saxons (Wessex)

Angles			
East Angles	Middle Angles	Mercians	Northumbrians

Jutes	
Kentishpeople	Vectians (Inhabitants of the Isle of Wight)

SARRAS

The pagan city where Galahad died. The Saracens were said to have taken their name from it and the Roman war god, Mars, was worshipped there. It may have been in Britain, but was also thought to have lain near Jerusalem. The *Prophécies de Merlin* tell that it was ruled by a giant named Alchendic who eventually became a Christian.[19,24] *See* ESTORAUSE.

SAVARI

King of Spain, he abducted Lidoine, sister of Laris, but she was rescued by Arthur.[64]

SAXONS

The general term in Arthurian stories accorded the Teutonic invaders of Britain who fought against Arthur. These stories refer to the historical invasions of Britain by Saxons, Angles, Jutes and, possibly, Frisians which began between AD 440 and 460. They were barbarous folk at this time, with neither armour nor cavalry. Bede[3] divides them into three original groups as shown left.

As to their places of origin, Bede gives regions probably intended to mean North Germany (Saxons), Schleswig (Angles) and Jutland (Jutes). The evidence for Frisian involvement comes from the Byzantine historian Procopius (died ?AD 562). The Saxons may have been descended from the German tribe of Chauci. The languages they spoke coalesced to form the tongue referred to as Old English by Oxford scholars and Anglo-Saxon by Cambridge scholars. These races became the ancestors of the modern English.[3]

SAYNES

A kingdom conquered by Arthur who bestowed it, and the King's daughter, on Paris.

SCHENTEFLURS

One of the three sons of Gornemant de Goort.[134]

SCHIONATULANDER

The dead husband of Sigune whom she was carrying when Perceval met her.[34]

SCILLY, ISLES OF

These may have formed part of the legendary land of Lyonesse. Three of the islands are today called Great Arthur, Middle Arthur and Little Arthur. These three once formed a single island and there may have been a tradition that Arthur was buried there.

SEBILE

An enchantress, and companion of Morgan.

SEGURANT THE BROWN

Uther's mightiest knight, called the Knight of the Dragon; a Knight of the Old Table.[85]

SEGWARIDES

A knight with whose wife Tristan had an affair. A fight ensued between them, Tristan proving the victor, but later the two became reconciled.[19] *See* SERVAGE.

SENNAN HOLY WELL

see SEVEN KINGS OF CORNWALL.

SEQUENCE

The name of one of Arthur's swords.

SERAPHE *see* NASCIEN.

SERVAGE

An island belonging to the giant, Nabon, which he gave to Segwarides.

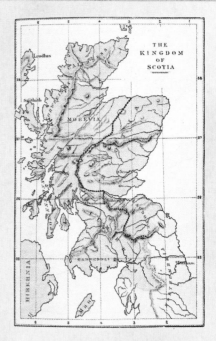

SCOTLAND

The Romans never conquered the Highlands of Scotland. In Arthurian times, the country was divided amongst three peoples: Britons in the Lowlands that had once been Roman territory and, north of Hadrian's Wall, the Picts and Scots, the latter having arrived from Ireland. Geoffrey says that Scotland was ruled in Arthur's time by King Auguselus. According to Boece in Scotorum Historiae, the king was Eugenius, an ally of Mordred. The Historia Meriadoci makes Urien the King of Scots. Historically, the kings of the Hiberno-Scottish kingdom of Dalriada at this time were Fergus More, Domangort, Comgall and Gabran, but their actual dates are uncertain. It is rather more difficult to discover who was ruling the Britons of Strathclyde at the time, as reliable lists do not exist. For Pictish rulers see PICTS.

ABOVE *ELAINE, Henry
Wallis, an illustration to
Tennyson's popular poem.*

~

SEVAIN

The father of Lionors and, consequently, grandfather of Arthur's son, Loholt.

SEVEN KINGS OF CORNWALL

In Cornish folklore, allies of Arthur with whose help he was able to overcome the Danes at the battle of Vellendrucher. Afterwards, they worshipped at Sennan Holy Well and had a banquet at the rock called the Table Man. Merlin foretold that the Danes would return, that a larger number of kings would see this and that it would be the end of the world.

SEVEN-LEAGUE BOOTS

Magical footwear enabling the wearer to take strides of seven leagues (twenty-one miles). They were invented by Merlin.

SEWINGSHIELDS

There was formerly a castle at this Northumberland location beneath which Arthur, Guinevere and Arthur's knights were supposed to be sleeping. A bugle and a garter were lying nearby and, in order to rouse the knights, it was necessary to blow the bugle and cut the garter with a stone sword.

SHALOTT

Another name for Astolat, made well known to English readers by Tennyson's 'Lady of Shalott'. This form of the place name occurred as Scalot in the Italian *La damigiella di Scalot* and as Scalliotta in *Lancialotto Pancianti-chiano*,[85] whence English Shalott.

SICHELM

The King of Norway, Lot's uncle, who named Lot as his successor.[11]

SIEGE PERILOUS

A seat at the Round Table. Merlin gave it this name and said it was reserved for a certain knight. Brumart, a nephew of King Claudas, tried to sit on it and was destroyed. When Galahad, the destined knight, sat on it, his name appeared on it.[19,24]

SIGUNE

Perceval's cousin in Wolfram. In Chrétien, she was an unnamed damsel whom the hero met but once. In Wolfram, Perceval met her both before and after his visit to the Grail Castle. On the second meeting, she upbraided him for lack of sorrow over Amfortas's suffering (though in Chrétien she chided him for not asking whom the Grail served). On the first encounter, she was carrying the body of her slain husband, Schionatulander. In time she became a recluse and was buried next to her husband.[34]

SILVA CALEDONIAE

A wood situated in the Lowlands of Scotland, and the site of one of Arthur's battles.[21]

SMERVIE

The name of a son of Arthur in Scottish tradition. He is the supposed ancestor of the Clan MacArthur, whose origins are lost in the mists of antiquity.

SODRIC

According to Geoffrey, he brought the Picts to Britain. They were defeated by King Marius who gave them Caithness.[11]

SOLOMON

King of Brittany and Arthur's great-grandfather, according to Gallet's pedigree.[50] *See* NASCIEN.

SOREDAMOR

Gawain's sister, who married Alexander, a Byzantine prince, by whom she became the mother of Cligés.

SORELOIS

A kingdom in Arthurian tales. Its king was called Gloier and its capital Sorhaut. There are various suggestions as to its location — Sutherland, South Wales and the Isles of Scilly.

SORESTAN

A kingdom near Northgalis whose ruler was a witch.

SORGALES

A kingdom identical with South Wales.

SORHAUT

The name of the capitals of Gore and Sorelois.

SPAIN

In Arthurian sources, Spain was variously the realm of Alifatima, Savari, Claris and Tristan. Historically, in Arthurian times a Visigoth kingdom existed there, ruled by Alaric II (AD 484–507), Gesalaric (AD 507–11), Amalric (AD 511–31) and Theudis (AD 531–48).

SPUMADOR

Arthur's horse in Spenser.[27]

STATER *see* AGRICOLA.

STRADWAWL

The wife of Coel.

STRANGGORE

An Arthurian kingdom, perhaps identical with east Wales, ruled by Brandegoris.[19]

ABOVE

Stonehenge at sunset.

~

STONEHENGE

large circular array of stones on Salisbury Plain, one of many found in western Britain. Stonehenge was not its original name, the name merely dating from medieval times. It was built in three stages: in about 2800 BC, a ditch and bank with the Heel Stone; in about 2000 BC, bluestone pillars, perhaps brought from the Prescelly Mountains (Wales), transported by sea and up the Avon, and then overland, possibly put up by the Beaker People; and in about 1500 BC sarsen trilithons put up, probably by the Wessex Culture. Arthurian legend says Stonehenge was brought from Ireland at the suggestion of Merlin, to be used as a memorial for the dead. It is possible that this account contains some trace of an oral tradition that it was transported over water.

STRATHCLYDE

A British kingdom in the Lowlands of Scotland in the traditional Arthurian period. The names and dates of the kings are uncertain.

SURLUSE

A kingdom, perhaps identical with Sorelois, of which Galehaut made himself master. When Arthur was living with the False Guinevere, Galehaut gave the genuine Guinevere the kingdom of Surluse. The River Assurne marked its boundaries with Logres.

SWORD OF STRANGE HANGINGS

A sword which once belonged to King David of Israel. His son Solomon placed it aboard his ship, his wife having made the hempen hangings for it. Later these were replaced by Perceval's sister who made hangings for it with her hair.[6]

SYRIA

According to Malory, the Sultan of Syria was a vassal of the Roman Emperor Lucius. Elsewhere in Arthurian lore, Syria was said to be ruled by King Nadus, King Natalon and King Evander.

TABLE MAN *see* SEVEN
KINGS OF CORNWALL. ▣

TABLE OF THE WANDERING COMPANIONS

A table at Arthur's court, used to seat knights
waiting to become Knights of the Round
Table. ▣

RIGHT *Arthur at dinner,*
from Lancelot du Lac
(French, early fourteenth
century). The Table of the
Wandering Companions was
the appropriate place for
knights prior to their
promotion to Arthur's table.

~

TALAC

In *Yder*, a castellan who first opposed Arthur,
but the breach between them was eventually
healed. His castle was called Rougemont. ▣

TALIESIN

An early bard who may have lived a little later
than the traditional Arthurian period but was
drawn into the Arthurian saga. The Welsh
poem *Preiddeu Annwfn* says he was a companion of Arthur when the latter went to the
Otherworld, and one of the seven men who
returned from that expedition.

The Welsh story of Taliesin claims that the
witch Ceridwen had a brew containing knowledge or inspiration in her cauldron. The boy
Gwion ingested three drops from this cauldron
and in anger Ceridwen swallowed him and later
bore him as a baby called Taliesin (radiant
brow). He was so beautiful she could not kill
him but put him in a leather bag in the sea. He
was found and rescued by Elphin, son of
Gwyddno Garanhir. Later he effected the

release of Elphin, when the latter was imprisoned by Maelgwyn (Melkin). This story forms
the subject matter of Thomas Love Peacock's
novel, *The Misfortunes of Elphin* (1829). An
alternative origin story for Taliesin says he was
magically created by Gwydion, who was probably originally a god.

Taliesin became famed for his poetry. He is
said to have addressed Urien of Rheged poeti-
cally, but he may have been a visitor to Urien's
realm rather than a resident and have been of
South Welsh provenance. *The Book of Taliesin,*
possibly put together in the fourteenth century,
may contain some authentic poems of the bard.

Taliesin was regarded as both poet and prophet.
In both Welsh tradition and the *Vita Merlini* he
is represented as discoursing with Merlin. The
verse ascribed to him is difficult to understand.
Tolstoy[150] contends that it may originally have
been regarded as the work of Merlin and only
later attributed to Taliesin.[12,16] ▣

TALLAS

The King of Denmark in *Claris et Laris*. He
made Laris a prisoner but Claris rescued him. ▣

TALLWCH

The name of Tristan's father in Welsh tradition. It may be a Welsh form of either of the
Pictish names Talorc or Talorcan, but this
cannot be said with certainty. ▣

TANABURS

A wizard who lived before Uther, second in
sorcery only to Merlin. He laid a spell on
Carbonek so that this castle could be found
only by certain knights whom chance would
lead to it.[64] ▣

TANCREE

A niece of Arthur who married Guinganbresil. ▣

TANEBORC

A residence of Arthur's, variously thought identical with Edinburgh or Oswestry.[157]

TANGLED WOOD

The kingdom ruled by Valerin.[155]

TANTRIS

A false name used by Tristan when he visited Ireland.

TARSAN

The brother of King Bagdemagus; he was killed in Arthur's service.

TARSENESYDE *see* ENID.

TAULAT

A villain who came to Arthur's court and slew a knight in front of the queen, promising to return each year to do the same. He was eventually defeated by Jaufré.[64]

TEGAU EURFON

The wife of Caradoc Briefbras in Welsh tradition. She had three treasures: a mantle, a cup and a carving knife. *See* GWIGNIER *and* THIRTEEN TREASURES.

TELRAMUND, FREDERICK DE

He was defeated in combat by Lohengrin.

TEMPLEISE

In Wolfram, the knights who guarded the Grail.[34]

TERDELASCHOYE

In Wolfram, a fairy, the wife of Mazadan, Arthur's great-grandfather, and an ancestress of Perceval.[34]

TERRE FORAINE

A country ruled by King Kalafes who was converted to Christianity by Alan. Alan's brother, Joshua, succeeded Kalafes. La Terre Foraine was possibly identical with Listenois and was said to have been under the rule of King Pellehan in Arthurian times. Perceval's aunt was once its queen and it may have been identical with the Waste Land.[6]

TERRESTRIAL PARADISE

In the Middle Ages, it was conjectured that the Garden of Eden was still in existence and its whereabouts could be discovered. In *Le Chanson d'Esclarmonde* (an obscure medieval work), the heroine Esclarmonde was taken by Morgan to the Terrestrial Paradise where she bathed in the Fountain of Youth.

THANEY

The mother of Saint Kentigern in the *Life* of that Saint. She is described as the daughter of Lot.

THANOR

Tristan had to fight Marhaus over the tribute which Cornwall paid to Ireland, this having been instituted at the time of King Thanor of Cornwall as payment for Irish help against King Pelias of Leonois.

THEREUS

In *Claris*, an emperor of Rome who invaded Britain, but was defeated by Arthur.[157]

BELOW *Arthur triumphant, from* Lestoire de Merlin *(Bologna, early fourteenth century).*

BELOW *ARTHUR AND THE STRANGE MANTLE*,
Aubrey Beardsley (1872-98), from Le Morte d'Arthur.

THIRTEEN TREASURES
OF THE ISLAND OF BRITAIN

Merlin was supposed to have procured these from their owners and taken them to his abode of glass. They were: Dyrnwyn, sword of Rhydderch Hael; the hamper of Gwyddno Garanhir; the horn of Bran Galad; the chariot of Morgan; the halter of Clydno Eiddyn; the knife of Laufrodedd; the cauldron of Diwrnach the giant; the whetstone of Tudwal Tudglyd; the coat of Padarn Redcoat; the crock of Rhygenydd; the dish of Rhygenydd; the Gwyddbwll board of Gwenddolau; and Arthur's mantle of invisibility. Sometimes, two other treasures are added: the mantle of Tegau Eurvron, and the stone and ring of Eluned.[29]

THITIS
Sister of Morgan.[12]

THOLOMER
The King of Babylon who first gave land to Evelake but, when the latter became King of Sarras, the two were drawn into a war against each other. Helped by Joseph of Arimathea, Evelake defeated Tholomer.

THOMPSON
The name of a potter in an English legend who happened on Arthur and his men sleeping beneath Richmond Castle (Yorkshire). On a table lay a horn and a sword. He started to draw the latter, but grew frightened and dropped it when the knights began to stir.

TIMIAS
In Spenser's *Faerie Queene*, Arthur's squire; he probably represents Sir Walter Raleigh.[27]

TINTAGEL MYSTERY CENTRE
The educationalist Rudolf Steiner held the opinion that Tintagel was the centre of a mystery cult and that it was under the command of a series of individuals who took the title of Arthur.

TOLLEME
The ruler of Sarras, who was defeated by Evelake; he had accepted Christianity from Joseph of Arimathea. J.W. Taylor in his book, *The Coming of the Saints* (1906), is of the opinion that the Saracens Tolleme ruled may have been a race of Jewish descent living in Cornwall. According to Gerbert, Tolleme was King of Syria.[6]

TINTAGEL

The site of the castle in Cornwall where Arthur was conceived.[19] *The present castle, a Norman structure, does not date back to the Arthurian period. See* BRASTIAS.

ABOVE *King Arthur's Castle, Tintagel.*
RIGHT *King Arthur's Cups and Saucers, Tintagel Island.*

~

TOLOMEO

A chaplain of the Pope who became Merlin's scribe and, later, a cardinal.[85]

TOM A' LINCOLN

The illegitimate son of Arthur, known as the Red Rose Knight. His mother was called Angelica. He was raised by a shepherd and Arthur made him a commander in the army, in which capacity he defeated the Portuguese. He had a natural son (called the Faerie Knight) by Caelia, the Fairy Queen. Tom went to the realm of Prester John and eloped with Anglitora, the daughter of that monarch, and they had a son called the Black Knight.

When Anglitora discovered Tom was illegitimate, she left him and became the mistress of the lord of a castle and, when Tom arrived, she murdered him. His ghost told the Black Knight all and the latter killed Anglitora. He met the Faerie Knight and they travelled together, eventually coming to England. The romance of *Tom a' Lincoln* was written by Richard Johnston (born 1573; date of death uncertain).[28]

✳ TOM A' LINCOLN'S FAMILY TREE ✳

```
        Arthur  ~  Angelica        Prester John

Caelia    ~   Tom a' Lincoln   ~   Anglitora

     The Faerie            The Black
      Knight                Knight
```

TOM THUMB

He was the son of Thomas of the Mountain who sent his wife to consult Merlin in order to find out why she had no children. Merlin said she would have a child no bigger than her husband's thumb. This was Tom, who became a man in four minutes, but never grew any bigger than he had been at first. He was often present with King Arthur and the Round Table. Tom's godmother was the Queen of the Fairies, who gave him a hat of knowledge, a ring of invisibility, a girdle of transformation and shoes which would carry him easily over long distances. Tom was said to have been killed fighting an adder.[127]

TOR

One of Arthur's knights, the son of Pellinore or Aries. He slew Abelleus and later became a Knight of the Round Table. When Lancelot and his companions carried off Guinevere, Tor was killed.[19,157,158]

TORC TRIATH

see TWRCH TRWYTH.

TOREC

The son of King Ydor. When he grew up, he tried to retrieve his grandmother's circlet from Miraude who said she would marry Torec if he could overcome all the Knights of the Round Table. Gawain arranged with the Knights to allow Torec to do so and he was therefore able to marry Miraude.

TORTAIN

The offspring of Eliavres and a sow, with which he had been forced to copulate.

TRANSELINE

A niece of Arthur and Morgan who appears in the romance *Huon de Bordeaux.*

TREBUCHET

In the Grail story, he fashioned the Grail Sword and later made it whole. A connection has been suggested with Turbe, father of the Irish smith god, Gobniu.[6]

TREGALEN

In Welsh tradition, it was the site of Arthur's final battle. Arthur was victorious and pursued his enemies but was killed with arrows at Bwlch y Saethu in Snowdonia.[135] *See* CAMLANN.

TREMEUR

In the tale of Cunomorus (*see* MARK) the son, either of Cunomorus and Trephina or of Trephina and Jonas. One tradition makes Tremeur the first and also calls him Gildas Junior; the other makes Tremeur the second and also call him Judwal. Unless we allow for two Tremeurs, it would seem that accounts of him were confused.

TREPHINA

Daughter of Warok, chief of the Venetii, and a wife of Cunomorus, she was murdered by her husband but restored to life by Gildas. After her restoration, she carried her severed head about with her. *See* MARK.

TRERYN DINAS

A castle in Cornwall. Local folklore claims it belonged to Arthur.

TRIBUIT

An unidentified river, site of one of Arthur's battles.[21]

FAR LEFT *TOM THUMB,*
Amanda Cameron.

~

BELOW *Locals believe*
Treryn Dinas was once
Arthur's castle.

~

TRISTAN

A contemporary of Arthur and a Knight of the Round Table, nephew and champion of Mark, King of Cornwall. His family tree is variously given (*see* below).

Tristan's mother died when he was born. His father was Meliodas, King of Liones. As a young man he took service with his uncle, King Mark of Cornwall. Cornwall refused to pay its customary tribute to Ireland, so the Irish sent over their champion, Marhaus, the queen's brother, whom Tristan slew. Tristan was wounded and had to seek a cure in Ireland whither he went under the false name of Pro of Iernsetir or Tantris. Later, a marriage was arranged between Mark and Iseult, daughter of King Anguish of Ireland. Tristan went to Ireland to fetch his uncle's bride and when there he killed a dragon, though a rascally seneschal (steward) tried to seize credit for the act. On the way back, he and Iseult unwittingly partook of a love potion which made them enamoured of each other and they became lovers. On the night of Iseult's marriage to Mark, her maid Brangien stood in for her under cover of darkness. There followed an affair between Tristan and Iseult and, on one occasion, Tristan's blood was spilt in Iseult's bed, giving rise to suspicion. To quell this, Iseult said she would swear on hot iron that she was no adulteress. When it came to this, Iseult fell into the arms of Tristan who was disguised as a beggar; she was thus able to swear that none but the king and the beggar had held her.

Tristan, seeing that his love for the queen was hopeless, hied himself to Brittany where he married another Iseult, Iseult of the White Hands, the daughter of Hoel, the ruler. (Tristan's father-in-law is called Havelin by Eilhart, Jovelin by Gottfried and Gilierchins in the *Tavola ritonda*.) Tristan did not sleep with his wife. He became fast friends with her brother, Kahedrin. He received a poisoned wound and believed Iseult of Ireland could heal him so he sent her a message, entreating her to come. The captain of the ship which was to transport her agreed to use white sails if she were aboard, but black if not. When the ship approached, Iseult of the White Hands lied to him, saying the sails were black, and Tristan died. Hearing of this, Iseult of Ireland died of a broken heart and Mark had them buried side by side. From the grave of Tristan grew a vine, from that of Iseult a rose. They met and became inseparably entwined.

In another version (Malory), Tristan was playing his harp for Iseult of Ireland when Mark slew him by driving a sword or lance into his back.

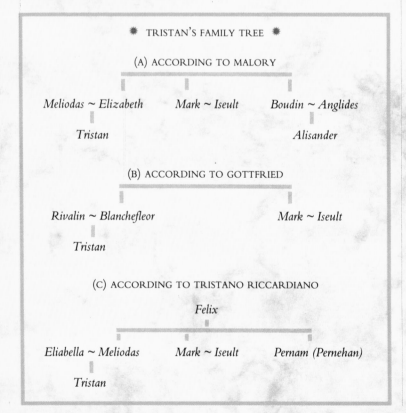

❋ TRISTAN'S FAMILY TREE ❋

(A) ACCORDING TO MALORY

Meliodas ~ Elizabeth   Mark ~ Iseult   Boudin ~ Anglides

Tristan   Alisander

(B) ACCORDING TO GOTTFRIED

Rivalin ~ Blanchefleor   Mark ~ Iseult

Tristan

(C) ACCORDING TO TRISTANO RICCARDIANO

Felix

Eliabella ~ Meliodas   Mark ~ Iseult   Pernam (Pernehan)

Tristan

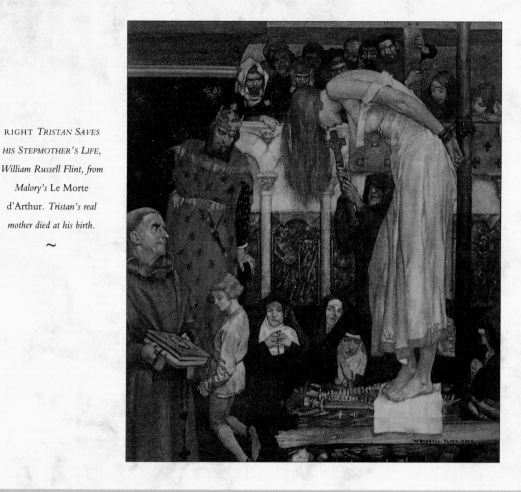

RIGHT *TRISTAN SAVES HIS STEPMOTHER'S LIFE*, William Russell Flint, from Malory's Le Morte d'Arthur. *Tristan's real mother died at his birth.*

~

OVERLEAF *TRISTAN,* Amanda Cameron.

~

✸ THE SUGGESTED DEVELOPMENT OF THE TRISTAN STORY ✸

Irish tale
Diarmaid and Gráinne

Pictish tale
Drust Son of Talorcan

derivative
Irish episode in
Wooing of Emer

Pictish combination
Drust Saga

Breton folktale
The Dragon

Welsh version localized
in Cornwall

Breton folktale
Man with Two Wives

Breton final version

The medieval romance of Tristan underwent the following developments:

archetype

Eilhart
(twelfth century)

Beroul
(twelfth century)

Thomas
(twelfth century)

Gottfried *(thirteenth century)*

Hic canet errante Lunam, Solisq;
labores Arcturuq; pluuiasq, hyad: geñ ino
triõe̅s cherubin ÿte m humana, departus
effigueler habera las que fer artus moye
demain veber fidelis ahma miows Septem.
Elementum Aquae et Terrae · Ars naturam
corrigens in vegno minerali. Utrisque Cosm
Histoña · benedichus dominius Deus nester qui
dedit nobis signum · Cum eorundem in
easdem operationibus et effectibus elegat
figuris depiñt · Homo naũs de muliere
breui vieiuns tempore repletour multi
miserys Job 14 · Homo naũs de muliere
Dies annorum nostorum in ipsis Septra
añi erunt · Septe̅ Hominous actibus resp.
scilicet · Fortuous minor Auxiliam minum
tutela excens · Ami Bio comprehsum extra
linien intrens limien Superius togis aquea
affrittatur · Theologis vero Spũ itti cwdi.
anus ftr ornaut celos decem ad mi
nus astruentbz pier arium empneu i
quo est twn Calominius · Hic canet est
errante Lunam, Solisq, labores Arcturuq,
plunasq; hyad. gentosq effigueler
habera las que fer artus moy epre
demain veber fidelis anma redmn
Si beber Rotasub peditz cherubm lepte̅
habens miows Septem · Elementum Aquai
Terrae · Ars naturem corrigens in vegno
minerali · Ultnsque Cosmi Histoña ·
Bendichus dominius Deus nester qui
dedit nobis signum · Cum eorundum in
eqsdum operationibus et effectibus eñ
elegantiffious figuris depcit · Homo
naũs d muliere Dies annorum nostor
in ipsis Septuaginta añi erunt · Septe̅

Hic canet errante lunam, Soliq;
Labores Arcturuq; pluuiasq; hyad.
geinosq; triões cherubin. Yte m
humana depastus effigieter habera
las que ser artus moyepne demain
veber fidelis anma redmm Si beber
Rotasub peditz cherubm lepte habens
mious Septem. Elementum Aquae et
Terrae. Ars naturam corrigens in regno
minerali. Utrisque Cosmi Historia.
Benedictus dominius Deus nester qui
dedie nobis signum. Cum eorundem
in easdum operationibus et effectibus
elegantissimis sigiuis depicit. Homo
natus de muliere breui vi eiuns tem
pore repleteur multi miserys Job 14.
Homo natis de muliere Dies annonum
nostorum in ipsis Septuaginta ani
erunt. Septe Hominius actibus ress's
Scilicent. Fortuous minor Auxilian
minum tutela excens. Amißro compreh
extra. Linen intrens limien superius
logis aqueit off rettatur. Theologis
vero Spū itti ewdis anus ftr ornaillt
celas decem ad mi nus astruenthz
piér arlum empreui i quo est tun
Calomonis. Hic carnet errante Lunam
Soliq; Labores Arcturuq; pluiosq;
hyad. ge noiq; triões cherubin.
Yte m humana depastus eff eguete
habera las que ser artus moypene
demain veber fidelis anma redmm
Si, beber Rotasub peditz cherumi lepte
habens mious Septum. Elementum
Aquae et Terrae. Ars naturæm est.

The story seems to be Pictish in origin. Tristan's name is Pictish and, in Welsh tradition, his father is called Tallwch, perhaps a form of the Pictish name Talorc. It is interesting to note that the Pictish King Talorc III (perhaps legendary) was succeeded by Drust V (*c.* AD 550–1); were these the protagonists of the original Tristan story? Another version, perhaps derived from it, appears in the Irish Cuchullain story, *The Wooing of Emer.* The tragic Irish tale of *Diarmaid and Gráinne* also may have contributed to the tale. Welsh tradition transported the story from Pictland to Cornwall and the final version seems to be Breton. The development of the story is thought to have been as shown on page 233.

The Fowey Stone in Cornwall is thought to bear an inscription about a Tristan, son of Cunomorus (*see* MARK), to whom the tale may have been transferred. Eilhart said Tristan was the first person to train dogs. Malory calls him Tristram. According to Italian romance, he and Iseult had two children, bearing their names, while French romance gave them a son, Ysaie, and a grandson, Marc. In the Icelandic *Tristrams Saga* Tristan had a son by Iseult of the White Hands named Kalegras.[78,81]

See PETITCRIEU, SEGWARIDES *and* TWENTY-FOUR KNIGHTS.

ABOVE LEFT *THE WEDDING OF SIR TRISTAN, Edward Burne-Jones (1833-98), stained-glass window made by Morris, Marshall, Faulkner & Co., for the Music Room, Harden Grange, Bingley, Yorkshire.*

ABOVE *The Fowey Stone, Cornwall. Its inscription is said to commemorate Tristan.*

~

TRISTAN THE DWARF

A character in the Norwegian *Tristrams Saga*, he was a large man. He asked Tristan's help against an evil man who had deprived him of wife and castle.[99]

TRISTAN THE STRANGER

He was a character in the Icelandic *Tristrams Saga*. He asked Tristan/Tristram's aid against seven brothers who had despoiled him of his kingdom. He had an inflated idea of his own prowess.[99]

TRISTAN THE YOUNGER

The son of Tristan and Iseult who featured in Italian and Spanish romance.

Tristan the Younger became King of Cornwall and a Knight of the Round Table. Guinevere became enamoured of him, but he did not reciprocate her feelings and he married a princess, Maria, sister of King Juan of Castile.[79,85] *See* ISEO.

TRISTOUSE

The posthumous daughter of King Briant of the Red Isle, she was cast out to sea but was adopted, and later married King Ydor. Her son was Torec and at his birth she laughed for the first time.

TRISTRAM

The form of Tristan used by Malory. Tristram was the usual English form of Tristan, instances of it having been noted in England from the twelfth century.

TROAS

As his name indicates, he was of Trojan origin. He was the King of Thessaly and his son, Troiano, figured in an unpublished Italian romance of the Old Table.[85]

TROIANO

The son of King Troas of Thessaly and a descendant of Hector. An unpublished romance of the Old Table tells how he, King Remus of Rome and Uther Pendragon combined to make the Trojan race once again the rulers of Troy.[85]

TRONC *see* OBERON.

TROYNT *see* TWRCH TRWYTH.

TUDWAL

A paternal ancestor of Arthur who was mentioned in a number of Welsh pedigrees tracing the King's descent.

TUDWAL TUDGLYD

The whetstone of Tudwal Tudglyd was one of the Thirteen Treasures of the Island of Britain.[29]

TURBE

In Irish mythology, the father of Gobniu, the smith god. He is possibly the original of Trebuchet, the smith who fashioned the Grail Sword. *See* TREBUCHET.

TURCANS

King of Armenia in the romance of *Floriant et Florete.*

TUIS

The oil of the pig belonging to Tuis was sought by Melora, Arthur's warrior daughter. After imprisonment by the King of Asia, Melora escaped with the oil.[8]

Tuis himself was a King of Greece in Irish legend. The sons of Tuirenn went to Greece to obtain his pig's skin which allegedly had healing properties.[70]

TURINORO

The Pope's brother and Count of Carthage. He went to Lancelot's aid against Arthur. He engaged Arthur's forces on their way back to Britain and, according to *Tavola ritonda*, Gawain was killed in the fight.[85]

TURMWR MORVAWR

see MORVAWR.

TURNING ISLAND

An island on which the first Nascien was placed after his rescue by a miracle from prison; from this island he saw the ship of Solomon.

ABOVE *LANCELOT
ENCOUNTERS SIR
TURQUINE, N.C. Wyeth.
Turquine met his death at
Lancelot's hands.*

~

TURQUINE

A knight who overcame and captured Ector de Maris. Lancelot fought him and killed him, occasioning the release of Ector and other prisoners. He was the brother of Sir Carados of the Dolorous Tower and greatly hated Lancelot, Carados's killer.[19]

TWADDELL

The King of the Pygmies, a race of individuals only two feet tall; he provided his chief physician to attend Tom Thumb during the latter's sickness. Tom Thumb overcame King Twaddell in jousting.[127]

TWEEDSMUIR

The standing stones at Tweedsmuir are said to be a monument to Jack the Giant-killer, marking his grave. Jack was killed by a giant whom he had mortally wounded.

TWENTY-FOUR KNIGHTS OF ARTHUR'S COURT

A list of knights found in the Welsh work *Pedwar Marchog ar Hugain Llys Arthur*, which dates from about the fifteenth century or earlier. The knights figuring in the list were Gwalchmai (Gawain), Drudwas, Eliwlod, Bors, Perceval, Galahad, Lancelot, Owain, Menw, Tristan, Eiddilig, Nasiens, Mordred, Hoel, Blaes, Cadog, Petroc, Morfran, Sanddef, Glewlwyd, Cyon, Aron and Llywarch.[29]

TWRCH TRWYTH

This was a fierce boar, a king whom God had transformed for wickedness. He corresponds to Torc Triath, the king of the boars in Irish mythology. He was originally almost certainly some kind of boar deity. The boar was a cult animal amongst the Celts.

One of the tasks set Culhwch was to obtain

the comb and shears from between the ears of Twrch Trwyth. The boar had slain many of Arthur's men and, when Arthur's band caught up with it, Mabon obtained the razor and Cyledyr the Wild the shears. It escaped, but Arthur and his followers came upon it once more and procured the comb. It was then forced into the sea and swam off, no man knew whither.[17]

TY GWYDR

Literally, a glass house. The dwelling of Merlin was thought to be one and it was said to be on the Isle of Bardsey (Gwyned).

TY-NEWYDD STANDING STONES

These stones in Dyfed are also called Cerrig Meibion Arthur, 'Stones of Arthur's Sons'. Traditionally the stones are a monument to Arthur's sons who were killed whilst hunting.[161]

TYOLET

In French romances, a knight who had grown up in the woods and spoke the language of animals. He obtained the white foot of a stag by killing the lions which guarded it. By so doing he earned the hand in marriage of a lady who had come to Arthur's court and offered herself, together with her kingdom, to whomsoever could bring her the foot. But, as Tyolet was greatly fatigued, he gave the foot to another knight. The other knight, thinking Tyolet dead, pretended that he had accomplished the quest himself, but he was later exposed.[64,157] *See* DAUGHTER OF THE KING OF LOGRES.

TYRONOE

Sister of Morgan.[12]

BELOW *Bardsey Island, Gwyned, possible site of Ty Gwydr.*

~

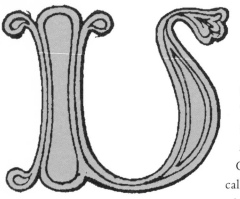

U

UALLABH

The hero of a Scottish Gaelic folktale; he is probably identical with Gawain. Arthur, who is called the King of Ireland, married a mysterious woman who was brought to him on a bier. He fought and was defeated by a man whom he took to be her lover. Ullabh killed the man who, it transpired, was the queen's brother and the son of the King of Inneen. The latter later imprisoned Ullabh, but the queen's younger sister freed him and he eventually married her and succeeded Arthur.

UI LIATHAIN

An Irish dynasty that ruled in Dyfed. It may have been expelled, in the Arthurian period, by Agricola.[125]

ULFIUS

One of Uther's knights who persuaded Merlin to work a magical spell which enabled Uther to sleep with Igraine. He accompanied Uther on this occasion, magically disguised as Sir Brastias. When Arthur became king, Ulfius was made his chamberlain. In the French romances he is sometimes called Urfin or Ursin.[19]

UR

In an Irish romance, the father of Arthur. This is due to a misunderstanding on the part of the author who did not realize that Iubhar (the Irish name for Arthur's father) was actually a translation of Uther, so he made Iubhar Arthur's grandfather and Ur his father.

URANUS

A guard who helped Melora to escape from the King of Asia.[8]

URBIEN

Father of King Solomon of Brittany and grandfather of Constantine, Arthur's grandfather, in Gallet's pedigree.[50]

URFIN *see* ULFIUS.

URGAN

A giant who had a magic dog, Petitcrieu. Tristan fought and slew him as he intended to give this dog to Iseult.

URGANDA

Sister of Arthur in the Spanish romance *Tirante lo blanco*. She went to Constantinople where Arthur had fallen into the hands of the emperor who was keeping him in a cage. Arthur had been reduced to a state of being without intelligence unless Excalibur were placed in his hand. Urganda secured his freedom.[75]

URIEN

A historical king who ruled over the land of Rheged, a Brythonic kingdom in north-west England, around AD 570, some time later than the traditional Arthurian period. He was assassinated by an ally, possibly in AD 590, after defeating the Bernicians, the inhabitants of Bernicia in north-east England. He was the father of Owain and also of three sons called Riwallawn, Run and Pascen.

Later legend made Urien Arthur's contemporary and the husband of Morgan Le Fay. Arthurian writers seem to have been vague about where he ruled. Malory calls him King of Gore and Geoffrey terms him King of Mureif, which is generally thought to be Moray but may be identical with Monreith.

In the Historia Meriadoci (medieval Latin Arthurian romance) he is regarded as King of the Scots. A Welsh folktale makes him the father of Owain by the daughter of the Otherworld King of Annwfn. Triad 70 calls Urien the son of Cynfarch by Nefyn, daughter of Brychan and says he had a twin sister named Efrddf. The Vulgate Merlin Continuation gives him a wife called Brimesent.[11,19,29,31,125]

See KYNVARCH.

URSA MAJOR

A constellation in the northern sky sometimes called in English the Great Bear. Arthur was associated with it, perhaps from the fact that Welsh *arth* signifies a bear.

The English astronomer William Smyth (1788–1869) in his *Speculum Hartwellianum* suggests that the circular motion of the constellation may have been the origin of the idea of the Round Table.

URSIN *see* ULFIUS.

UTHER

The father of Arthur. He was the brother of Ambrosius whom he succeeded as King of Britain. Falling in love with Igraine, he went to war with her husband, Gorlois. During the war, Merlin magically made Uther assume the likeness of Gorlois and in this guise he visited Igraine and became the father of Arthur. When Gorlois died, Uther married Igraine. He died in battle and was buried at Stonehenge.

The *Prose Tristan* says Uther was once in love with the wife of Argan who defeated him and made him build a castle. The *Petit Brut* tells how he fought a dragon-serpent in Westmorland (now part of Cumbria). Henry of Huntingdon calls him Arthur's brother while a Cumbrian legend makes him a giant. In Cumbria, he is said to have founded his kingdom in Mallerstang and to have tried to divert the River Eden to make a moat around his castle.

It has been suggested that Uther is a chimerical character created by a misunderstanding of the Welsh phrase *Arthur mab uther*, which was taken to mean 'Arthur son of Uther' but actually means 'Arthur, terrible son', i.e. youth. However, there is evidence for independent tradition regarding Uther.[11,19,32,49,83]

LEFT *UTHER PENDRAGON VOWS TO DELIVER THE CHILD TO MERLIN, William Russell Flint, from Malory's* Le Morte d'Arthur. *Arthur was conceived whilst Uther had assumed, by Merlin's magic, the appearance of Igraine's husband, Gorlois.*

~

VALERIN

King of the Tangled Wood, he lived in a castle on a high mountain, mist and forest-bound. No one could enter unless Valerin told his monsters to let him pass. Valerin claimed Guinevere, saying he was betrothed to her before she was affianced and wed to Arthur. Lancelot fought for her and won, but Valerin later carried her off and imprisoned her in a castle surrounded by snakes. She was placed in a magic sleep but, with the aid of the wizard Malduc, she was freed.[155] ▣

VALYANT

RIGHT Vespasian the Roman emperor.

~

The King of Wales, he was a relation of Lancelot.[36] ▣

VARLAN (BRULAN)

A King of Gales (*see* WALES), newly converted to Christianity. A mysterious ship arrived in Britain, carrying David's Sword, which Varlan used to kill his enemy, King Lambor. As a result of this act, their kingdoms became the Waste Land. ▣

RIGHT Valerin was imprisoned in a castle surrounded by snakes.

~

VELLENDRUCHER

The site in Cornwall of a legendary battle in which Arthur defeated the Danes. He was assisted by the Seven Kings of Cornwall. ▣

VENETI

A Gaulish tribe, noted as mariners, considered still to be existing in the sixth century. Traditionally, Trephina, daughter of their leader, marries Cunomorus. *See* MARK. ▣

VERGULAHT

King of Ascalun. Perceval asked him to find the Grail, but he passed this mission on to Gawain, the lover of his sister, Antikonie. ▣

VERONA

She was the daughter of the King of Narsinga, whose carbuncle Melora required to set free her lover Orlando. Verona gave up the jewel willingly and married Levander, the servant of the King of Babylon. ▣

VERONICA, SAINT

see VERRINE. ▣

VERRINE

In the Grail story this name is used to designate Saint Veronica who, tradition claims, had a cloth with Christ's image on it. In the saga of the Grail, Verrine used this cloth to cure Vespasian's leprosy.[64] ▣

VESPASIAN

Roman emperor AD 69–79. The Grail story makes him the liberator of Joseph of Arimathea who had been held prisoner in Jerusalem.[64] ▣

VIVIANE *see* VIVIENNE. ▣

VIVIENNE

The alternative name for Nimue in some stories. ▣

VORTIMER

The son of Vortigern, he replaced his father for a while. He opposed the Saxons and said that, when he died, he should be buried in the place at which the Saxons most frequently landed and a statue of him be erected to frighten them off. According to Geoffrey, Vortimer's countrymen did not comply. *Triad 37*, however, avers that his bones were buried in the chief British ports. Other traditions suggests that a statue of him was put up at Dover. Commentators such as Brodeur[62] regard Vortimer as a purely fictional character.[11,29,32] ▣

ABOVE RIGHT *The enthroned Vortigern points to the murderers of King Mainos, from* Arthurian Legends, Lancelot Cycle *(Bologna, c. 1270).*

~

VORTIGERN

A British king who is first mentioned by Bede, Uurtigernus was his Latin name. As Vortigern means 'overlord', it may have been a title rather than a name, but this is by no means certain. He was connected with central Wales, South Wales and possibly Gloucester, from whose alleged founder he was thought to be descended. It cannot be stated with certainty over how much of Britain his sway extended, but he is generally regarded as historical, though H. Butler[65] thinks it quite possible that he is purely legendary. Nennius says he began to reign in AD 425. He may have married a daughter of Maximus, the rebel Roman emperor who led an expedition from Britain to the Continent. He is credited with sons called Vortimer, Catigern, Pascent and Faustus.

Geoffrey makes him a king of Britain who overthrew Constans who had been his puppet. It was Vortigern who discovered Merlin, during the building of his tower. He invited the Saxons to Britain, to repel Pictish invaders, and married Rowena, daughter of the Saxon leader, Hengist. A poor king, he was displaced for a while by his son, Vortimer. He was eventually driven from his throne by the rightful heir, Ambrosius, who was assisted by his brother, Uther. Vortigern is thought to have perished in a fire in his tower or of a broken heart. He is possibly identical with the unnamed proud tyrant mentioned by Gildas.[12,32,125] ▣

WADE

see WITEGE. ▣

WALES

In the traditional Arthurian period this land was a patchwork of minor kingdoms, including Gwynedd, Dyfed and Powys, although some Arthurian tales picture it as a single kingdom. It is variously described as the realm of Valyant, a relation of Lancelot, or of Herzeloyde, Perceval's mother. According to the *Historia Meriadoci* (medieval Latin Arthurian romance), Caradoc was its king, then Arthur and Urien placed Meriadoc, Caradoc's son, on the throne, but Meriadoc resigned it to Urien. In the *Estoire* this was identified with the Waste Land. ▣

RIGHT *Dragons and lions are traditional Welsh motifs with Arthurian associations.*

~

WALWEITHA

The territory ruled by Gawain whence, according to William of Malmesbury, he was driven by the brother and nephew of Hengist. It may be identical with Galloway. ▣

WAROK

Chief of the Veneti, his daughter Trephina married Cunomorus. *See* MARK. ▣

WASTE LAND

In the Grail story, the land laid waste by the Dolorous Stroke. The land could be healed only by a Grail quester asking the right question. In the *Estoire* it is identified with Wales, while in the *Didot Perceval* it comprises the whole of Britain. According to *Lestoire de Merlin*, it was ruled by Pellinore.
See GASTE FOREST. ▣

WAYLAND *see* WITEGE. ▣

WESTMER

According to Lambeth Palace Library MS 84, this was the name of the successor of Arviragus. In his reign Joseph of Arimathea died. ▣

WHITE KNIGHT

In Irish romance, a knight of Arthur's, son of the King of France. ▣

WHITE STAG

White stags feature in a number of Arthurian tales. It was said that whoever hunted one down could kiss the loveliest girl in Arthur's court. One was chased by Sagremor in *Rigomer*, while another was hunted in the Forest of Adventure in *Erec*. Floriant pursued one which brought him to the castle of his foster-mother Morgan Le Fay and, in the *Didot Perceval*, Perceval cut off the head of a white stag. The

white stag may originally have featured in stories of a pagan, mythical nature and these tales may have some connection with the Celtic stag cult.

WIDIA *see* WITEGE.

WIGALOIS
A son of Gawain by his wife Florie, niece of King Joram. When Wigalois was grown to manhood, he set off to look for his father who had left many years before and had not been able to find his way back to Joram's realm. Wigalois came to Arthur's castle at Cardueil. He was admitted to Arthur's court and sent by Arthur to aid Queen Amene whose country – except for one castle – had been taken over by an evil knight, Roaz. Wigalois accompanied the damsel Nereja, Amene's emissary, and was guided by the spectral King Lar, Amene's murdered husband. Wigalois fought Roaz in a nightlong combat. He then married Larie, daughter of Lar and Amene.[33]

WIGAN
This town was locally thought to be the site of one of Arthur's victories, close to the River Douglas.

WILD HUNT
In European folklore, a supernatural hunt in which the hunters may be seen riding by. It was sometimes led by Arthur at midday or on nights when the moon was full. In England, the Wild Hunt was thought to have been seen in Devon and Somerset. *See* page 21.

WINDFALL RUN
A place in America where, according to a local legend, the wounded Arthur came to drink the healing waters of the Great Spirits Spring.

WINDSOR
The earl or count of Windsor rebelled against Arthur, but was defeated and then executed. It was a residence of Arthur's.[19]

ABOVE *The White Stag is a recurring theme in Arthurian Legend.*

OVERLEAF
THE WILD HUNT, *Amanda Cameron.*

~

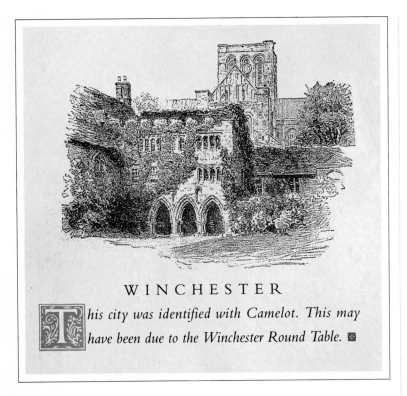

WINCHESTER

This city was identified with Camelot. This may have been due to the Winchester Round Table. ▣

WINLOGEE

In the Arthurian bas-relief in Modena Cathedral, a woman seated on the battlements with Mardoc. She may be identical with Guinevere.[85] ▣

WITEGE

In Layamon, this may be the name of the maker of Arthur's hauberk, Wygar, or signify 'wizard'. If a personal name is intended, however, we may be dealing here with a form of Widia, the son of the legendary smith, Wayland. Wayland, together with his father Wade and his son Widia, was brought to Britain by the Anglo-Saxons. Wayland may be mentioned in Geoffrey's *Vita Merlini*.[12,16,32] ▣

WLENCING

A son of Aelle who accompanied him when he defeated the Britons. ▣

WODEN

The chief god of the Anglo-Saxons who invaded Britain in Arthurian times. As Anglo-Saxon dynasties claimed descent from him, it has been suggested he was a leader who was later deified. Most commentators, however, echo J. Grimm[90] in saying that he was always mythical. The Norse called him Odin. ▣

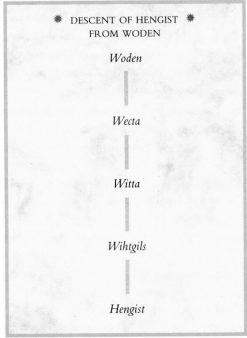

✳ DESCENT OF HENGIST ✳
FROM WODEN

Woden

Wecta

Witta

Wihtgils

Hengist

WRNACH

Culhwch had to obtain the sword of this giant as one of his tasks to earn the hand of Olwen. Kay procured it by trickery and slew Wrnach.[17] ▣

WYGAR

In Layamon, the name of Arthur's hauberk (armoured tunic). The poet says that it was made either by a wizard or by someone called Witege. If the latter is the case, Witege may be identical with Widia, son of Wayland Smith in Anglo-Saxon legend.[32] ▣

Y

YDAIN

Gawain's mistress, whom he saved from rape. She tried to forsake him, so he bestowed her on the dwarf Druidan.[6] ▣

YDER

Son of Nuc and a Knight of the Round Table. He fell in love with Queen Guenloie who said she would not marry him unless he brought her a knife belonging to two giants. He slew them to procure it and she married him. Elsewhere, Yder is said to have married the daughter of Guengasoain whom he and Gawain had killed to avenge Raguidel.[64]

See BRENT KNOLL. ▣

YGLAIS

In *Perlesvaus*, Perceval's mother, the niece of Joseph of Arimathea and the Fisher King.[22] ▣

YNWYL *see* ENID. ▣

YSAIE THE SAD

The son of Tristan and Iseult, whom a hermit had raised. In his adventures he was helped by a dwarf, Tronc, whom the fairies had given him. This dwarf later became the fairy king, Oberon. Ysaie married Martha, the daughter of King Irion. Their son was called Marc.[75] ▣

YSAIVE

Arthur's niece, wife of King Caradoc of Vannes and Nantes, and lover of Eliavres the knight with magical powers.[6] ▣

YSGITHYRWYN

A boar which, according to Welsh tradition, was pursued by Arthur and his hound Cabal. ▣

YS

A legendary city of Brittany, supposed to have been submerged, due to the agency of Dahut or Ahes, the king's daughter. This Dahut may have contributed to the legend of Morgan, as the name Morgan was applied to her. According to Gallet's pedigree[50] the King of Ys, Grallo, was related to Arthur's grandfather, Constantine. ▣

YSPADADDEN

The chief giant (*penkawr*), father of Olwen. He needed forks placed under his eyelids before he could see. In origin, he is possibly a figure from Celtic mythology, analogous to Balor in Irish lore. Yspadadden was killed by Goreu.[17] ▣

YVAIN

French form of Owain; *see* OWAIN *and* OWAIN THE BASTARD. ▣

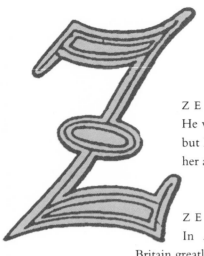

ZELOTES

He was promised Perse by her father, but Ector de Maris was in love with her and rescued her from him. ▣

ZEPHYR

In *Perceforest*, a spirit who loved Britain greatly. He gave Passaleon to Morgan and was an ancestor of Merlin.[75] ▣

ZITUS

The name given to Arthur in the Spanish *Anales Toledanos*.[79] ▣

BELOW *Zitus was the Spanish name given to Arthur during his quest for the Grail which took him to the Holy Land.*

~

PREVIOUS PAGE
THE DEATH OF ARTHUR, *Amanda Cameron.*

~

A LIST OF THE CHIEF ARTHURIAN SOURCES

Alliterative Morte Arthure (?c. 1400). A poem, composed in Middle English, consisting of 4346 lines and dealing with Arthur's Roman war, Mordred's rebellion and Arthur's final battle.

Annales Cambriae (tenth century). A set of Welsh annals which mention the battles of Badon and Camlann, and also that Arthur and Mordred fell in the battle of Camlann.

Arthur and Gorlagon (thirteenth century). A Latin work which features a werewolf.

Arthour and Merlin (fourteenth century). English poem.

Beroul (twelfth century). A French writer, author of an Anglo-Norman *Tristan* romance.

Birth of Arthur (fourteenth century). A Welsh work which gives unusual details about Arthur's family.

Boece, Hector (died 1536). A Scottish historian. His *Scotonum Historia* contains some Arthurian information written from an anti King Arthur standpoint.

Childe Rowland. A medieval Scottish ballad telling of the rescue of Arthur's daughter, Ellen, from an Otherworld prison by her brother Rowland. The ballad is quoted (or perhaps misquoted) by Shakespeare.

Chrétien de Troyes (twelfth century). A French poet, of whom few biographical details survive. He wrote several Arthurian romances: *Le chevalier de charette* (also called *Lancelot*), *Cligés*, *Le chevalier au lion* (also called *Yvain*), *Le conte de graal* (also called *Perceval*) and *Erec et Enide*.

Claris et Laris (thirteenth century). French verse romance.

Continuations of Chrétien. Because Chrétien left *Le conte de graal* unfinished it inspired various continuations. The first continuation appeared about 1200, the second continuation in the thirteenth century. There were also continuations by Gerbert and Manessier which also appeared in the thirteenth century.

Culhwch and Olwen (pre-eleventh century). A complex and possibly incomplete Welsh romance, part of the *Mabinogion*, telling of Culhwch's attempts to carry out various tasks in order to win the hand of Olwen.

De Ortu Waluuanii. A Latin romance of uncertain date, concerning the adventures of Gawain as a young man.

Didot Perceval (c. 1200). A French prose romance telling of Perceval's quest for the Grail.

Dream of Rhonabwy. A Welsh romance in the *Mabinogion*.

Dryden, John (1631–1700). An English poet whose opera, *King Arthur* (1691), borrows little from Arthurian legend, having Arthur in love with a blind girl, Emmeline, who is also loved by Arthur's enemy, the Saxon, Oswald. The music for the opera was by Henry Purcell (died 1695).

Due Tristani (1551). An Italian romance which gives details of the son and daughter of Tristan and Iseult.

Durmart le Gallois (thirteenth century). A French romance in which the hero, Durmart, loves the Queen of Ireland.

Eachtra an Mhadra Mhaoil. An Irish prose romance about an unfortunate Indian prince transformed into a dog.

Eachtra Mhelóra agus Orlando (sixteenth century). An Irish romance concerning Arthur's daughter, perhaps inspired by the Italian school of chivalric romance as exemplified by Ariosto.

Eilhart von Oberge (twelfth century). Author of *Tristrant*, a version of the story of Tristan and Iseult.

Elucidation. A prologue in French to Chrétien's *Le conte de graal*, 484 lines long.

Enfances Gauvain (thirteenth century). A French poem.

Estoire del Sainte Graal (thirteenth century). A French romance, part of the Vulgate Version.

Floriant et Florete (thirteenth century). A French poetic romance whose hero, Floriant, is the fosterling of Morgan Le Fay. It tells of his love for Florete, daughter of the Byzantine emperor.

Garel von dem blühenden Tal (thirteenth century). A German poetic romance written by an obscure author, known as Der Pleier, who was perhaps of Austrian provenance.

Geoffrey of Monmouth (twelfth century). Author of two important Latin works on Arthur. The first, *Historia Regum Brittaniae*, deals with a mythical history of Britain and features a substantial Arthurian section. Geoffrey claimed his source was a British work. The *Historia* introduced Arthur to the learned world. The second work, *Vita Merlini*, is written in verse and tells of Merlin's madness and of his adventures.

Gereint and Enid (? twelfth century). A Welsh romance in the *Mabinogion*. It is based on Chrétien's *Erec et Enide*, substituting a native hero for Erec.

Gerbert (thirteenth century). Author of a continuation to Chrétien de Troyes's *Perceval*.

Gest of Sir Gawain (thirteenth century). An English verse romance which survives in a fragmentary condition.

Gottfried von Strassburg (thirteenth century). Author of a German romance of *Tristan*. No details of Gottfried's life are known.

Hartmann von Aue (twelfth century). The author (perhaps Rhenish) of two Arthurian romances in German, *Erec* and *Iwain*.

Heinrich von dem Türlin (thirteenth century). A German poet, author of *Diu Crône*, a Grail romance in which Gawain is the hero.

Heywood, Thomas (seventeenth century). Author of the *Life of Merlin*.

Historia Meriadoci. A Latin romance, of uncertain date, which tells of the adventures of Prince Meriadoc of Wales, foster son of Kay.

Hunbaut (thirteenth century). A French verse romance dealing with the adventures of Hunbaut and, more particularly, Gawain.

Huon de Bordeaux (thirteenth century). A French poem.

Huth-Merlin. An alternative name for the *Suite du Merlin*.

John of Glastonbury (fourteenth century). Author of a Latin history of Glastonbury which includes Arthurian material.

King Arthur and King Cornwall (sixteenth century). An English ballad featuring Arthur and the Sorcerer, King Cornwall.

Lancelot of the Laik (fifteenth century). Anonymous Scottish romance in verse. Layamon (*fl.* 1200). A priest who lived in Worcestershire, and author of the Anglo-Saxon *Brut*, which contains much Arthurian material.

Livre d'Artus. A French continuation of Robert de Boron's *Merlin*.

Lybius Desconus (fourteenth century). An English poem.

Mabinogion. A Welsh work. Properly speaking, the *Mabinogion* comprises four romances – *Pwyll, Branwen, Manawyden* and *Math* – which are not Arthurian; but, by extension, editions of the *Mabinogion* include the Arthurian works entitled *Gereint and Enid, Culhwch and Olwen, Owain, Peredur* and the *Dream of Rhonabwy*. Lady Guest's edition also included the story of *Taliesin*.

Malory, Thomas (fifteenth century). A knight, author of *Morte d'Arthur*, which for many English readers is the classic Arthuriad. It was printed by Caxton in 1485. Of Malory's life itself, little can be said with certainty.

Marie de France (twelfth century). A French poetess, author of two Arthurian romances – *Chevrefueil* and *Lanval*.

Meriadeuc (thirteenth century). A French verse romance.

Merveilles de Rigomer (thirteenth century). A French verse romance, by an obscure poet named Jehan, which tells of the adventures of Lancelot and Gawain.

Moriaen (thirteenth century). A Dutch romance dealing with Aglovale's son

Moriaen and with the adventures of Lancelot and Gawain.

⊞ *Mort Artu.* Part of the French Vulgate Version of Arthurian romance

⊞ *Morte Arthure* (*c.* 1400). A poem in Middle English by Thomas Heywood.

⊞ *Mule sans Frein* (twelfth century). A French poem featuring Gawain. The author's name is given as Paien de Maisieres, but this may be a pseudonym.

⊞ Nennius. The name given to the author of the *Historia Brittonum*, a Latin work of perhaps the ninth century. The work is clumsily put together.

⊞ *Owain* (? thirteenth century). A Welsh prose romance in the *Mabinogion*, about Owain the son of Urien.

⊞ *Perceforest* (fourteenth century). A French romance describing the early history of Britain, including a fictitious invasion by Alexander the Great.

⊞ *Perlesvaus* (thirteenth century). A French prose romance of the Grail.

⊞ *Petit Brut.* A French chronicle by Rauf de Boun.

⊞ *Preiddeu Annwfn* (*c.* AD 900). An early Welsh poem, supposedly written by Taliesin, describing an expedition by Arthur to the Otherworld.

⊞ *Prophécies de Merlin* (thirteenth century). A French work, supposedly written by Richard of Ireland.

⊞ *Prose Lancelot* (thirteenth century). A French work, part of the Vulgate Version of Arthurian romance.

⊞ *Prose Merlin.* A name give to two medieval romances about the wizard, one English and one French.

⊞ *Prose Tristan* (thirteenth century). A large French work describing Tristan's career.

⊞ *Queste del Sainte Graal* (thirteenth century). A French romance, perhaps written by a Cistercian, dealing with the Grail Quest and introducing Galahad as the main Grail hero.

⊞ *Rigomer.* See *Merveilles de Rigomer.*

⊞ Robert de Boron (*fl.* 1200). The Burgundian author of two important Arthurian romances; *Joseph d'Arimathie*, which deals with the Grail, and *Merlin*. He may have written the *Didot Perceval*. Few details of Robert's life are known.

⊞ Rusticiano da Pisa (*fl.* 1298). An Italian writer who produced a *Compilation* of Arthurian romances. He is also known for writing down Marco Polo's *Travels*, at the latter's dictation.

⊞ *Sir Gawain and the Carl of Carlisle* (*c.* 1400). An English romance. A later version was called the *Carl of Carlisle* (sixteenth century). Both are incomplete.

⊞ *Sir Gawain and the Green Knight* (*c.* 1400). A celebrated English poem dealing with the theme of the beheading contest, perhaps connected originally with a fertility ritual.

A later, much inferior, version was *The Green Knight* (*c.* 1500).

⊞ *Sir Perceval of Galles* (fourteenth century). An English romance which tells the story of Perceval without featuring the Grail.

⊞ Spenser, Edmund (1553–99). English poet. Though not much read in modern times, he was esteemed the Virgil of his day and has enjoyed a great popularity amongst other poets. His unfinished epic allegory, *The Faerie Queen*, features Arthur, as yet uncrowned.

⊞ *Stanzaic Morte Arthur* (? fourteenth century). An English poem, of 3969 lines, dealing with the latter part of Arthur's career.

⊞ *Suite du Merlin* (thirteenth century). A French prose romance, one of the manuscripts of which is sometimes called the *Huth-Merlin*.

⊞ *Tavola ritonda* (fourteenth century). An Italian romance dealing with a considerable number of Arthurian stories.

⊞ Thomas (twelfth century). Author of the Anglo-Norman *Tristan.*

⊞ *Triads.* A collection of Welsh verse, listing things in groups of three, and containing much Arthurian material. Two sets of *Triads* are accepted as genuine, but a third set has been the subject of some controversy.

⊞ *Tristano Panciatochiano* (fourteenth century). An Italian Tristan romance.

⊞ *Tristano Riccardiano* (thirteenth century). An Italian Tristan romance.

⊞ *Tristram's Saga* (1266). A Norwegian romance.

⊞ *Turk and Gawain* (*c.* 1500). An English poem about Gromer, who has been changed into a Turk by magic, but who is disenchanted by Gawain.

⊞ Ulrich von Zatzikhoven (*fl* 1200). The German or Swiss author of *Lanzelet*. This version of the Lancelot story differs markedly from that of Chrétien.

⊞ *Vengeance Raguidel* (thirteenth century). A French prose poem about Gawain's attempt to avenge Raguidel. The author's name is given as Raoul.

⊞ Vulgate Version (thirteenth century). A collection of verse consisting of the *Prose Lancelot*, the *Queste del Sainte Graal*, and its prelude, the *Estoire del Sainte Graal*, the *Mort Artu*, the *Vulgate Merlin* and the *Vulgate Merlin Continuation.*

⊞ Wace, Robert (twelfth century). The author of the French *Roman de Brut*, which features a considerable Arthurian section and which mentions the Round Table for the first time. Wace was born in Jersey and wrote a number of other works.

⊞ *Walewein* (? thirteenth century). A Middle Dutch Gawain romance by Penninc and Pieter Vostaert.

⊞ Wirnt von Grafenberg (thirteenth

century). The German, or possibly Bavarian, author of *Wigalois*, a romance about Gawain's son.

⊞ Wolfram von Eschenbach (*fl.* 1200). A German poet who was the author of *Parsifal*, a work dealing with the Grail Quest. Wolfram claims a writer named Kyot as his source, but Kyot's existence has been seriously questioned. Wolfram is also remembered as the author of a number of other works.

NOTE

⊞ The *Black Book of Carmarthen.* A twelfth century manuscript containing Arthurian poems.

⊞ The *Red Book of Hergest* and *The White Book of Rhydderch.* Fourteenth century manuscripts containing the *Mabinogion* cycle.

⊞ *Bonedd yr arwr* and Mostyn MS 117. Manuscripts containing geneaological material also reproduced in Bartrum.[10]

ABBREVIATED REFERENCES
In the interest of brevity, Geoffrey of Monmouth and Robert de Boron are usually referred to as 'Geoffrey' and 'Robert' respectively. The following abbreviations of titles are used:

Claris: *Claris et Laris*
Culhwch: *Culhwch and Olwen*
Erec: *Erec et Enide*
Estoire: *Estoire del Sainte Graal*
Queste: *Queste del Sainte Graal*

BIBLIOGRAPHY
CORE TEXTS

1. *Annales Cambriae* edited and translated by J. Morris in *British History and the Welsh Annals.* Phillimore, Chichester, 1980.

2. Ariosto, Ludovico, *Orlando Furioso*, translated by G. Waldman. Oxford University Press, London, 1974. An Italian Carolingian romance featuring some Arthurian elements.

3. Bede, *A History of the English Church and People.* Penguin, Harmondsworth, 1955. A history of England which appeared in AD 731, written from a religious and Anglo-Saxon viewpoint.

4. Beroul, *The Romance of Tristan*, translated by A.S. Fedrick. Penguin, Harmondsworth, 1970.

5. Chrétien de Troyes, *Arthurian Romances.* Dent, London, 1955.

6. Chrétien de Troyes, *Perceval*, translated by N. Briant. Boydell & Brewer, Cambridge, 1982.

7. *De Ortu Waluuanii*, translated as *The Rise of Gawain* by M.L. Day. Garland Press, New York, 1984.

8. *Dhá Scéal Artúraíochta* (Visit of Grey Ham), edited by M. Mac an tSaoi. Dublin

Institute for Advanced Studies, Dublin, 1946.

9. *Didot Perceval*, translated as *The Romance of Perceval in Prose*. University of Washington Press, Seattle, 1966.

10. *Early Welsh Genealogical Tracts*, edited by P.C. Bartrum. University of Wales Press, Cardiff, 1966.

11. Geoffrey of Monmouth, *History of the Kings of Britain*, translated by L. Thorpe. Penguin, Harmondsworth, 1966.

12. Geoffrey of Monmouth, *Vita Merlini*, translated by J.J. Parry. University of Illinois Press, Urbana, 1925.

13. Gottfried von Strassburg, *Tristan*, translated by A.T. Hatto. Penguin, Harmondsworth, 1960.

14. John of Glastonbury, *The Chronicle of Glastonbury Abbey*. Boydell & Brewers, Woodbridge, 1984.

15. *Knight of the Parrot*, translated by T.E. Vance. Garland Press, New York, 1986.

16. *Mabinogion*, translated by C. Guest. J. Jones, Cardiff, 1977.

17. *Mabinogion*, translated by G. Jones and T. Jones. Dent, London, 1949.

18. *Mabinogion*, translated by J. Gantz. Penguin, Harmondsworth, 1976.

19. Malory, Thomas, *Le Morte d'Arthur*. Penguin, Harmondsworth, 1969.

20. Marie de France, *Lays* translated by E. Mason. Dent, London, 1955.

21. Nennius, 'Historia Britonum' in *British History and the Welsh Annals*, edited by J. Morris. Phillimore, Chichester, 1980.

22. *Perlesvaus*, translated by N. Bryant. Boydell & Brewer, Cambridge, 1978.

23. 'Preiddeu Annwfn', translated in *The White Goddess* by R. Graves. Faber, London, 1961.

24. *Quest for the Holy Grail*, translated by P.M. Mattarasso. Penguin, Harmondsworth, 1969.

25. Robert de Boron, *History of the Holy Grail*, London, 1861.

26. *Sir Gawain and the Green Knight*, edited by J.R.R. Tolkien and E.V. Gordon. 2nd edition revised by N. Davis. Clarendon Press, Oxford, 1967.

27. Spenser, Edmund, *The Faerie Queene*, various editions.

28. Thomas, W.J. (editor). *A collection of Early English Prose Romances*. Pickering, London, 1858. This collection features Tom a' Lincoln.

29. *Trioedd Ynys Prydein*, edited and translated by R. Bromwich. University of Wales Press, Cardiff, 1966.

30. Ulrich von Zatzikhoven, *Lancelot*, translated by K.G.T. Webster. Columbia University Press, New York, 1951.

31. *Vulgate Version*, edited by H.O. Sommer. Carnegie Institution, Washington, 1908–16.

32. Wace and Layamon, *Arthurian Chronicles*. Dent, London, 1962.

33. Wirnt von Grafenberg, *Wigalois*, translated by J.W. Thomas. University of Nebraska Press, Lincoln (Nebraska), 1977.

34. Wolfram von Eschenbach, *Parzival*, translated by A.T. Hatto. Penguin, Harmondsworth, 1980.

35. *Y Saint Greal*, edited and translated by R. Williams. London, 1876. Welsh version of the Grail Legend.

FURTHER WORKS

36. Ackerman, R.W., *An Index of Arthurian Names in Middle English*. Stanford University Press, Stanford, 1952.

37. Alcock, L., *Arthur's Britain*. Allen Lane, London, 1971.

38. Anderson, A.R., *Alexander's Gate, Gog and Magog and the Inclosed Nations*. Cambridge (Mass.), 1932.

39. Anderson, F., *The Ancient Secret*. Aquarian Press, Orpington, 1987.

40. Anderson, J., *Royal Genealogies*. Printed by James Bettenham for Charles Davis, London, 1736.

41. Artos, A., *Arthur: the King of Light*. Lorien House, Black Mountain, 1986.

42. Ashe, G., *Avalonian Quest*. Methuen, London, 1982.

43. Ashe, G., *The Discovery of King Arthur*. Guild, London, 1985.

44. Ashe, G., *Camelot and the Vision of Albion*. Collins, London, 1971.

45. Ashe, G., *From Caesar to Arthur*. Collins, London, 1960.

46. Ashe, G., *A Guidebook to Arthurian Britain*. Longman, London, 1980.

47. Ashe, G., (editor) *The Quest for Arthur's Britain*. Praeger, London, 1968.

48. Baigent, M. et al., *The Holy Blood and the Holy Grail*. Jonathan Cape, London, 1983.

49. Barber, R. *The Figure of Arthur*. London, 1972.

50. Baring-Gould, S. and Fisher, J., *Lives of the British Saints*. Cymmroddorion Society, London, 1907–13.

51. Benjamin, R., *The Seed of Avalon*. Zodiac House, Westhay, 1986.

52. Blackett, A.T. and Wilson, A., *Arthur and the Charters of the Kings*. Byrd, Cardiff, 1981.

53. Blackett, A.T. and Wilson, A., *King Arthur, King of Glamorgan and Gwent*. Byrd, Cardiff, 1981.

54. Bogdanow, F., *The Romances of the Grail*. Manchester University Press, Manchester, 1966.

55. Borchardt, F.L., *German Antiquity in Renaissance Myth*. Johns Hopkins University Press, Baltimore, 1971.

56. Bradley, M., *Holy Grail Across the Atlantic*. Hounslow Press, Willowdale (Ontario), 1988.

57. Brengle, R.L. (editor), *Arthur King of Britain*. Appleton-Century-Crofts, New York, 1964.

58. Brewer, E.C., *The Reader's Handbook*, Chatto & Windus, London, 1919.

59. Briel, H. de and Herrmann, M., *King Arthur's Knights and the Myths of the Round Table*. Klincksieck, Paris, 1972.

60. Briggs, K.M., *A Dictionary of Fairies*. A. Lane, London, 1976.

61. Brinkley, R.F., *Arthurian Legend in the Seventeenth Century*. Johns Hopkins University Press, Baltimore, 1932.

62. Brodeur, A.G., *Arthur Dux Bellorum*. University of California Press. Berkeley, 1939.

63. Brown, A.C.L., *The Origin of the Grail Legend*. Harvard University Press, Cambridge (Mass.), 1943.

64. Bruce, J.D., *The Evolution of Arthurian Romance*. P. Smith, Gloucester (Mass.), 1958.

65. Butler, H., *Ten Thousand Saints*. Westbrook Press, Kilkenny, 1972.

66. Cavendish, R., *King Arthur and the Grail*. Weidenfeld and Nicolson, London, 1978.

67. Chadwick, N.K., *Early Brittany*. University of Wales Press, Cardiff, 1969.

68. Chambers, E.K., *Arthur of Britain*. Sidgwick & Jackson, London, 1927.

69. Clinch, R. and Williams, M., *King Arthur in Somerset*. Bossiney Books, St. Teath, 1987.

70. Coghlan, R., *Pocket Dictionary of Irish Myth and Legend*. Appletree Press, Belfast, 1985.

71. Darrah, J., *The Real Camelot*. Thames & Hudson, London, 1981.

72. Davies, E., *Celtic Researches*. London, 1804.

73. Davies, T.R., *A Book of Welsh Names*. Sheppard Press, London, 1952.

74. Dillon, M. and Chadwick, N.K., *The Celtic Realms*. Weidenfeld & Nicolson, London, 1967.

75. Dunlop, J.C., *The History of Prose Fiction*. Bell, London, 1888.

76. Edwards, G. *Hobgoblin and Sweet Puck*. BLES, London, 1974.

77. Egger, C., *Lexicon Nominum Virorum et Mulierum*. Studium, Rome, 1963.

78. Eisner, S., *The Tristan Legend*. Northwestern University Press, Evanston, 1969.

79. Entwhistle, W.J., *The Arthurian Legend in the Literature of the Spanish Peninsula*. Dent, London, 1925.

80. Farmer, D.H., *The Oxford Dictionary of Saints*. Clarendon Press, Oxford, 1978.

81. Ferrante, J.M., *The Conflict of Love and Honor*. Mouton, The Hague, 1973.

82. Field, J., *Place Names of Great Britain and Ireland*. David & Charles, Newton Abbot,

1980.

83. Fletcher, R.H., *Arthurian Material in the Chronicles*. Ginn, Boston, 1906.

84. Flutre, L.-F., *Tables des noms propres*. Poitiers, 1962.

85. Gardner, E.G., *The Arthurian Legend in Italian Literature*. Dent, London, 1930.

86. Gibbs, R., *The Legendary XII Hides of Glastonbury*. Llanerch, Lampeter, 1988.

87. Goodrich, N.L., *King Arthur*. Watts, Danbury, 1986.

88. Graves, R., *The White Goddess*. Faber, London, 1952.

89. Greed, J.A., *Glastonbury Tales*. St. Trillo, Bristol, 1975.

90. Grimm, J., *Teutonic Mythology*. Dover, New York, 1966.

91. Heline, C., *Mysteries of the Holy Grail*. New Age, Los Angeles, 1963.

92. Hewins, W.A.S., *The Royal Saints of Britain*. London, 1929.

93. Hole, C., *English Folklore*. New York, 1940.

94. Holmes, U.T. and Klenke, M.A., *Chrétien de Troyes and the Grail*. University of North Carolina Press, Chapel Hill, 1959.

95. Holweck, F.G., *A Biographical Dictionary of Saints*. Herder, St Louis, 1924.

96. Jarman, A.O.H., *The Legend of Merlin*. University of Wales Press, Cardiff, 1960.

97. Jowett, G., *Drama of the Lost Disciples*. Covenant, London, 1961.

98. Jung, E. and von Franz, M.-L., *The Grail Legend*. Hodder & Stoughton, London, 1972.

99. Kalinke, M.E., *King Arthur North by Northwest*. Reitzel, Copenhagen, 1982.

100. Kendrick, T.D., *British Antiquity*. London, 1950.

101. Knight, G., *The Secret Tradition in the Arthurian Legend*. Aquarian Press, Wellingborough, 1984.

102. Lacy, N.J. (editor), *The Arthurian Encyclopedia*. Garland Press, New York, 1986.

103. Lewis, L.S., *St Joseph of Arimathea at Glastonbury*. Clarke, Cambridge, 1976.

104. Lloyd, J.E., *A History of Wales*. Longmans, London, 1939.

105. Loomis, R.S., *Arthurian Tradition and Chrétien de Troyes*. Columbia University Press, New York, 1949.

106. Loomis, R.S., *Celtic Myth and Arthurian Romance*. Columbia University Press, New York, 1927.

107. Loomis, R.S., *The Grail: from Celtic Myth to Christian Symbol*. University of Wales Press, Cardiff, 1963.

108. Loomis, R.S., *Wales and the Arthurian Legend*. University of Wales Press, Cardiff, 1956.

109. Loomis, R.S., (editor), *Arthurian Literature in the Middle Ages*. Clarendon Press, Oxford, 1959.

110. Luttrell, C., *The Creation of the First Arthurian Romance*. London, 1974.

111. Mac Niocaill, G., *Ireland Before the Vikings*. Gill & Macmillan, Dublin, 1972.

112. Markale, J., *King Arthur King of Kings*. Gordon & Cremonesi, London, 1977.

113. Matarasso, P., *The Redemption of Chivalry*. Droz, Geneva, 1979.

114. Mathias, M., *Glastonbury*. David & Charles, Newton Abbot, 1979.

115. Matthews, C, *Arthur and the Sovereignty of Britain*. Arkana, London, 1989.

116. Matthews, C, *Mabon and the Mysteries of Britain*. London, 1987.

117. Matthews, J., *The Elements of the Arthurian Tradition*. Element, Shaftesbury, 1989.

118. Matthews, J., *The Elements of the Grail Tradition*. Element, Shaftesbury, 1990.

119. Matthews, J., *Gawain: Knight of the Goddess*. Aquarian Press, Wellingborough, 1990.

120. Matthews, J., *The Grail*. Thames & Hudson, London, 1981.

121. Matthews, J., and Green, M., *The Grail Seeker's Companion*. Aquarian Press, Wellingborough, 1986.

122. Miller, R., *Will the Real King Arthur Please Stand Up?* Cassell, London, 1978.

123. Millican, C.B., *Spenser and the Table Round*. Harvard University Press, Cambridge (Mass.), 1932.

124. Moorman, C., and R. *An Arthurian Dictionary*. University of Mississippi Press, Jackson, 1978.

125. Morris, J., *The Age of Arthur*. Weidenfeld & Nicolson, London, 1973.

126. Newsted, H., *Bran the Blessed in Arthurian Romance*. Columbia University Press, New York, 1939.

127. Opie, I. and P., *The Classic Fairy Tales*. London, 1973.

128. O'Rahilly, T.F., *Early Irish History and Mythology*. Dublin Institute of Advanced Studies, Dublin, 1946.

129. O'Sullivan, T.D., *The 'De excidio' of Gildas*. Brill, Leiden, 1978.

130. Owen, D.D.R., *The Evolution of the Grail Legend*. Oliver & Boyd, Edinburgh, 1968.

131. Paton, L., *Studies in the Fairy Mythology of Arthurian Romance*. Boston, 1903.

132. Ratcliffe, E., *The Great Arthurian Timeslip*. O.R.E., Stevenage, 1978.

133. Reid, M.J.C., *The Arthurian Legend*. Edinburgh, 1938.

134. Reiser, O.L., *This Holyest Erthe*. Perennial, London, 1974.

135. Rhys, J., *Celtic Folklore*. Clarendon Press, Oxford, 1901.

136. Rhys, J., *Studies in the Arthurian Legend*. Clarendon Press, Oxford, 1891.

137. Roberts, A. (editor), *Glastonbury: Ancient Avalon, New Jerusalem*. Rider, London, 1978.

138. Robinson, J.A., *Two Glastonbury Legends*. Cambridge University Press, Cambridge, 1926.

139. Ross, A., *Pagan Celtic Britain*. Routledge & Kegan Paul, London, 1967.

140. Ruoff, J.E., *Macmillan's Handbook of Elizabethan and Stuart Literature*. Macmillan, London, 1975.

141. Rutherford, W., *The Druids*. Aquarian Press, Wellingborough, 1983.

142. Saklatvala, B., *Arthur: Roman Britain's Last Champion*. David & Charles, Newton Abbot, 1967.

143. Senior, M., *Myths of Britain*. Orbis, London, 1979.

144. Spence, L., *The Minor Traditions of British Mythology*. London, 1948.

145. Stewart, R.J., *The Prophetic Vision of Merlin*. Arkana, London, 1985.

146. Stewart, R.J., (editor) *The Book of Merlin*. Blandford, Poole, 1987.

147. Stewart, R.J., (editor), *Merlin and Woman*. Blandford, London, 1988.

148. Stuart-Knill, I., *The Pedigree of Arthur*. Kingdom Revival Crusade, Sidmouth, 1977.

149. Tatlock, J.S.P., *The Legendary History of Britain*. University of California Press, Berkeley, 1950.

150. Tolstoy, N., *The Quest for Merlin*. Hamish Hamilton, London, 1985.

151. Treharne, R.F., *The Glastonbury Legends*. Cresset, London, 1967.

152. Vendryes, J. *et al.*, *Lexique étymologique de l'irlandais ancien*. Paris, 1959.

153. Vickery, A.R., *The Holy Thorn of Glastonbury*. Toucan Press, Guernsey, 1979.

154. Waddell, L.A., *The British Edda*. Chapman & Hall, London, 1930.

155. Webster, R.G., *Guinevere: a study in her abductions*. Milton (Mass.), 1951.

156. Wentz, E., *The Fairy Faith in Celtic Countries*. C. Smythe, Gerrards Cross, 1977.

157. West, G.D., *An Index of Proper Names in French Arthurian Verse Romances*. University of Toronto Press, Toronto, 1969.

158. West, G.D., *An Index of Proper Names in French Arthurian Prose Romances*. University of Toronto Press, Toronto, 1978.

159. Weston, J.L., *From Ritual to Romance*. Doubleday, Garden City, 1957.

160. Weston, J.L., *The Legend of Sir Gawain*. NUTT, London, 1897.

161. Westwood, J., *Albion*. Granada, London, 1985.

162. Whitehead, J., *Guardian of the Grail*, Jarrolds, London, 1959.

163. Wildman, S.G., *The Black Horsemen*. John Baker, London, 1971.

164. Wright, R. *A History of Castle Eden Lore in search of King Arthur*. Published by the author, Hartlepool, 1985.

165. *Etudes celtiques* Vol.8. (periodical).